THE LANDED GENTRY

Other books by Sophy Burnham

THE ART CROWD
BUCCANEER (Fiction)
PENELOPE (A Play)

The——
LANDED GENTRY

by
SOPHY BURNHAM

G.P. Putnam's Sons
New York

Library of Congress Cataloging in Publication Data

Burnham, Sophy.
   The landed gentry.
   Includes Index.

   1. United States—Social life and customs—
1945-1970. 2. United States—Social life and
customs—1971- 3. Upper classes—United States.
4. Country life—United States.
I. Title.
E169.02.B86   1978   973.92   78-1464

PRINTED IN THE UNITED STATES OF AMERICA

to Elinor

CONTENTS

Tell Tale Tit
Your tongue shall be slit
And all the dogs in town
Shall have a bit of it
          —anon. nursery rhyme

THE LANDED GENTRY

INTRODUCTION

I left my home, my landed home, soon after going to college, and I have never returned to that life. Some people may say that I have no right, therefore, to write of it, to disclose its secrets and hold it up to public view. But this book represents not just a description of a way of life, but my personal journey back to my own beginnings, and to the people I had left, in an effort to understand ... what? Myself, my people, my land, my economic system, my character, my country.

My country. Our country. Never has such a land been seen, I think, never has one been found so rich in the plenty of the earth. Take a plane. Fly over it. Take a car. Drive across our beautiful country. The golden plains of midland wheat, rolling horizon-wide. The primordial black swamps of the alluvial deltas, where the alligators bask loglike in a hot ooze, the silence broken only by the high whine of mosquitos and the dull chunkalunk of a bullfrog. The horse country, pastern-deep in emerald grass and whistling with winds and cheerful creeks

that burble over their stones, glittering, flashing, chirruping on
the journey to the sea. Exalted mountains rearing to the skies,
all crag and cliff; and then the deserts, flat and salt. Travel the
rivers of our land, sweeping south and west and east, joining
into great roaring bodies of rushing fluid, moving tons of rich
silt earth for thousands of miles and darkening the ocean itself
with its spill. Walk in the forests, the stinging scent of pine
and redwood ... dear God! What a country is ours! Cross the
lakes in our land, and not all are clear and green, but some are
dead lakes, oleaginous and glaucous with the chemical effluvia
from our high, rich, oily life. We stab the earth with our
machines, tear out its flesh to reach the minerals within, and all
in the name of corporate wealth. We speak of, long for, a
mystic unity with the land, and we are helpless to avoid destroying it. We are so very small.

This book is about many who are rich and some who are
quite poor. It is about those who own land, and how they live,
and how they see themselves as living (for the two are not
always the same), and what values they hold, and why they live
as they do, mutilating themselves and each other (helpless to
avoid it) and their lands, mutilating our lands.

> Ill fares the land, to hast'ning ills a prey
> Where wealth accumulates, and men decay.

That is from Oliver Goldsmith, and it has something to do with
the themes of this book, for corporations too often control our
lands today, even when disguised as private owners. And
corporations have no soul, are responsible to no one but their
boards of directors—and who are they? You will find the answer
to that too in this book, if you care to puzzle the question out.

* * *

I did not know when I began this book what I would find or what directions it would take. I was surprised to discover halfway through that it veered around to my own recollections. There are many themes: of class, land use and conservation, economics and psychology. Well, the book is flawed, the subject vast. No apologies are made.

I am, however, grateful to the many people who supported me in this project out of interest or friendship. To my agent, Lois Wallace, caustic and striving, needling me on; my editor, Phyllis Grann, smiling and nodding gently at my irresolution and then in a businesslike way sending me away to write; and another editor, Eleanor Rawson, now at Rawson Associates, who let me talk for hours and who gave the title to this book; to Kevin Kaplan, a student from Drew University, who worked on the research; to my typist, Liz Ogata.

I am also grateful to three newspapers, the *New York Times,* the *Los Angeles Times,* and the *Chicago Daily News,* which generously allowed me use of their clips and files.

Finally, there are the friends and acquaintances whose curious questions encouraged me, whose stories and suggestions led me to new paths: the Stanley Petters, who run a weanling farm in Lexington, Kentucky; the Reeds of Virginia; the Richard Crowleys in Rhinebeck; Bobby Ferguson of Cumberland Island; and Elizabeth Aldrich, Bill Jones, Ann Hobson Freeman, Tom Wolfe, Arthur Gelb of the *New York Times*—there are too many to name. Moreover, some cannot be named. They spoke anonymously. Many are they and to you all who opened your hearts to me, I thank you humbly, not only for the life stories poured out so generously, but also for the insights that you lent me of myself. And especially I wish to thank my mother, whose guidance and companionship have shaped my life and and whose wit entertained me for so many years.

This book developed out of conversations with my dear friend Elinor Fuchs Finkelstein, who first asked me to write about what it was like when I was growing up, to which I answered: "But what's unusual about that? Nothing happened."

Her devotion, encouragement, confidence in my efforts, and unflagging interest are equalled only by that of my beloved husband, David, who together with my daughters, Sarah and Molly, bravely withstood my fits of despondency and the inconvenience of my travelling.

This book has not been easy for me to write. Just breaking down the barriers of social convention and caste, the scabs of ancient wounds, both of which combine to enforce a code of silence, militate against its execution. You can see that the first pages are tentative, a few drops of water seeping from a mountain spring, and, as each chapter unfolds, running swifter, gathering strength, freshening, flowing, until by the last portions, they have turned into a stream. The dikes have burst. Lay that initial slow seepage, however, to my caste.

Are these stories true?

Either I have witnessed these events myself over thirty years of observation, or they were told to me, usually by the person who experienced them.

Two practical problems evolved in writing this book, especially in the latter half, which departs from routine journalism. One: the problem of how to tell these stories without hurting friends and acquaintances. I would not hurt them for the world. Or hold them up to ridicule. Yet even to write about what happened to them is to expose them publicly. A style was required that would permit depiction without inflicting harm. Which brought me to the second problem: the question of truth. Did things really happen as I saw them? Or is this my own perception of a fact? And is an emotional truth larger than mere factual detail?

So I have taken liberties. Sometimes I have disguised names and sometimes twisted and shaped the details of a story to hide the identity of the person involved. Occasionally I have moved people around our continent, so that a story said to have occurred in South Carolina may have happened, instead, in Tennessee. More often, however, I have simply told the story placelessly, for the propertied class are a mobile set, roaming the world, weaving happily in and out of each other's lives (though always restricted to their own narrow perimeters, their limited social set: to that extent they are deprived and isolated). Regional variations, nonetheless, occur in our country to a remarkable extent, despite the physical ease of jet plane travel and the homogenizing effects of television. Today a man on Long Island lives differently from one in Minnesota, even when they have the same amount of money and share a common value, class, and education. A Westerner is distinct in walk and gesture, not to mention the bend of his brain. His landscape has burned into him, superimposing a Western cant, just as a Southerner's land remains in him long after the accent is lost.

There is a Japanese saying: To know yourself, you must go out the front door, travel around the entire world, and return by your own back door. This book for me has been a journey of exploration, and I have been required to do much travelling and hold many interviews to reach my own back door. I approach. I am not sure I have arrived there yet.

The Landed Gentry

When I was growing up, we lived in an area of the landed gentry. The highest achievement was to be a "gentleman farmer." The young men worked off their high spirits with horse racing, cockfighting, fox hunting, or bassetting, and life seemed hardly removed from eighteenth-century England: hard-drinking, hard-driving, hard-sexed. I don't remember anyone ever having a pit dog fight, but these were talked about as if they had just passed out of fashion. Bennie Thomas, at seventeen, got picked up by the police on gambling charges for fighting his cocks, and most people in the Valley felt the police were the dumb ones there, when all he was doing was showing his pluck. Ours was a violent, physical life.

Later there were debutante dances, at which the "boys," growing older every year until they were twenty-five and twenty-six, were still attending the deb parties and looking over the new crop of eligible girls. We went skeet shooting, dove shooting, married incestuously into the same families for generations. We were the landed gentry, so certain of our power that the young men often saw no need to go to college (or for that matter to graduate from prep school), and neither did the girls. The ambitions of a girl and that girl's mother were fulfilled with marriage. One classmate of mine exemplifies the point.

She was a plain child, Irish by extraction, and raised by governesses and English nannies, she and her sister, on a huge estate. She rode to hounds on her pony, swam under the sparkling sun in the Olympic-sized outdoor pool, played tennis on her own courts; but who was there in that tractless land to play against except the servants or her sister? She was a lonely, gawky, awkward, and utterly arrogant, unpleasant girl. Still, she was bright and, after boarding school, she attended college and was an "A" student, ready to graduate with honors, when, in the middle of her junior year, her mother called her home—her beautiful mother, who always hunted sidesaddle in elegant black habit and veil.

"Dear," she said, "your little sister is coming out in another year, and I can't afford both a wedding and a debut in the same year. Pick one of your beaus and we will arrange a wedding in June."

"But Mummy," she argued, "I want to finish college. I don't like any of the boys I know." I have this story from her senior advisor at college, to whom she tearfully turned for help. But no help was available. In the end, she dutifully left college, married, and retired to her own estates to continue the tradition of the landed gentry.

It seems incredible in 1977 to talk in such terms of old, old families, often of enormous wealth, rooted to the land. Their names do not fall into the glittering celebrity set. If they once dominated the newspapers, they have passed now into obscure respectability. Pells, Gerrys, Guests, even du Ponts. Their modern generations are no longer hungry, either physically or emotionally. They lust for no money and God knows they want no renown. Indeed, having known for generations what it is to live at a stable, comfortable—or occasionally stupendous—economic level, they consider discussion of money, even within a family around the dinner table, as vulgar. Desire for it is suspect, the worship of false idols, the Baal of materialism.

"Money is the root of all evil," said Thomas W. Lamont to J. Pierpont (Jack) Morgan, Jr., in 1936.

"No," he shot back. "If you read your Bible, you'd know, it said the *love* of money is the root of all evil."

If discussion of money is avoided as poor taste, publicity is so much avoided that putting one's name on the mailbox at the end of the drive is cause for apprehension; it seems so ... pushy. As if the name of the estate should not suffice—for houses have names among this group. So that you may find a Weyanoke Plantation, or Rokeby, or Rippon Lodge, while the owner's name remains discreetly blank. Anyone with business with the owner, you see, knows where he lives, and anyone else would merely intrude.

In each area of the country the life-style differs, customs vary. The Virginia and Maryland hunt countries differ from each other and both from the Long Island estates or the diamond-studded plantations of South Carolina. In the Chateau country of Delaware, the du Ponts hold sway. . . . and in Michigan, Kentucky, California, Mississippi, other species of the genus *gentry* are to be found, each with its own particular set of characteristics.

Yet what is curious is that they all form one group. They move fluidly back and forth between all these areas. They know each other. When I was young, this amazed me, that everyone seemed to know everyone else. How was it possible? If a schoolmate's name came up, my father would know that girl's father, or my mother would begin tracing her parentage:

"Isn't she Kitty Sonso's niece?"

"No, that would be the Sonsos of Kentucky. This girl comes from Chicago."

I watched as a child with awe and admiration my father who knew everyone. Now I understand there is a group, a single class, tossed like a silver skein across the entire United States. A network interlocked by a thousand cobwebbed knots. It doesn't matter what you call them: the upper class, the propertied class, families of established wealth, the right people. They are tied by blood. They are tied by class, which is based, to a large degree, on property and wealth. They are tied especially by a shared lifestyle, shared values, education, interests, and an emotional attachment to the land, to property, which constitutes, yes, one form of wealth but also more than that: at times the land becomes synonymous with self.

How can I begin to tell you about this life? the landed gentry, the aristocracy. The very concepts are antique. The comfort, the self-satisfied provincialism, the reactionary (and sometimes startlingly liberal) political views. For that matter, the sheer size of the spaces to be described. Can you imagine how large is 1,280 acres? It is two square miles. Or 12,000 acres? Or 64,000—which is ten miles by ten. Do the math yourself. Throughout this book I will talk of size. One "section" equals one mile square. There are 640 acres to a square mile.

Outside of Chicago, the Drakes (of the hotel family) have a style of life more reminiscent of Russian nobility than anything we think of on America soil. My husband visited his friend Bill Drake once when they were both at Harvard. The air-conditioned interstate train left Chicago and swept out into the prairie, endless fields of golden corn baking under a cloudless sky. After several hours, the train suddenly slowed and halted. One car was opened. A metal stepladder was dropped to the grass by the side of the track, and the college boys stepped into the prairie heat. It was the Drakes' private stop.

The train pulled away and almost simultaneously there appeared in the distance a station wagon bouncing over the fields. The house itself was grand. The wooden blades of a single fan swung noisily overhead, moving the hot air around. They sipped absinthe until they felt no heat.

The estate had its own Episcopal chaplain attached to its private chapel. The employees were expected to attend Sunday services. The farmers on the place were maintained by the Drakes: Mrs. Drake (who died last year) chose the curtains for their houses, bought the bedspreads, oversaw their children's schooling, and ran her lands in all respects like a feudal estate.

This is not unusual in this class. When I went to the wedding of Emily Astor Harding to Michael Zimmer in Rhinebeck, New York, in the mid-1960s, the members of the wedding were housed in the farmers' cottages. The tenants were moved out for us—who knows where?—but so completely was their presence removed that no clothes, no personal possessions remained behind. We hung our clothes in the closets, filled the empty bureau drawers, and asked the maid to make coffee for us in the well-stocked kitchens. When we swam at the magnificent indoor pool at the Big House (formerly the Little House), with its wide arches looking out across the lawn and the life-sized porcelain leopards lying on the marble floor, we were provided with our choice of dozens of bathing suits of all sizes and types. Michael, the bridegroom, who had hurt his foot, leaned on the gold-headed cane of John Jacob Astor and looked properly dignified throughout the two days of festivities, until the limousine whisked the newlyweds to the helicopter waiting in a field.

I am told this way of life is dying out. Vanishing. We don't have a class of Established Wealth any longer, and quasi-feudal estates are a thing of the past: everything has changed. Yet hidden among the motels and french fry stands are these enclaves of landed wealth.

Avery Island, for example, in Vermillion Bay, Louisiana, has been held by the same family since 1818. It has its own post office, deputy sheriff, justice of the peace, public grammar school, and a publicly maintained state road that runs across the flat moist marshes of this utterly flat salt land right to the island itself: a seigneurial domain. You turn a corner and there it is, a hill, a verticle slope rising like a wart on the plain: Avery Island. Twenty-five hundred acres of green English hillsides, surrounded by another ten thousand acres of marsh. It supports two company stores and one thousand workers with three industries: the salt mines that run for miles beneath the earth, the red-pepper fields that produce the chief ingredient for Tabasco sauce, and 150 oil wells.

This is private land. As Walter McIlhenny,* the *parrain*, explained in his soft, firm drawl: "You don't tell me you want to come to Avery Island." He smiled thinly. "You ask if you may."

"How do you get a deputy sheriff?" he was asked.

"I tell the sheriff of New Iberia Parish whom I want," he answered simply, "and he appoints him."

---

* "Mister Walter" is president of Avery Island, Inc., and the McIlhenny Co., Inc. It was he, as head of the family and business, who decided in 1967 whether the public grammar school on the island should be integrated according to federal law or closed—and chose to integrate.

Can you imagine how it affects a man to have such control over the course of his life? How does he perceive the world? Yet Avery Island is by no means the only private island in the United States. Nor even the largest. There is Cumberland Island, off the coast of Georgia, which is owned in part by Mrs. R. L. Ferguson, granddaughter of Thomas Carnegie. Raised to sumptuous wealth, she lives there still, a woman in her seventies, struggling to keep her land out of the hands of developers—or the federal government.

There is Naushon, owned by the Forbeses of Boston, with its thirty-six great houses and its soft dirt carriage drives. (No cars are allowed on the island.) Or Santa Catalina Island in California, owned by the Wrigleys of the chewing gum company. Or Niihau in Hawaii, owned by the Robinsons, who are so determined to maintain the ecological balance there that, according to reports, no visitors are allowed on the island to disturb the pure Hawaiians, and any Hawaiian who leaves, I have heard, does so at the pleasure of the Robinsons and must ask permission to return.

A private island creates a particular psychology of privacy, but the fact of island-ship is not the necessity. Merely space. Water and land stretching out as far as the eye can see, field and forest, valley and hillside, yours from one horizon to its end; or, if not owned entirely by you and your family (and this is an important point), then owned by such good friends that you share the same ideals. You hold the land in common, as it were, and to a common end.

The psychology of inherited wealth, the love of land, the sense of continuity, a stubborn rootedness that explains both provincialism and complacent prejudice, a class system rigid as caste, and an economic reality that puts into question our highest ideals of democracy and social mobility all dominate this class. One woman I know provides a perfect example of

the traits that so often drive me to despair. I shall call her Mrs.
Baldwin. She lives in Maryland in a handsome house high on a
hill, overlooking what I consider the most beautiful country in
the world, all valleys and hills and plowed fields and gentle
streams and unpretentious pasture.

A while ago we fell into conversation.

"Did you hear what Hereford County has done?" She was
indignant. "They've passed a law stating that hereafter no one
can graduate from high school unless he can read, write, and do
minimal mathematics. Isn't that appalling?"

"Well, I've been trying to tell you," I crowed. "Our
educational system stinks. Kids graduate all the time who can't
read or write."

"Well, *don't* you think that's awful?" she pursued.

"Of course I do! It's outrageous. But maybe I'm not as
surprised as you because I've known about this system for a
long time and—"

"Did you hear what I said?" she interrupted me. "I said
Hereford County has passed a law stating that every child must
read and write and do mathematics before he can graduate."

"Yes?" I was uneasy.

"Well, don't you think that's awful?"

"Um," I said. "Why do you think that's awful?"

"Why, they don't need to know how to read and write!" she
burst out. "Charlie Hoff, who rakes the leaves for me and chops
wood and mows the lawn, supports a wife and four children,
and he can't read or write!"

Stop right there. You assume Charlie Hoff is black, don't
you, Maryland being a Border State. He's not. Mrs. Baldwin
treats all people, black or white, with equal respect, according
to her principles of the inequality of class. Charlie comes of
good, solid, country family, well liked and well respected. His
mother cleans house two days a week for Mrs. Baldwin, who

wouldn't know what to do without her, not only in maintaining a minimal attack against the dirt and dog hairs, but also as a devoted friend. There's no one can tell a story like Mrs. Hoff, for which Mrs. Baldwin loves her dearly.

Her comment is founded in bedrock conservatism, shared by the country folks themselves, and it is derived from fearless self-reliance. It takes expression in derision for all urban life (especially of New York), combined with contempt for all external government.

"A law!" she continued. "They'd pass a law!"

Country folk are perhaps the ultimate anarchists.

Me Myself

It seems necessary to say a word about myself and where I fit into this geometry of money and class. This is hard to do, not only because of my own ingrained, well-trained revulsion at revealing a personal matter (lest, revealed, I too am vulnerable to attack), but also because no one in my family will agree with whatever I say. (Further attack.) If I say we were poor when I grew up, my aunts will rise in outrage, flailing me as if I were the Elephant's Child and insisting I am wrong. *"Poor in relation to what?"* they will shout and point out that they managed to keep their horses and their places and send their children to good schools and "hold up their heads" in society. Wasn't one aunt's great friend the first Mrs. Nelson Rockefeller—Mary Clarke of Philadelphia? How could I be so crude as to accuse my family of poverty?

If, on the other hand, I were to state we were well off, I'd call down on my head even harsher abuse. Well off? What does that mean? Rich? Rich in relation to whom? We were never rich, and if I understood anything, surely I would understand that. My mother would then turn to me in scorn to remind me that she spent her life juggling bills, scrimping, saving, parcelling out her pieces of eight among the tradesmen and supplying the house always (despite the vagaries of the stock market) with the cheapest items on the grocery store shelves: the white Wonder Bread, the tradebrand imitation mayonnaise. What did I know of rich? Go away and don't come back till you grow up, they'd say.

Money is relative, you see, and to a degree much less important to the question of class than some sociologists seem to think. You can have no money and belong to a propertied class, and you can have buckets and never have a prayer of belonging. Basically, class is a matter of shared values.

Money is an interesting topic, though. It is treated differently, you'll find, in different families and geographic areas of the country. I had not realized until I began this book the extent of the geographical distinctions. People in the West, for instance (Texas being the exaggerated example), are quite open about money, about how much they pay for an object, what income they have, how much property they own. Those in the East among the propertied class would slit their tongues before they'd tell. To ask is a mortal insult. This explains the embarrassment of one Rockefeller (and of certain people I knew who were not even related to the Rockefellers but were mortified for them) when Nelson disclosed his fortune in his lust for the vice-presidency. It is one reason why "nice people" in many areas in the country, from Louisiana to New York, avoid going into politics—lest they be required to reveal the sanctified.

Years ago, I met an ebullient New York Jew, the son of an underwear manufacturer, who held me spellbound with his talk:

"I made sixty thou last year," he poked me with one finger. "I'll knock 'em dead this year. I made twenty on one deal alone!" I was fascinated. It was so forbidden. I found his cockiness exhilarating, his attitude in such contrast to that of my own family, where money was—and is—simply never mentioned. To this day, I do not know how much money my parents or aunts or grandparents have or had. I would never ask.

When I say money was not mentioned, I mean it was not used as a measure of esteem, except perhaps negatively, as in: "I hear Johnson sold Mr. Krolberger a horse for $50,000. He wanted a hunter, and damned if he didn't buy a horse blind in one eye!" (Bursts of laughter.)

Another story exemplifying the thriftiness of the established rich occurred after Miss Jesse Ball, of a fine old Virginia family, married Alfred du Pont, thereby raising her status in a single day from that of a modest schoolteacher to one of the richest women in the country. One day, she was out shopping with Mrs. J. Robert Massie, Jr.* Mrs. du Pont tried on a very expensive twenty-five-dollar hat (This was in the days when you could buy a hat for twenty-five dollars), then put it back: "Oh, no," she said. "It's much too expensive. I don't need a new hat."

On the way home, she dropped into her friend's lap an envelope "with a little something" for the hospital. It was a check for five hundred dollars.

The question of money itself is too vast, too filled with ramifications to easily comprehend. We were not rich. Certainly not in terms of the kind of money I was to see later in life, not in relation to the kind of money I describe in this book. On the other hand, we had Family. As children, we were never

* Charlotte Massie is a former society editor for the *New Leader* in Richmond and was executive director of the Garden Club of Virginia when she told me this story.

allowed to forget it, just as we were not allowed to forget our place, our class. We were Peytons and Cochrans. We were Tayloes (who clucked their tongues at the British Royal Family: "They're so *middle-class*," they would complain).

One day my husband and I were sailing on the Chesapeake Bay and found ourselves anchored, during a terrible rainstorm, about thirty miles from the Tayloe plantation. The rain slashed down in sheets, dripping right through the cabin walls, and rather than remain in the leaky boat we decided to visit Mt. Airy. I was involved in writing this book by then, and curious. I had never been to Mt. Airy, though I had read that it was "perhaps the finest example of Palladian architecture in America," and I had studied the black and white lithographs of it in my grandmother's house. The Tayloes were the Rockefellers of their time. When the White House was burned by the British in the War of 1812, it was to a Tayloe townhouse that President Madison moved. The family fell on hard times after the Civil War, and my sister once described her visit there with the three ancient Tayloe sisters like the old crones in the fairy tale, living in the downstairs parlor without heat while the place fell into dilapidation.

We hired a car and a boy to drive us over. The boy was the son of the boatyard owner, a strapping, country kid in his late teens, pimply-faced and fat, and as proud of his mufflerless, tail-dragging chariot as he was of the dirty tapes that he played for our delectation along the way. He chuckled approvingly at each joke. The windows steamed up and the moisture dripped from our foul-weather gear, as we rocketed across the country. Approaching our destination, the boy slowed down, eyeing various modern brick ranch houses.

"Is that it?"

"No, it's a big place. I'm sure there'll be a gate."

A highway had cut across one piece of the property, destroying the entrance, but two pillars still guarded Mt. Airy.

"This is it."

"This is the house?" the boy answered in surprise.

"Well, at the end of the drive...."

The drive was a long, curving, dirt road. Signs declared a speed limit, enforced by the misanthropic injunction:

"Rising dust draws gunfire."

The boy drove through the muddy potholes with extreme care. Across the hillside stood the house, built of soft red stone. A curving staircase descended between giant urns to the pebble circle.

"Wow!" he said. "It really is big."

I was impressed myself. I'd been raised on stories of the Orangerie, of the gardener who never let Miss Tayloe plant what she wanted in the garden, of the slave who in anger at her masters set fire to the house (and was removed to the cotton plantation in Alabama rather than hanged, so kindly were my ancestors, her masters). Somehow, I had not expected it to be handsome.

Col. Gwynne Tayloe met us at the door. He had already looked us up in the Family Book.

"Your grandmother gave me my first pony," he told me graciously, "when I was a little boy."

Then he showed us the portrait of the horse that Cousin Arthur had left Mt. Airy in his will, and the refurbished dining room with the chandelier that "Aunt Polly" had found at a church sale, and the redecorated modern kitchen with his work shoes and shotguns leaning in one corner. I came away filled with conflicting emotions of annoyance and pride–the former due to my scorn for ancestor-worship, the latter from a sense of belonging to such a house. It is a conflict I shall probably never reconcile.

The boy drove us to our boat in silence. He did not play his tapes.

People in my family believe that merely to mention the

Family in public is to brag; and they are careful therefore not
to make anyone feel sad or inferior by bringing up Family
Roots, though there's little enough to be done about the
general unhappiness at not being part of it. (For people in my
family also think that no one is so much fun as another
member of the family, an opinion they are convinced is
universally shared.) You understand, however, the necessity for
my mentioning all this in order to show where I fit into our
discussion of land and class. I'd guess we are Old Family of
Decaying Means.

The Valley

Years ago there used to be three shanties on the hill leading to
our house—old slave quarters for the Fisher place. When I was
about four, my sister Anne and I would trot down the hill to
visit our cleaning woman there. Lillian was white, and she and
her husband lived in one of the houses for a while, the only
white family I remember living there.

It was an unpainted board shack, like those you see on
television in Mississippi today. It had two rooms on the ground
floor and two above. Lillian, big and fat, spread honey on bread
for us. We also drank water from a bucket set on a plank shelf,
there being no running water in the house. We drank from a
tin ladle that hung on a nail on the wall. Anne and I thought
it was wonderful. Then we would go out to the outhouse, and
back in the kitchen we would look at each other, my sister and
I, and shudder with delight when Lillian said she had to go out
there at night. "Aren't you afraid?" we'd ask.

Afterwards we would climb up on the hill past Irv's house

(Irv was black and had about ten children, if I remember correctly, in a similar though much larger shack) to our own brick house on the hill.

The three slave quarters burned down some years ago, but as I drive up Red Hill to our house, I am always surprised to see the woods grown over the property and the houses gone, the absence of the shacks being a continual reminder of their presence.

The Valley lies twenty miles north of Baltimore, forty-five minutes from Washington, an oddity in Megalopolis. It consists of 44,500 acres of country estates, horse and cattle farms. Geographically, there are four valleys, running roughly east to west and separated by high ridges. But call them one, for they form a spiritual unity–the Green Spring Valley.

The manor houses stand imposingly on the tops of the hills, with sweeping views of cattle and horses grazing in the pastures. The woods are filled with mountain laurel and dogwood. In the hollows are abandoned springhouses, built of yellowish stone and mortar. The area was settled in the 1740s, and though almost no one knows the exact site of the old Garrison Fort, used to ward off the Indians in the French and Indian Wars, the place names echo the frontier: Garrison Forest, Garrison Road.

The Lower Valley is fast becoming suburbs now, with groomed lawns and flower beds and new $300,000 houses hidden in the developments in the woods; and though the inhabitants still often stable a pony behind the house and Garrison Forest School for Girls vans horses upcountry to hunt, the young bankers, lawyers, and insurance brokers prefer golf and tennis at the Lower Club.

The upper Valley is undeveloped. Miles of neat, white fencing mark the Alfred Gwynne Vanderbilt farm, Sagamore, home of Native Dancer. Farther up the road is the estate of former senator Danny Brewster (charged with taking a bribe while in Congress–thus ruining his political career). And still farther upcountry is St. John's Episcopal Church, where the hounds are benevolently blessed before the Thanksgiving Day Hunt.

("What you don't understand is that this is America. This is the way people live everywhere. You don't think New York or Washington is representative, do you?")

Twenty-five thousand people inhabit the four valleys, but in an area where 355 families own 40 percent of the land, "The Valley" can properly be limited to 1,000 people or less, mostly members of the Green Spring Valley Hunt Club.

("What's it like living in the Valley now? Same as ever?"

"Oh, God, you wouldn't recognize it. The Jews are moving in everywhere.")

I used to ponder the fragility of life, the transience that led Heraclitus to write: "There is only one absolute, and that is change." But the events I am about to describe occurred ten years ago, with a terrible force. And do you know, the result was ... nothing changed. Incomprehensible.

The Valley is still rural enough to mark the visible changes of seasons, the parched grass of summer, the drifts of snow in a winter sun. The fox hunting season goes from October to March, after which four races are held, one on each Saturday in April. The last is the Maryland Hunt Cup. The Maryland Hunt Cup is the fastest, toughest race over timber fences in the country. It is comparable to the Grand National in England, where the horses jump brush; Mr. Noel Traing, whose horse was killed under him in one Hunt Cup, said: "I would look forward with the greatest pleasure to another ride at Aintree, but shudder at the thought of riding in the Maryland Hunt Cup again."

The solid post-and-rail fences are so high and the pace so fast that usually only a few horses finish. This is a "gentleman's race": the horses are hunters, the riders mostly amateurs, and the prize traditionally a silver cup. But that year, 1968, the Hunt Cup Committee added a small cash prize to attract more entries, and it caused a certain amount of discussion.

("What do you think of the prize?"

"Oh, I'm in favor of it. Isn't everybody?"

"Oh, no! This is a gentleman's race. You want to keep it that way.")

Most people in the Valley don't have much to do with the race now, as the area grows more suburban, but everyone is ready to quote the story of the five gentlemen who were sitting on the steps of the Elkridge Club in the spring of 1894 discussing their horses. A race was organized on the spot. There were nine entries in that first race. All the horses fell once and Kildare fell twice, but the race was so successful it was made an annual affair.

In the Valley, it is the excuse for parties—three days of lunches, cocktail parties, dinners, and dances, attracting people from all over the country: Washington diplomats, the Long Island and Palm Beach millionaires, the horsey set from Virginia and Pennsylvania.

In 1968, the atmosphere of the race was different, for two weeks before the race Martin Luther King was murdered; riots erupted in Baltimore; 6 people were killed and 5,400 arrested.

Three days before the race, Mr. Janon Fisher was grazing Mountain Dew on a halter on the lawn of his eighteenth-century pink brick house. Mr. Fisher was about seventy-five then, lean and hard in his khaki pants and waterproof rubber shoes. His wiry hair was stark white, and he was very handsome. Mrs. Fisher was heaving at a power mower near the house. She stopped the noisy machine, smiling cordially and wiping her hands on her apron at her approaching friends.

"Did you hear what happened to Murray and Lucretia?" she asked. "They got caught in the riots coming back from Fell's Point. Everyone thinks it's so funny, because they're so liberal."

"And what do they say now?"

"Oh, well, now they're against all those radicals."

Everyone laughed, but then turned serious.

"Well, whatever were they doing driving down there in the riots?"

"They didn't know about it." She pushed at the straying wisps of gray hair, pushing them futilely back toward her bun. "Lucretia was driving. Murray was hit by a rock–"

The Fisher house combines those peculiar smells of country dirt and dogs, familiar to farmhouses in the hunt country of Maryland and Virginia. The chair springs sag, and the faded pink slipcovers are dirty with the traffic of seven children and sixteen grandchildren and their dogs (one being Lulu, a black bulldog, her hind legs twisted under her, crippled by a car).

Everywhere you look are works of art, paintings of stables and horses, pit dogs and fighting cocks. The tables and window ledges are covered with silver cups, horse magazines, and Victorian bronzes of stag hunting and fighting dogs. Mrs. Fisher led us through a back room (with a saddle on its wooden tree), past a greenhouse, to the huge kitchen, where she had made a tub of butter that morning. The dining room and parlor are formal rooms, with the quiet feel of disuse.

This year one daughter, Kitty, was running a horse against her father, and it was splitting the family. Kitty stood in the living room in jeans and a pink shirt and told how her younger sister, Annie, had grabbed her passionately by the shirt collar a few days before:

"If you find them coming down the stretch together, you better pull back," she'd said, shaking Kitty. "This is *Daddy's* race."

It was just as likely that Kitty's mare would fall, for she had run in only two small races before.

"Why didn't you enter her in some of the Virginia races?" someone asked. She tossed her head. "Virginia! Who cares?"

The Fishers are an exception to the Valley, first because they are not rich (their beautiful possessions are inherited), and second, because they raise horses for a living. Most of the Valley is composed of lawyers, bankers, brokers, and businessmen who commute each evening from Baltimore to their stately houses.

There is, for example, Charles Fenwick, secretary of the Hunt Cup Committee (Cuppie, as he's called, for the Valley abounds with nicknames: Poopsie, Bootsie, Sissie, Squeaky, Pudge, Snood, and Ubas. "You've heard of Sabu the Elephant Boy; this is Ubas the boy elephant.")

Cuppie is about 45, blond, fit. Three days a week he leaves his insurance office in Towson to fox hunt over the Maryland hills with the Green Spring Hounds. He is whipper-in.

Cuppie had a horse in the race, ridden by his son, a senior at Gilman School for Boys.

"Brucie's done it all," he smiled. "All I've done is the familial duty of putting up the money. Brucie's the one. He gets up every morning before school to train the horse."

Usually there are a couple of horses from out of state. This year it was a Valley race. Everyone was related. Janon Fisher's horse was ridden by his son; his daughter's by young Paddy Smithwick, seventeen years old. Paddy is the nephew of Mikey Smithwick, who rode Pine Pep to three victories in the 1950s. Redmond Stewart's horse was ridden by his son-in-law; Fife Symington's by his nephew. (Symington is a relative of Senator Stuart Symington of Missouri. He was Master of Fox Hounds. He married a Frick and has run three times, unsuccessfully, for Congress as a Republican considerably right of Goldwater. The last time he ran, his slogan was "Symington, a Name You Know." Since his district included the steel mills of East Baltimore, it evidently was.)

Mountain Dew was favored to win. He had already run in the race six times and won it three. No horse had ever run in the race seven times or tried for a fourth win.

"Ah, remember Blockade." Which brought up that other Fisher-trained horse, a son of Man o' War, who won the Hunt Cup three times and set a record of 8:44 that stood for twenty-five years. Blockade was killed in the Virginia Gold Cup in 1942, broke his neck.

But Mountain Dew was not another Blockade. Two years before, Jay Trump from Lancaster, Pennsylvania, had beaten Mountain Dew in the Hunt Cup and broken Blockade's record by one and a half seconds (and later gone on to win the Grand National at Aintree). Jay Trump, having won the Hunt Cup three times, retired the challenge cup that year, so that while Mountain Dew, with his name twice inscribed on Jay Trump's cup, won the race for the third time the following year, all it got him was his name on a new cup. He would have to win that cup two more times to keep it.

Now all of this seems very arbitrary, quite dull, even. But horses are remembered like people in the Valley, only with more affection.

For as long as I can remember, there has been a cockfight on the Friday night before the Hunt Cup. This is just a hack fight, a fight among friends, nothing like the big derbies and tournaments that can bring in twenty thousand dollars to the winner. It is held at night. Bales of straw form the ring, tiered to make a step. A bare yellow bulb hangs over the center of the ring, lighting the flashing movements of the cocks on the green April grass. A brindled mongrel is stretched on the yellow straw, oblivious to the activity, and a few children sit beside him, solemnly watching, hands on knees. Most people are socializing in jeans and khakis, drinking beer and talking and watching the fights.

In the lighted ring, the handlers hold the cocks, run them across the grass, blow on their ruffs and spit on their heads to excite them, all the while making friendly cracks at each other, until the referee says:

"Ready . . . pit."

And the two birds fly at each other, a blaze of red, yellow, blue, slashing with their spurs, cutting, going for the eyes. Soon they are bleeding and tired, with torn wings, and maybe have an eye ripped from its bleeding socket—"blinked" as it's called. They flop on the grass with the blood dripping down their feathers, the referee trying for a count.

"Count. One . . . two . . ." The cock must lie motionless for a count of ten. If he pecks at his opponent, he breaks the count.

"Count here."

"No, he was pecking at a straw."

The cocks fight with one-and-a-quarter-inch spurs, the two-and-a-half-inch "jaggers" rarely being used.

The year before the vice squad had raided the Hunt Cup weekend fight. The Valley had gotten word of the raid and was ready for it, so when the detectives came winding across the fields in the dark, talking softly over their walkie-talkies and moving in on the lighted ring of straw and the crowds of people silhouetted against the light, all shouting and cheering round the ring, they found—nothing. A few babies had been placed in the ring. It was a "love-in," the Valley proclaimed, and someone held up a guitar. But the raid busted up the fight that year.

"It was just some detective out to make a name for himself," said Mr. Fisher scornfully.

Cockfighting is not illegal in Maryland, and the Valley is annoyed at the persistent interference in their sport. The feds get them on gambling charges, and the county on cruelty to animals, although, as one of the Valley points out, "What's cruelty to a bird when all he wants to do is fight?"

"The government doesn't care as long as it gets its cut. Thing is, it just hates to think of all that money going untaxed." The speaker is an insurance broker. This weekend morning, dressed in khaki work clothes, he carries a bucket of dog food and mash to his fighting cocks. The birds are kept in long pens behind the house, not far from the swimming pool.

He feeds them when he gets home from the office, spurs the stags (muffed, so they won't hurt each other), and breeds his seven purebred families. On Hunt Cup weekend, he was taking his fighting cocks from the regular pens to the "scratch" pens (watching for "game" birds, good "cutters," birds with stamina and "bottom," which is strength) to get them ready for a tournament two weeks later. The Valley doesn't publicize the fights, though, because you don't go looking for trouble. It's a matter of privacy.

The Valley is a simple place, and quite simply private. Or snooty. Baltimoreans have a name for it: The Green Spring Stare—a cold, open snub of distaste. Many people from the suburbs of Ruxton or Riderwood or from Baltimore city itself have been made uncomfortable by that look. It expresses a real emotion, which is occasionally put into words.

Once four women were playing golf:

"Something should be done for the new members of the club," said one. "No one speaks to them. No one knows them. A party, perhaps, to introduce them to the other members. What do you think?"

"I think they should be shot," her partner answered. She was not entirely joking. It no more occurred to her to "do something" for the new members than to speak if she met one in the bar. Membership entitles one to use of the facilities of the club and to stare back at the cold stare of the other members.

This sense of privacy explains to some degree the secrecy of the Hunt Ball. The Hunt Ball is held on the Saturday night after the race. The men wear traditional fox hunters' pink coats (which are actually scarlet) or the dark green of the basset hunts. The ladies wear long dresses. It is very much a Valley affair, and opinions about it vary from "boring" to "exclusive," the two not being necessarily contradictory.

"Absolutely no publicity. There is no publicity about the Hunt Ball ... particularly with the riots."

The statement is passed off, swallowed under the speaker's breath, almost as an afterthought and explained no further; yet nothing happens at the Hunt Ball. It is just a dinner dance.

"It is *not* just a dance. It is a very elegant affair."

But the allusion to the riots demonstrated the ripples of uneasiness that flowed this weekend into the Valley.

The five hundred guests (at twenty dollars a ticket) are seated at tables of ten in the Stanford White Ballroom at the top of the Sheraton Belvedere Hotel in Baltimore. On each table is a bottle of scotch and bottle of bourbon, and during the course of the evening the waiters pass four or five bottles of fine French champagne to each table. Dinner traditionally has been shad roe. This year it was to be chicken.

The weekend began well. Friday was a soft, beautiful day. The sky was blue. The dogwoods glittered like snow, deep in the woods. That night the houseguests would arrive. Meanwhile, hostesses were preparing for their lunches on the morrow, finishing marketing, getting their cars washed. Some people were playing golf at the club.

The owners and riders were walking the course. The Hunt Cup is run on the Gary Black and Senator Brewster estates.

There is some confusion about this, because the Black estate is sometimes known as the Martins'. The young men in the Valley would shoot skeet in the summer, up behind the Martins', to get ready for the dove season. Property having totemic value in the Valley, these things are important. Mr. Black married Mrs. Martin after the divorce from his first wife—and, subsequent to our story, they were divorced themselves.

The owners' and riders' four-mile walk is a ritual act to check each solid chestnut fence, like stroking a rabbit's foot twenty-two times. There is the seventeenth fence, where Trouble Maker is buried. There is the third (which is also the thirteenth) known as the "Union Memorial" after the Baltimore hospital: four panels of five rails standing four feet ten inches straight up and down. Spain and Amalgo were both killed at the third in 1950; War Gold broke his neck at the thirteenth in 1953.

As dusk falls this Friday night, the cocktail parties begin. The guests gather in the dining room at the oval mahogany table, a turkey at one end, a roast of beef at the other. The level of voices rises.

This weekend blacks have supplanted Jews in the Valley as the main topic. Only here, as in many rural areas, blacks are still politely known as Negroes, the urban radical terminology not having taken root.

"You know," says one lady, "if the police had *shot* the people in the cities where they first started rioting, this wouldn't have happened here."

"Did you hear about Carrie Ramsey organizing a penance march down Charles Street after the death of Martin Luther King? And stopping in at every church on the way to pray for their sins. Can you imagine?"

No one can. Mrs. Ramsey is from Baltimore.

This was the weekend of student rioting at Columbia over a

gymnasium in Harlem, the weekend that Senator Brooke's daughter announced her engagement to a white man. The Valley pondered the incomprehensible, cataclysmic dimensions of the events, then returned to the everyday world.

The talk was of golf, azaleas, the Compton wedding the previous weekend (and Mrs. Compton, her eyes magnified behind her glasses, describes, half-proud, half-dismayed, her daughter's friend, who smokes pot). But the Valley finds most satisfaction in gossip—joyous gossip—all the more savory because everyone knows not only the adulterous parties but (with Homeric love of lineage) the parents and children as well.

Even the Valley has limits of delicacy. Some things are too obscene to discuss—like a play then popular in New York.

"Oh, it's the best play in New York. *Scuba Duba*. It's terribly funny. It's about a man in a French chateau whose wife has just run off with a Negro scuba diver."

There was an embarrassed silence.

"Please. Remember where you are."

Later this Friday night, a Northerner—yes, a newcomer to the area—would lean forward over her Irish coffee, so filled with emotion that she emphasizes her words with one hand pounding the white tablecloth. "If God had meant Negroes and whites to live together, he'd have made them the same color."

It is an argument rarely voiced in the Valley—the name of God being invoked there principally in profanation. Besides, in an area where the only blacks are the country folk, who have lived there as long as the whites, the need for such justification is not pressing. The country blacks agree, according to the Valley, wanting no equality with the Valley whites.

The Hunt Cup is run on Saturday afternoon. By noon, the St. John's Horse and Pony Showgrounds are filling with cars (at five dollars a ticket) and people picnicking on the grass, with hot dog vendors and balloon men and souvenir stands hawking cowboy hats, Confederate flags, and black monkeys bouncing on strings. It is very gay as toward three o'clock the spectators wind across the lush field to watch the race, balloons flying in the air.

The Valley parks, at ten dollars a car, along the line of locust trees on the Martin estate and partakes of tailgate picnics on china plates and silverware. There is much wandering along the triple row of cars, chatting with friends, sipping champagne.

Two race stewards in black hunting costumes canter stylishly past on their horses. An illicit bookie passes down the cars: "Here you go. Choose a winner."

Up on the hill, a busy, buzzing crowd of ten thousand is gathering. Two children roll down the hill, laughing dizzily, while their parents settle themselves on the grass beside their plaid ice-coolers.

The Valley jams the paddock, talking and watching the jockeys weigh in and the horses walk around and around in the pastern-deep green grass.

Young Janon is sitting on the grass, his back to the red snow fence. He picks at the blades of grass. He is dressed in his silks—blue and gray halves, one sleeve blue, one sleeve gray.

Big Janon hunkers down on his heels to speak to Paddy Smithwick, riding Kitty's mare. Paddy looks up, apprehensive, a young boy in pale gold silks with lavender sleeves. Big Janon says something, grips his shoulder, grins, pushes himself to his feet. Snatches of conversation float on the air of the paddock.

"How old are you?"

"Thirteen."

"I hear Haffaday's the horse to beat."

"Hello, Harry. I think you know my daughter—"

The paddock crowd breaks, moves up the hill. It is a perfect grandstand. From here you can see the entire Valley. Kitty, dressed in an unfashionably long blue coat, is climbing the hill beside her sister, Annie.

"Kitty, you're so calm."

"Don't talk to me. You'll find out." The tension sounds in her voice.

"This is my fiftieth Hunt Cup," proclaims big Robb Tyler happily. "I remember when Brose Hover won, and he came in at about twenty to one. I saw my bookie down there. I started runnin'. I was runnin' so fast down that hill I couldn't stop. But I got him," he says, remembering. "I was afraid he'd scoot off with m' money."

The horses travel twice around the circuit, twenty-two jumps, some exceeding five feet in height. A small crowd has gathered ghoulishly at the third (or thirteenth) fence, waiting for a horse to fall. But they are not the Valley crowd. The Valley watches from Snow Hill, where they can see from start to finish.

The start of the race lies behind a rise, so that the beginning always takes you by surprise. There is a surge in the crowd as the horses come over the hill, over the first fence, the second (and the crowd stands, seems to rise on tiptoe, urging, willing the horses safely over the jumps). At the third fence, Kitty's mare falls. A gasp runs through the crowd.

"Paddy's just lying there."

"Is he all right? He's just lying there."

And some people remember that his father, a professional jockey, had been paralyzed for a time by a fall at Monmouth Park.

The horses continue around the Valley. They are tiny dots, like toys. They seem to be running very slowly because of the distance. It is Mountain Dew's race all the way, and then

suddenly at the nineteenth fence something happens. A horse
leaps forward. He is lengths ahead. As he comes up the finish,
his colors are green and white. It is Haffaday, followed by the
Symington horse.

"What happened? What happened to Mountain Dew?"

"He broke."

"What happened?"

The crowd separates, begins to spill down the hillside, some
toward their cars, some to the wagon at the finish line, where
the winner will receive his cup. It is all over, and a sense of
disappointment follows, a mild depression, as if there should be
something more than a ten-minute race.

"Well, that's horse racing."

"Hey, where did the Lindsays put the liquor?"

Mrs. Stuart Janney is on the wagon, smiling, holding out the
antique $1,500 silver challenge cup that she was sent to New
York to buy, smiling at the owners of the horse and at the
jockey, who is beaming from ear to ear. The judges are milling
about. There is no established ceremony at this point, so that
no one quite knows the order of procedure. The newspaper
photographer explodes a flashbulb. It is the first time a Stewart
has won the race since Gough Thompson rode Mazarin in 1921.

The Fishers give a mint julep party every year after the race.
The house is filled with guests, but it is quiet, in mourning.
Voices are low.

"Don't talk, don't speak," says Johnny Elder, embracing Mrs.
Fisher. Her eyes are red and sore. She pats the soft skin of her
throat, shakes her head, smiling:

"I can't speak. My throat is sore."

The silver mint julep bowl arrives. Each person puts it to his
lips, passes it around the room.

"Where's Janon?"

"He's with the horse. He stayed with him."

In the kitchen, Kitty is doing something at the sink, full of crushed ice.

"Kitty, how's your horse?"

Her eyes are filled with tears, as she looks directly at the speaker.

"He'll be all right. He'll never race again, but he'll be able to hunt."

"No, I mean the mare."

"Oh." She tosses her head impatiently. *"She's* all right."

As for Mountain Dew, the story eventually comes out. The horse bowed a tendon. He was pouring on speed. Janon took him over the nineteenth fence and heard a crack like a broken leg, and he felt him go soft under him, lame. He tried to pull him up, but the horse took one more fence before Janon could pull him off the course.

"He has so much courage," says Annie fiercely. All the Fishers speak of the horse as a person.

Outside the house, the grandchildren are laughing and tumbling over a hammock on the lawn. Mr. Fisher, head down, walks soberly across the grass with Dr. Gadd, the vet.

Mountain Dew earned his cup. He won the race three times, and he never kept the challenge cup. But you can't retire a $1,500 challenge cup the first year it's been bought. So the Fishers have three silver tankards with the Maryland Seal for triple-winner Mountain Dew—and Mountain Dew's name is twice inscribed on Jay Trump's challenge cup and once on the present cup. But Mr. Fisher has no challenge cup.

Ah, it's so sad. Everyone is sad, because Janon Fisher, with his Princeton education, lives honestly—honorably—the way life used to be lived in the Valley fifty years ago, up on his farm raising horses, his big, comfortable house filled with dogs and tack and grandchildren; because he doesn't commute to an insurance or law office in town to make the money to live in the Valley; and because (though no one dares consider why it matters) there were riots in Baltimore two weeks earlier.

The party at the Gordon Whitings' is gayer.

"What do you think of the turkey dressing? I made it myself."

Tasting. Smacking of lips.

"Mmmm. No. Too much seasoning."

"Too much seasoning! Your mother thinks there's too much seasoning. My God!"

Across the room are the young daughter's friends from school. One is a white girl from Senegal. After an initial surprise at someone coming all the way from Africa, no one is really interested, though the girl holds up her hyena-skin handbag.

"He was the youngest MFH Green Spring ever had," the voice booms across the dining room table. "And a damned good one. But they didn't like him. He wouldn't write letters to the farmers when the hunt ran across their fields, or replace broken fences, or all the things an MFH has to do."

"I want to show you a beautiful dog," says Mr. Whiting, calling his pointer from the basement. "Come here, pup. Now this is a beautiful dog."

The white-ticked pointer leaps and twists, excited at being the center of attraction.

Everything seems the same, but the world, they felt, was breaking over them, and, bewildered, they felt helpless against the intrusion of a civilization they did not want to understand.

"I don't think there's a house in the Valley that doesn't have a gun by the front door. Armed." Her voice is breaking with tears. "I've never had a gun armed in a house in my life. The other night there was a knock at the front door, late at night, and we took out a gun to answer the door. Ah, that's a terrible thing."

The events described here—the riots, that race—took place some time ago. Yet you go back to the Valley today and it hardly seems changed. New houses have been built and property values have risen. And taxes. Mr. Fisher had a stroke that forced him to retire up on his farm. Tommy Smith, who had ridden Jay Trump to victory in the Grand National at Aintree, was lionized from Newport to Hobe Sound, gave lectures on his great ride, drank as one does in such societies and circumstances, until he gave up the horsey set altogether and settled in the Midwest.

And Ubas, whom I used to date years ago—Ubas died. It was a horrible death. He had a little boy whom he adored, his third child. The little boy was only two when he blew out the candles on his birthday cake and took such pleasure in the flames that soon after, his mother heard him screaming, and rushed in and found his bathrobe all afire, a box of matches nearby. The baby died two weeks later, despite the skin grafts, and two weeks after that his father had a heart attack.

My mother forgot to tell me about it. A year passed before I heard, and by then too much time had gone by to extend my sympathies. I am left with the memory dangling unfinished.

Today, the pressure of development is strong, and along the Reisterstown Road, tacky Pizza Huts and Burger Kings, gas stations, massage parlors, and drive-in movies sprout like toadstools fertilized by the generous lack of strict zoning ordinances. Yet the Valley remains—threatened, yes, but protected to a certain extent by its own internal social pressure.

Life-Styles

We have some friends, Mr. and Mrs. William Reed III, who live in Goochland County outside of Richmond on a beautiful place, Chastain. Not long ago a friend of theirs, Ben Hardaway, visited them for a week. He brought with him his wife, his two daughters, nine horses, his private pack of foxhounds, and his "whip" to tend the hounds.

The Reeds are not old, old Virginia family, but they have lived for fifty years or so in Goochland County. Their money came from mines and brokerage houses, and they are the most charming people you would want to meet.

Once they gave a house party in their castle, Royal Orchard, which stands on a mountaintop above Charlottesville. The house has stained-glass windows, suits of armor, and heavy oak bannisters as big around as a weightlifter's biceps; a Gothic pile. It was a lovely weekend, and as we sat on the terrace overlooking the Valley of Virginia, we were told how in the 1930s the government was planning to run the Skyline Drive right through Royal Orchard. Bill's grandfather, Mr. Reed, who built the place, made a point of being introduced to one high government official in the Department of the Interior, and the friendship flourished to the point that the official was invited to Royal Orchard for a weekend, where he too sat (as we were then) on the stone terrace with the rough stone castle at his back, watching the evening cast long green shadows across the woods.

"What a beautiful place," he said.

"Yes," came the answer. "It's too bad it will be torn down soon."

"Torn down! Why?"

"Oh, the government's putting in a highway here.... It's too bad, too, because the road could easily detour down into that parcel of land over there and across the ridge. If it were moved to the back side of the mountain," Mr. Reed continued, "I'd give a scenic easement and leave that land undisturbed...."

When the official returned to Washington, he asked for the maps of the Skyline Drive and pencilled in the changes himself, according to the family story; so that if you look at a map of the drive today, you see it winds along the mountaintops all the way to the Great Smokey Mountains—except at one place near Charlottesville, where the highway fish hooks around Royal Orchard and then back up again. It was one of the first scenic easements ever worked out in the country, and about ten years ago, when the Reeds were cutting timber in that area, they had to keep in mind their promise to the Park Service to retain the public's right to a view.*

---

* Today more and more scenic easements are being worked out, one of the best known being that stretch of land opposite and across the Potomac River from Mt. Vernon.

Ben Hardaway, their friend, owns the Hardaway (Contracting) Company of Columbus, Georgia, which was ranked by *Engineering News and Record Magazine* as 129th out of 400 companies in 1975, doing $75.2 million worth of heavy and highway construction work. But Hardaway's passion is fox hunting. He is Master of the Midland Fox Hounds of Georgia and has bred an amalgamated cross-bred strain of English and American Fell hounds so fine that he tours the country to demonstrate his breeding and hunting techniques. Did I say earlier that nothing seemed to change? Well, things do, for his whipper-in, Jefferson "Tot" Goodwin, is black. This deserves remark.

The Green Spring Valley was the first hunt to invite Hardaway to demonstrate his hounds. This was a couple of years ago, and you could see the field was a little taken aback when, as he unloaded his hounds and horses, it was discovered that his whip was black.

No one said a word, and it took only one hunt, Hardaway says, for them to get comfortable with him. After that they were crazy about him. A marvelous little guy, says Hardaway, so easy and quiet. It helped that Hardaway "gave 'em a good hunt," there being nothing better to put a dedicated fox hunter in a good mood than a hell-for-leather chase and to hell with the company. Tot has his own fifteen couple of hounds that he hunts for himself, in addition to handling Hardaway's Midland Hounds, and he's also hunted in Ireland, so he's more knowledgeable than most. Even so, people joke some and wonder if a horseman will someday ride up as Hardaway is unloading his baying hounds from the van for an invitational demonstration hunt (the field mounting in a creak of leather, the horses pacing, reins slack on their necks), and say with an imperious wave toward the pink-coated Tot: "We don't allow people like that to ride with our Hunt." Then Hardaway will

look up good-naturedly and drawl, "Oh, ah didn't know that.
Come own, Tot. Load up the hounds. We're not huntin'
heah."

I think almost the only renowned Virginia hunt they
haven't joined is the Middleburg Hunt. You'll hear a lot
among the gentry about Middleburg in Facquier County.
Population 833. This is the seat of the *Chronicle of the Horse.* It
counts among its citizenry such autochthons as Paul Mellon
and various du Ponts and the McGhees of Texas and Joan
Irvine Smith of the 80,000-acre Irvine Ranch in California and
another 100,000-acre ranch in Montana. I suppose it has as high
an average income as any township in the United States. Jackie
Kennedy rented a place in Middleburg for the fox hunting
when she was in the White House, and her old friend John
Warner, who was formerly married to Cathy Mellon and is
now the husband of Liz Taylor, took his new bride to
Middleburg last year,* where J. Carter Brown, head of the
National Gallery of Art, moved with his second wife at just
about the same time. The Best People keep a foot in
Middleburg. Foxcroft School is there, and Tommy Smith, who
rode Jay Trump to triumph at three Hunt Cups and at Auteiul
in France and the Grand National in England—the first
American to win that race—Tommy Smith grew up in
Middleburg. If you get the book by Peter Winants, *Jay Trump:
A Steeplechasing Saga,* privately printed in Baltimore (1966), you
can see pictures of little Tommy at age four, hunting his own
pony (at six months he was tied in a basket to hunt behind his
father). There's a picture also of his patron, Mrs. T. A.
Randolph,† dressed in splendid riding habit, taking a stream

---

* It was Warner who, when asked why he was becoming the seventh husband of
Miss Taylor, responded seriously: "My children need a mother." The remark elicited
equivalent·blandness from one family friend: "It's true. They really do."

† When Tommy, racing a dog of a horse one day in 1956, fell three times before

on her strong, handsome horse, and there are numerous pictures of fresh, red-cheeked young boys, fine and fit, and of ripe, red-cheeked old men, fat and fleshy, eyeing the six-foot steeplechase jumps.

Tommy's father, Crompton Smith, was not one of the idle rich, however, due to the fact that *his* father, Harry Worcester Smith, had already dissipated the family fortune. Crompton, a dairy farmer, hunted every day possible. He won the first running of Mellon's Rokeby Bowl, but neither father nor son could match the old man, Harry, in passion for a horse.

In 1912, when Harry Smith went to Ireland, he brought with him: seventeen thoroughbreds, seven grooms, a yellow motor car, three Yankee four-wheel buggies and a trotting sulky, all painted yellow, countless trunks of tack and luggage, his twenty-two-year-old son Crompton, one game cock, and a pack of American foxhounds, left in quarantine in England. It was a life not far removed from Hardaway's in 1976—just as the Blessing of the Hounds hasn't changed since the time of John Peel. That takes place all over America.

I heard the bishop of the diocese bless the Iroquois Hunt in Lexington, Kentucky, one hot October morning. He was dressed in a crimson cassock with black sash around his ample belly, and he looked very splendid leaning on his tall staff tipped with a silver crook. Before the bishop some ten couple of hounds roamed round and round in a tight circle, held in check by the master (a fine, scarlet Toad of Toad Hall) and by the huntsmen and whips, and *they* were all dressed in formal pinks with black velvet collars indicative of their hunt.

---

the seventh fence and was lying groggily on the ground, Mrs. Randolph drove up in a blue Jaguar, picked him up, and without asking how he felt told him he should know better than to ride bad horses. She said she would send him to Mikey Smithwick in Maryland who trained her horses and who would teach Tommy what racing was about. Eventually he took her up on the offer.

Beyond the horses, the members of the hunt, each at his horse's bridle, bowed their heads.

"As nearly as I can figure it," said the bishop, beaming at his congregation in the unseasonable, steaming heat, "as nearly as I can figure it, and I'm not very good at figures" (appreciative laughter) "–as anyone who knows me can attest–"(more laughter) "–this is the thirtieth time I have blessed the hunt. In celebration of that happy event," he continued, "I'm going to read two short poems of mine that may be familiar to some of you assembled here today...."

One poem was called "The Choir Invisible," and began:

> One fine day in spring, as I walked out,
> I heard a wild bird sing.
> He sang so piercing clear and sweet
> As though an Angel sang.

It concluded that "The choir invisible I hear ... under the Greenwood Tree."

The other poem was about running the race until the day we join the Great Race.

Then he blessed the hounds and field: "Bless, O Lord ..."

The tradition of private packs of hounds dates back to the time when Lord Baltimore required each family settling in Maryland to bring in one dog (and Robert Brook, who arrived in June of 1650, only six years after the founding of this idealistic palatinate, brought with him his wife, eight sons, two daughters, twenty-eight servants, and a pack of hounds). The native gray fox was hunted in those days, the first red fox not being imported to the Eastern Shore from England until 1730, two years before the birth of George Washington.

For two hundred years, all hunting was done by private

hounds, each farmer bringing a few dogs to a hunt to make up what in England is called a trencher fed pack (meaning fed from a trough or trencher). And in Maryland, especially on the Eastern Shore, you can still walk through the woods and come on an open truck and a couple of cars with dog cages in the back, evidence that somewhere out there a hunt is taking place.

Most hunting today, however, centers around the 133 hunts in the United States recognized by the MFH Association, and another nine registered as starting up. Very very few packs, perhaps no more than six or seven, are privately owned anymore, and some can hardly be called private, for a man may own hounds, for example, as Hardaway does, but defray expenses with the income from the followers of his hunt. Most packs are owned by committees or clubs, and there are two reasons for this. First, keeping a pack is troublesome, for hounds must be exercised twice a day, trained, groomed, fed, and treated by a vet. Second, it is expensive. Depending on the size of the field and how well the country is maintained, a hunt can cost anywhere from a couple of thousand dollars to fifty or sixty thousand a year. I could not discover the cost of wholly maintaining a private pack. It's the sort of question that makes eyes slither to the far corners of a room, as occurred, for example, with Wilbur Ross Hubbard, who has kept his pack on the Eastern Shore in Maryland since 1931. Mr. Hubbard's hounds are maintained entirely as a private pack. His thirty-five couple are reduced to twenty-five couple now. A staff of three takes care of them.

Mr. Hubbard is nearly eighty years old, a short, stocky man who looks about sixty. He hunts three and sometimes four times a week. A bachelor, a Yale graduate, a lieutenant in the horse-drawn field artillery of World War I, he traces his family back ten generations on the Eastern Shore, his direct male ancestor having purchased land there, he says, in September of

1674. Mr. Hubbard lives now in the Georgian townhouse that his father bought early in the century, where the door handles and hardware are made of sterling silver and the formal gardens roll down to the river as if in eighteenth-century London. His mother was a Ross of Ballangow Castle, Scotland (recently bought by Arab oil, he says); of his father he is more reticent. For which his friends crow loudly, quick to report that the family fortune was made in the rendering business, grinding up horses for fertilizer. I won't swear that this is true. Mr. Hubbard wouldn't say.

Mr. Hubbard was a member of the Maryland legislature in his youth, studied and practiced law and eventually went to Baltimore, where he became president of a chemical business and an oyster-shell company, the latter being for chicken feed, to make the hens lay. In his sixties he retired to the Eastern Shore, dedicating himself, as is so often the pattern among this propertied group, to the historic preservation of old fine houses and a gracious way of life.

But his pride is his hunt. He is "the dean of the American Masters of Fox Hounds." For forty-five years he has owned hounds.

Mr. Hubbard is not the only master of a private pack. Others hunt from Long Island to Aiken, South Carolina. These Long Island and Aiken people, however, live in a more opulent style than that of Maryland and Virginia. I didn't meet them until I went away to school. If they startled me then, they remain unceasingly surprising. I have heard, for example (and hardly doubt the tale), of one Long Island dowager who periodically has the trees moved on her North Shore lawn—giant maples, full-grown oaks—lest she tire of the view. Or another Long Islander, this time a man, whose servants, when they lay out his clothes and turn his bed down each night, put the toothpaste on his brush for him. But this, by our Maryland or Virginia standards, seems as outlandish as ... as King Ak-Sar-Ben (Nebraska spelled backwards), who dances in his silver, bejeweled costume to promote that corn state at the annual Mardi Gras, a festival of rodeos, and Ice Capades, where little children dress up as pages and princesses, while diamond-tiaraed countesses escort the queen to the coronation citadel, dance at the cotillions, and win the contests that mark Ak-Sar-Ben events.

On Continuity

By now you're wondering who are the landed gentry and who we're talking about. A time for definitions.

Wealth relates to land in two ways. First, there is the fortune based on land, what Henry George termed the Basic Economic Unit. Second is the fortune based on commerce and manufacturing, on urban activities that provide the means to buy an estate, a tax shelter farm, a ranch, an island, a walled retreat.

The matter can be stated from a human point of view. Some people base their fortunes and derive their principal income from their land. Either they live on the land that has been in their families for generations, or, as absentee landlords, they own land whose purpose is to generate income—from grazing, oil, mining, timber, agriculture.

Other people live on estates that serve to represent their wealth in the Thorstein Veblen senses of consumption and display.

In America, both types may be "landed," and both are

bound by the shared values of established wealth. What they
are not (and therefore what this book is not about) is nouveau,
although most urban-based wealth eventually returns to the
country in the purchase of land, just as landed wealth turns
sooner or later to the city to increase and diversify its
investment base. There is, you understand, a certain inter-
change, a blurring of lines, because the bonds of the landed
gentry lie not in their differences but their similarities–their
sense of continuity and class. What we are talking about
encompasses two ideas. First is the reality of land, second is a
state of mind, an emotional tie to land, power, continuity, and
values that -form a direct handhold to the history of the
country. Implicit in the term is power. This point is often
overlooked or else obscured in a compulsive fog of ever-
narrowing definitions.

"The landed gentry?" people would say as I worked on this
book. "But we haven't any *land:* a few hundred acres–" (Or a
few thousand or a few tens of thousands of acres.) "You should
talk to Mr. C down the road. Now *he* has a big place."

And always, the half-curious, half-suspicious questioning:
"Who else are you seeing? Does Rockefeller belong?" I'd be
asked. Or, "Where is Whitney?" or "What about people like
the Fleishhackers of San Francisco, who gave that zoo to the
city. Do they belong?" You can see how too much can be
made of the size of land. What is large in the East at a few
thousand acres is pitifully small in the West, while for sheer
financial return the seventeen acres of Rockefeller Center in the
middle of Manhattan may be more profitable than a hundred
thousand acres of Western scrub. It is not land alone, then,
that we are talking about, for if our group is defined only in
terms of land and how large it is and where it lies, we end up
looking at larger and larger parcels owned by fewer and fewer

people until soon almost no one belongs to the group except perhaps the final questioner himself. No, what we are talking about is class. No blacks belong to this group at all. Occasionally–how rarely–we run across a Jew. We know him because everyone points him out, feeling altogether generous in expounding the mobility of our American social system.

Landed as opposed to urban. Gentry as opposed to farmers. *The London Observer* of 13 April 1806 reports that a gentleman was brought before a magistrate for "profane swearing," having "damned the clergyman's eyes." Facing a fifteen shilling fine, the man argued that he shouldn't have to pay more than one shilling, since he wasn't a gentleman. But the judge overruled him on the grounds that "he kept his spaniel dogs and took his wine at dinner."

The word "gentry" implies a certain pretension, an expectation of a way of life; which is why plain farmers do not come into the purview of this book, though some may own and lease more than most gentlemen could imagine possessing: a Nebraska farmer may till 100,000 acres, and a yeoman in South Carolina may own 800 acres and lease another 2,500 from the absentee gentry, but neither aspires to the state of mind, the style required of the propertied class.

One last group is worth mentioning in regard to land, even if we remain true to the English definition of gentry as anyone with 350 acres of land or more*–and that consists of those whose families once held estates but today have none at all. They live in apartments in large cities and mingle with the gentry to varying degrees, life being more complex and disorderly than the compulsive tidiness of writers and editors

---

* Burke's *Landed Gentry* listed 4,500 English families with such property in 1952–a figure that by the 1970s had grown to 21,000.

would prefer. Purists who would deny the dispossessed a place among the "landed" should remember that these are often more determinedly "gentry" and more dedicatedly "landed" than any of the types above, like flies frozen in amber memory.

Begin with memory, then, for memory was already exerting its pull when the first English adventurers sailed up the James River in 1607 or marvelled at the generosity of the Chesapeake Bay, so broad in places that no shore could be seen on any side. These first adventurers already brought with them a memory of sweeping English parks. Private parks they were. Memories of great houses built of stone and brick that stood rooted on hilltops surveying valley, woods, and lakes. Of crennelated towers and razor roofs, and of interiors with wide hallways and panelled rooms where liveried servants carried hot water and linens and sweets on silver trays. That this idea has persisted in the South is a cliché; that it took different form in New England is equally known. That it still exerts a fascination is less widely accepted. But here we are today, still a nation of immigrants, our dreams based on memories and our memories filled with dreams of a European aristocratic tradition, whether English or French or Russian or Polish. Yes, right to the present day they came to build a landed life.

We find, for example, Eric Kauders,* who arrived penniless in this country in 1932, made his money as a designer and inventor in manufacturing, and together with some twenty-five others bought shares in the Blue Mountain Forest Association, or Corbin Park, a club that owns 24,000 acres in New Hampshire. It has a chain-link fence around it and is stocked with game as a private shooting preserve, residuum of feudal Europe.

* His son, Andrew Kauders, recently bought a piece of land in the Tidewater of Virginia, title to which had never changed hands since the land grant.

Another immigrant, Thomas Wyman, went one better. Brought up in Czechoslavakia and educated in England, he came to America with the ambition of becoming a gentleman farmer: an ambition achieved moreover with his 1150 acres on the Eastern Shore, his private pack of foxhounds, his two-hundred-year-old house with the massive box bushes and formal gardens sweeping to the Wye River, his white Lippizaner stallions, his buffalo and fallow deer grazing under the huge trees in a park all neatly clipped and clear of undergrowth according to the European style. True, his ambition must be supported, as is usually the case in America, by a job on the side. But the motivating force of memory is not for that reason to be belittled.

Land was the first basis of wealth in America. Look back three hundred years to Virginia, when a few families owned miles. The names are still well known today: Byrd, Carter, Harrison, Lee. These families were all in the colony before the Cavalier influx of 1640–1660. They were hard-working, conservative, ambitious farmers, though when the modern descendant looks proudly back across the centuries, he tends to be stopped, pulled up short in his imagination around 1750, dazzled by the power and glory of that Colonial wealth.

A landed aristocracy was entrenched in Virginia by Bacon's Rebellion of 1676. Richard Lee of Northumberland County owned 20,000 acres; William Fitzhugh, 50,000. Robert "King" Carter, the richest man in Virginia in his time, acquired a staggering 300,000 acres and built five dynastic mansions for his sons (and still he could not come close to the Patroon van Rensselaer, who is said to have owned a million acres along the Hudson River in New York. Sailing ships dipped their flags as they passed van Rensselaer land and undoubtedly paid a toll as well).

An aristocratic political machine controlled the country. By 1770, membership in the House of Burgesses was virtually self-perpetuating, inherited even, since voting was done vocally in the presence of the candidates. It would take a brave freeholder to vote against the plantation master and colonel of the local militia while looking him smack in the eye.*

Memory, however, is mortal fickle, and when the Byrds, for example, look back on their family now, they do not pause fondly on the fact (indeed it is only human nature to forget) that William Byrd I, the most successful of the Indian traders, acquired 26,000 acres of land in his capacity as escheator and forgave himself all taxes. No, they remember instead that he donated the land on which to found the city of Richmond; that, except for two generations, a Byrd has sat for three hundred years in the state assembly; that the Byrds built Westover, the magnificent estate on the James River, driving the family into debt to do so. (But debt was not uncommon; when Mann Page, who married Judith Carter, daughter of "King" Carter, built Roswell in Gloucester County, the family was impoverished for two generations by the expense and ultimately forced to sell.)

They were very serious about acquiring property, our ancestors. When George Washington retired from the presidency, he was one of the richest men in the country, claiming not only Mt. Vernon, which he had inherited from his brother Laurence, but properties in Princess Anne and Westmoreland counties as well. He claimed 20,000 acres between the Allegheny and Ohio rivers. Some were earned as a bounty for fighting during the Seven Years' War; others were picked up at trifling prices from poverty-ridden soldiers forced to sell their

* To this day, the Virginia State Assembly has never ratified the Seventeenth Amendment to the Constitution, establishing in 1913 the direct popular election of senators.

shares. It was a sign of his wealth that he could afford to buy the lands and wait patiently, sometimes for years, to turn a profit. He knew also how to work a shady deal, as one would expect from a young man serious enough to order from London a book entitled *A Speedy Way to Grow Rich.*

Holmes Alexander, in his book *Washington and Lee,* recounts that when, by the treaty of 1763 between the British and the Indians, no whites were allowed into Indian territory, Washington "connived" with William Crawford to send him into the area with orders to pick out 2,000 acres of the best land "under the guise of hunting other game," and "to keep the whole matter secret."

If land, as Winston Churchill said, is the "mother of all other forms of monopoly," fraud in America was the basic method of obtaining it. At the end of the eighteenth century, in 1795, we find such wondrous deals as the Yazoo land frauds, the biggest land deal in our history, where some thirty million acres, consisting of nearly the entire area of Mississippi and Alabama, were sold by the Georgia legislature to four speculation companies for one-and-a-half cents an acre—and resold as prime farmland to thousands of gullible fools. Every member but one of the Georgia legislature had a personal interest in the speculation.*

Or we find Henry Miller, a German immigrant, who arrived in San Francisco in 1850 with six dollars in his pocket and, by the simple expedient of gaining control of water rights, amassed before his death an empire—a million acres in five

* The act was rescinded in 1796 in the face of popular indignation at the fraud, while influential Northerners urged the federal government to nullify the rescinding act itself. In 1802, Georgia surrendered the lands to the federal government. In 1810, the U.S. Supreme Court upheld the original 1795 act of sale, holding the rescinding act unconstitutional, this being the first time the Supreme Court had held any state law unconstitutional. In 1814, Congress indemnified the holders of the grants for their losses.

states—an area larger than Rhode Island. And on it were a
million head of cattle. The Miller & Lux Corporation today still
owns 93,058 acres.

Or we look at the partners, James Ben Ali Haggin and Lloyd
Tevis, who by stealthy manipulation of the Desert Land Act of
1877 acquired in one act 150 *square miles* of lush river valley in
California.

All of this has been written about in other publications. I
mention it merely to illustrate how values change, how, as Lord
Burghley said, "Gentilitie is naught but ancient riches."

Many of these vast landholdings are owned today as
corporations. The Haggin-Tevis partnership, expanding eventually to one-and-a-half million acres, was larger than the King
Ranch in its prime. In 1967 it was bought by Tenneco and is
still roughly intact. Continuity, gigantism: the two forces
combine.

In 1959, James Julian Coleman, Jr., bought 33,000 acres, or
fifty square miles, all within the limits of New Orleans. The
land had been held in the same family since the 1700s.

What we have, in effect, is still a land monopoly, as firmly
entrenched as ever, a nonresident landed aristocracy, often
under the guise of a company, which itself is owned by some
other corporation. The trend toward corporate ownership
surrounds us. Minute Maid, a subsidiary of Coca-Cola, and
Libby, McNeil & Libby together own 20 percent of the Florida
citrus groves. Half the agricultural land in California and three-
quarters of the best irrigated land is held by forty-five corporate
farms.

Statisticians point out the landholding patterns by corporations so frequently that we tend to overlook the corollary:
living people run them, diverting their income to living heirs.
It is these heirs who live as gentlemen in modest privacy,
abhorring publicity, rooted, unaware themselves, I think, of

their privileges. They are quiet, unflashy people. And since you do not see them on TV and certainly never read of them in the papers, since you cannot see their estates as you speed along the superhighways, and since you accept as true the proposition that all our lands are being swallowed by developments, the majority of our population now clustered in suburbs and cities, the fact of continuity is overlooked.

In part, this is the fault of the media that concentrate only on change—that being the definition of the news. We are bombarded by future shock, by changes in schools, in roads, in power, in transportation, in commerce, in fashion—each change demanding purchase of another paper—and also by changes in ideas, in how to think about women, about labor, about minorities, about economics, about whites. We see huge fortunes rising in the cities, and populations shifting to suburbs, and families crumbling, and sexual restrictions replaced by sexual license (though with no less danger of impregnation or disease)—and every day we proclaim the world a different place.

Do you remember the wonder and astonishment with which the media first "discovered" the background of Jimmy Carter, whose family had owned the same land in Plains since they came to Georgia 200 years ago, who himself, with his mother and brother in partnership, owned the town warehouse business, grossing two-and-a-half million dollars a year, whose uncle owned a worm farm in the same vicinity, whose brother ran the gas station, and another uncle the local antique store—whose family, in effect, controlled (to the awe of the urban press) the town of Plains?

They had not seen such rootedness before. Yet Joseph Lelyveld, a reporter on the *New York Times,* talked to a man on Smith Island, Maryland, who has not been off the island in thirty years, nor crossed it in five.

People like to stay in one place. Not long ago on the Eastern Shore, a lawyer, Philip Nabb, whose family had moved four generations ago from Talbot to the adjoining Dorchester County, was asked if he planned to return to be buried in Talbot County.

And still the media tell us all the time of change. When *Roots* was broadcast over TV in its marathon run in early 1977, the *Washington Post* ran an article on Judge A. (for Absalom) Nelson Waller, seventy-three, of Spotsylvania, Virginia, whose ancestors in that flat, rural farmland sixty miles from Washington, D.C., had owned author Alex Haley's ancestors. The reporter, Kenneth Avery Ringle, scion of Avery Island, had his own reasons, perhaps, for seeing only change in Spotsylvania County, where the population has nearly doubled in the past seven years, from 16,000 to 29,000, 20 percent being black, and where job training programs and a public welfare system are now installed. But Julia A. Thompson, eighty-four, remembers her grandmother telling about "being autioned off on a block in Charles Town, West Virginia," before coming as a slave to the Wallers. Mrs. Thompson's daughter-in-law, like her people before her, does housework for Waller, who has been general district judge for more than thirty years, and who traces his English ancestry back to the Battle of Agincourt; and Waller's family, two centuries later, still owns today the land that Kunta Kinte worked.

Virginia is our oldest colony, our best exemplar of the flow of social patterns. How curious to discover that many of the powerful families in Virginia today held power during the Civil War, that many of these could trace their power to the Revolution and their ancestry back another one hundred years to the Tidewater planters, whose lands formed the basis of the

Colonial economy and who held total oligarchical control in their time.

Think of that. Three ideas lie dormant in the thought, and all three go against the grain of modern democratic myth. One is the continuity of power once attained. Over the course of three hundred years, we see the sweep of generations, like billows rising, falling, on the sea, richer, poorer, stronger, weaker. But somehow the *families* do not drown. Old blood grows apathetic, thinned out with alcohol and debauchery, which is why "good, strong peasant stock" is so much praised in old families, good for marrying into old blood, revitalizing and preserving it. While power may pass, therefore, to new names, the old names do not die out entirely. They continue, sometimes without either money or power, to maintain a fragile position in "nice" society. An aristocracy of caste.

Second is the strength of family ties, even in times like ours of social strain. It is perhaps most evident in the South, where despite the periodic rallying cries about the New South rising, the Old South continues to trace cousins and kin, marriages and deaths, putting each person into place like a straying hairdo. Sorting out the cousins on meeting becomes a kind of soothing ritual, like two dogs wagging their tails as they sniff noses.

It is not to be laughed at. Strength is somehow drawn from these memories.

Third, perhaps most often missed in any discussion of family, is how close we are to the past. My own grandmother told me in the 1960s (when she was in her eighties) that she had shaken the hand of a soldier who fought at the Battle of Waterloo.

Harrison Tyler of Richmond, president of the Chemical Treatment Company, was only forty-six when I met him in

1974. He was handsome, athletic, an avid tennis player. Yet his father was born in 1853 and his grandfather in 1790. That was a *hundred and eighty years ago.* It hardly seems possible. His father was seventy-five in 1928 when Tyler was born (his mother, thank heavens, being a second wife). His brothers predate him by forty years.

One day a few years ago, Tyler's pretty South Carolina wife, Paynie, was walking with her brother-in-law in Annapolis, supporting the eighty-year-old gentleman on one arm, when an acquaintance came doddering toward them on a cane. "Have you met my brother's new young wife?" said the old man with malicious humor.

Harrison Tyler is the grandson of the President John Tyler, who ran on the 1841 Whig ticket with William Henry Harrison ("Tippecanoe and Tyler too"). William Henry, son of "The Signer" and three-time governor of Virginia, was born at the family plantation of Berkeley, but left Virginia to make his fortune in Ohio. In his campaign for president, thousands of handkerchiefs were printed showing the log-cabin birthplace of this scion of Virginia aristocracy. With free hard cider doled out to the crowds and a jingle about his opponent, Martin Van Buren ("Van, Van is a Used-up Man"), Harrison swept to Populist victory.

On his way to Washington, he stopped off at Berkeley Plantation. By then the manor house was decaying, owned outright by the Bank of the United States on a $20,000 debt. It was not to be much longer in the family. In his mother's bedroom, Harrison wrote his inaugural address, delivery of which constituted his sole act as president, for, having caught pneumonia during the inaugural parade, he died. The presidency fell to his running mate on this Populist ticket, John Tyler, whose family owned the neighboring Tidewater plantation of Sherwood Forest.

Tyler may be remembered for having eloped from the White House at the age of fifty with his ward, twenty-four-year-old Julia Gardiner (of Gardiner's Island off Long Island). Julia's father was a senator and a friend of the president, and when he died (blown up he was, together with other dignitaries, during dedication ceremonies for a new weapon), his daughter moved to the White House to distract the president from his executive duties.*

Later, during the War (which in the South always means the War Between the States), Julia found herself a widow with seven children at Sherwood Forest. She was alone during one Yankee raid and decided she would never be found there alone again. She packed a wagon with her silk and satin gowns and all the wine from the wine cellar (an understatement: it was a two-story house, chock-full of valuable vintages) and drove with her children to Richmond. There she sold her clothes and wine for five thousand dollars, invested the money in cotton, and sailed her cargo *herself* on a ship through the Union blockade to Bermuda to sell the cotton. After this, she returned through the blockade to Richmond, picked up her children, and escaped to the North.

Such memories form the very lifeblood of the Virginia aristocracy, and this one is only one of many, but unusual in having a Yankee for a heroine. Today, her great-granddaughter, Julia Gardiner Tyler, lives in Richmond. She appeared in *Town & Country* not long ago, dressed in riding habit and seated in the empty hallway of the derelict plantation, Sherwood Forest, which the Tylers have just brought back into the family and plan to restore.

Meanwhile, Gardiner's Island, from which she takes her

* It is said she was instrumental in securing annexation of Texas in 1845, just after Tyler left office, a feat she accomplished partly in the bedrooms of men other than her husband.

name, is likewise still in private hands, an American fiefdom held in the same hands for three-hundred-and-forty-some years, though Robert David Lion Gardiner, sixteenth Lord of the Manor, being himself without heirs, is trying now to have the 3,300-acre island declared a state or federal park. This is another characteristic of the propertied class. If taxes prevent the maintenance of private manors, they throw them to the public trust.

Gardiner's Island, which lies seven miles off the tip of Long Island, is seven miles long and three miles in breadth at the widest point. At one time, the Gardiners owned another 78,000 acres of Long Island as well, running from Montauk to Flushing. When Mr. Gardiner sold some land to create a shopping center and the lawyers asked to see the deed, Mr. Gardiner showed it—signed by the Indians.

Gardiner's Island, with its twenty-eight-room Georgian manor house, is closed to the public. At the private airstrip is a sign: PLEASE LEAVE, and three men patrol the island with shotguns. It is so private that Jock Mackey, chief caretaker, who has lived on the island since 1929, once ousted David, Laurance, and Nelson Rockefeller, whose yacht bobbed at anchor while they spread a picnic on the beach.

"I don't care if your name is Astorbilt," said Mackey in his Scottish accent. "Get off the island." The Gardiners rarely use the island now except on weekends or an occasional hunt in the fall. Otherwise, they are found at the $750,000 house in Palm Beach, Florida, or the mansion in East Hampton. Gardiner, a man in his sixties, has a portfolio of blue chip stocks, including some IBM stock that he bought for $14,000 in 1932 that is worth nearly $4 million today. He owns a Long Island shopping center that earns about $1.5 million annually, and he pays $460,000 a year in taxes.

"And then people ask what I do for a living. Don't they

realize the responsibility of administering that much money?" he said to a reporter from the *Baltimore Sun*. "If I had sat on my bottom I wouldn't be where I am today.

"The Gardiner family has always done that," he added, meaning watched their money. "That's the remarkable thing. We were into farming when that was profitable. We were into railroads when they were profitable, and we got out when they weren't."

So our propertied class have money often running out of their ears, and old places, and family roots; and the same education and an outlook that is only slightly left of Louis XIV, and a preference for an eighteenth-century life. It is only natural, therefore, to find them gathering imperiously into the 134 societies and genealogical orders that mark our democratic way of life. There is the DAR, the Sons of the American Revolution, the General Society of Mayflower Descendants, the Sons of the Cincinnati, Descendants of the Signers of the Declaration of Independence, the Order of Three Crusades 1096–1192, the Descendants of Illegitimate Sons and Daughters of Kings of Britain, and the Society of the Whiskey Rebellion, to name only a few. There is also the Order of the Crown of Charlemagne in the U.S.A. and the Baronial Order of the Magna Carta. Of them all, my favorite will always be the Order of First Families of Virginia.

The Order of the F.F.V.

Not long ago, I was working on an article for *Town & Country* on what are called the First Families of Virginia.

All my life I had heard of the F.F.V. I had finished my research and written half an article, based on the premise there is no official organization, when I learned of the Order of First Families of Virginia. Immediately, I made some calls, and one day the president, Mrs. Guy Withers, came to my house in Washington, her arms filled with books and pamphlets, to tell about it. A gentle, dignified, elderly lady she was. On her wrist was an antique gold watch that I took to be her grandmother's, around her neck, a lavalliere.

"I think it is so nice of *Town & Country* to send you to do an article about our order," she said shyly. "How did they hear of us?"

"Well, it isn't *entirely* on the order exactly," I answered.

This surprised her: "But I thought you said the article was about First Families of Virginia?"

"Yes."

"But then—I don't see. . . ."

Nonetheless, she told me about the order, which is composed of those people who can prove their descent from the 120 settlers in Virginia who arrived between 1607 and the first census, or Muster, of 1625 and who left children. The order was instituted in 1912, "for the specific purpose of reviving and preserving for the honor of the Nation, its unique distinction of having been founded by men and women 'of dignity and consequence. . . .' "

Mrs. Withers would not divulge the names of the members of the order, for that would be indelicate, an invasion of privacy. But she did not object to my asking how many members there were.

"We have twelve hundred and fifty," she smiled.

"Twelve hundred and fifty! That's a lot." I admit I was surprised.

"Oh," she added quickly. "But not all of them are still living."

"Oh."

"They come in," she nodded, "and they go out." We thought about that for a moment quietly.

"Well, how many members do you have who are still alive?"

"Seven hundred and fifty," she answered, "in *all* the states of the Union." Some of the members are charter members and, therefore, you can see, no longer in good health.

We talked for an hour, I suppose, with Mrs. Withers recounting the horrors of those early adventurers, before Virginia was even a Colony, and a little bit, modestly, about her own family, who came to Virginia from the Eastern Shore and who are omitted for some reason from the 1625 Muster, although other records show (and therefore eligibility in the order is permitted) that the family was in Virginia at the time.

Mrs. Withers is also a member of the National Society of Colonial Dames (which split with Colonial Dames of America over the question of whether the illegitimate children of Ben Franklin could join), as well as of the DAR, "a very democratic organization," she approved. "Not like some of them."

Suddenly I was struck with a thought so bold and daring in its conception that it took my breath away: the conclusion of my researches!

"But isn't it wonderful, just think! What does it say about the mobility, the social fluidness of our system—isn't it wonderful!—that of all the people who came over before 1625— and they were nobody—merchants and grocers and had no money at all, that *all* of their descendants became ... um ... nice people."

"What do you mean?"

"Well, I don't know—do you think—have you ever heard of a ... what would you do," I finally stumbled on the phrasing, "if a laborer, a bricklayer, came to your order and could prove that his ancestors were here before the Muster?"

"A laborer!" She reeled back against the couch. "A laborer! Do you believe in having a laborer in your organization? This is a very select group. Of course we would not have a laborer!"

"Oh." I was confounded. "I thought you said that the order was based on descent, and—"

So then she explained how each member must be recommended by an existing member and seconded by two others (though the seconds may live in other states), and how if the initiate could prove her (or his, for the organization plays no favorites by sex) ancestry, then an invitation to join would be extended.

I was disappointed. I told her how the very first person I'd

met on moving to Washington was the gardener who worked
next door, who had regaled me for twenty minutes on how his
family had come to Maryland in the 1630s. Mrs. Withers was
very interested and wondered who he was.

I asked, "Have you ever heard of ... of ... a commoner [for
by then my language had taken on the same archaic flavor as
her own] who...." Whereat she told the following story:

"When General MacArthur left the Pacific, he had a
parade," she said, sitting erect and fine on the sofa, "and he was
going to speak at the DAR. I wanted to see him. I don't
usually go to parades, but there were two I wanted to see—
MacArthur's and Eisenhower's—and I saw them both. Now I
am a member of the DAR, but I was not a delegate and so I
couldn't sit in the auditorium for his talk, but I went to stand
on the steps to see him pass. And while I was there I heard a
man nearby say something. He was just a ... a man of the
streets, you know, with no coat or tie. A man of the streets. I
don't remember what he said, but afterwards he added: 'And I
should know, because my family came over in 1618!' "

"What did you do? Did you ask him who he was?"

She shook her head. "No. I didn't say a word."

"Oh, Mrs. Withers," I laughed. "You chicken. How could
you resist!"

"I am *not* a chicken." She drew herself up.

"Oh yes," I teased. "You were afraid. You were afraid he
might be related ... to a friend...."

"To my family," she blushed. "Well, I didn't say a word. I
would do it *now*," she defended herself. "But I was much
younger then."

Who Owns Our Land?

Once Ralph Nader asked the U.S. Department of Agriculture for information on the percentage of people who own land in the country. He was asking, in other words, for figures showing the concentration of land ownership in America. He was told no such figures were available. It seems no one knows who owns the land in America.

"Well, do you have them for Gambia?" Nader asked. "Or Guatemala?"

Oh yes, the Foreign Agricultural Service had these at its fingertips. Nader was astonished.

"But why aren't there figures like these for the United States?"

"It would be very embarrassing," came the response. "Because in some areas of the country, the concentration of land ownership is comparable to that of South America."

There has never been a census of land in the United States.

The information simply does not exist. Not in the Department of Agriculture, which formulates and oversees our policy concerning land. Not in the Internal Revenue Service, which collects our taxes, not even in the Bureau of Census, which provides the other agencies of government with the information needed to make laws and administer them.

Moreover, to collect information on who owns land, even in a single state, would be a massive undertaking, for no single source for such data exists. To collect it for the country would require all the resources of Congress and much more courage and dedication than our elected officials can afford to demonstrate. You would have to go to every courthouse in every one of the 3,141 counties of the United States and trace each tract of land to determine the owner. Even then the information would not be complete, because some owners are hidden under trusts and corporate entities disguised, in turn by other corporations. Forty out of fifty states have no information on land ownership, and what there is, according to one spokesman at the U. S. Department of Agriculture, "isn't worth a damn."*

I do not mean that we don't know a lot about land ownership in our country—the general characteristics of owners, the number of owner-operated and non-owner-operated farms. We know about the size of farms and the produce they yield and the values of land. We know the pattern of farm and ranch ownership—individual or family or corporation or partnership or "other." We know that the "average" farm in the United States is about 440 acres. In some states, we know the sex of farm owners, their age, income, and place of residence. Information such as this has been collected by the Department of Agriculture since the 1880s, and it is updated every five years

---

* The Economic Research Service of the U. S. Department of Agriculture began in late 1977 a projected two-year sample survey of 60,000 owners of land randomly selected across the country by a "pin-point" system. But it is not a land census.

and distributed in long, blinding computer printouts. So we have a good idea of ownership patterns.

What we don't know are the names of those who own the land or how much each man owns.

If no land census has ever been taken in the United States, two have been made in England. The first was made in 1086 by William the Conqueror. It is the famous Domesday Book, the name and date of which are reverently memorized by school-children in many an English-speaking country around the world.

The second was ordered 800 years later in 1873, when Lord Derby decided to demonstrate to a skeptical public the relatively widespread ownership of English farms. And guess what he found. Land ownership had hardly changed at all. The same families owned the land in 1873 who had owned it around 1086.

The New Domesday Book disclosed more than that. Four-fifths of the land was owned by 7,000 people in England. Ninety percent of the peers owned sizeable sections of the country and about twenty peers owned lands in the quantum of 100,000 acres or more.

The census was not repeated.

Since that time hardly a nobleman has managed to maintain his former estates, yet "[t]he lordly classes," according to Roy Perrott in *The Aristocrats*, a 1967 study of the British aristocracy, "remain easily the biggest private and individual landowners in the country." *

Before trying to sketch–at least impressionistically–some patterns of land ownership in America and some characteristics

---

* One-third of the peerage, about 350 lords, "still own enough land to provide a significant element in their income and outlook." We find the Viscount Bolingbroke, who had 3,300 acres listed in 1873 and now lists 4,000; and the Duke of Beaufort with 52,000 acres (up from 51,000 in 1873), and Lord Bolton with

of those who own the land, I offer one caveat: I am not a
radical. Nor have I any coherent position on the redistribution
of money and land. I'm obliged to tell you this because so
many people bring the subject up.

"Well, what would you suggest? You want a massive
redistribution of land, I suppose? Is that what you want?"

Actually, I have nothing to suggest. Except a census. We
should have that. As for reform, I've never noticed it to work,
given the knack of human beings to work any situation around
to their own advantage. It's a virtue, this characteristic. Or it
can be. Useful for survival. But hell on reform and change.

All right. The land.

In New York City, down in Greenwich Village, there's a
little triangular park at the Women's House of Detention, all
prettily landscaped and laid out with walks and shrubbery and
grass. Around it rises an eight-foot chain-link fence to keep the
people out. Because they'd destroy it. You can link your fingers
through the holes in the fence and peer through at the
greenery. That's how precious is space in the city. Land, our
scarcest urban resource.

Once, walking down the street in New York, I was passed
by a gang of teenage boys, swinging loose and easy down the
cement sidewalk.

"Have you ever been in the country?" asked one.

18,500 acres, or the Duke of Northumberland with 80,000 acres, or the Earl of
Durham with 30,000; and in Scotland the Countess of Sutherland, whose land has
been reduced to 138,000 from 1,358,000 acres. In Scotland, the land is held in larger
increments than in England and Wales. There is also the Duke of Buccleuch with
220,000 acres (reduced from 460,000), Lord Lovat with 160,000, the Earl of Cawdor
with 50,000. Run your startled eye down the list of figures compiled in 1967 and you
are filled with awe at such acreage in areas so small as England, Scotland, and Wales.
Eleven thousand acres, 7,000 acres, 10,000, 24,000, 99,000. In London itself property
is listed in acres: 300, 100, 90, 30.

"Yeah. I was there once. Up near Van Cortlandt Park. There was a lot of grass and stuff. It was creepy."

If no one knows the names of the landowners in the United States or the amount of land they hold, one thing we do know: the total number of owners of agricultural land. They are fewer than 4.3 million people. Out of a population of 216 million, they represent therefore about 2 percent of the population (and eight percent of the households). Many, it appears, are nonresidents of their land, composed of such diverse types as Robert Orville Anderson, son of a prominent Chicago banker and chairman of the Atlantic Richfield Company (ARCO), who individually owns more than a million acres of working cattle ranches in New Mexico, Texas, and Colorado; or George Weyerhauser, president of the $1.7 billion Weyerhauser (timber) Corporation, which alone owns 1/500th of the land mass of the continental United States—it owns 5.7 million acres, or 8,124 square miles of forest in the United States and foreign countries, including investments in Southeast Asia.

Oh yes, periodically we catch a glimpse of property ownership, like the white spume flashing off a wave. One half the states of Maine is said to be owned by paper companies. Fly from Palm Springs to New York, runs one adage, and you are never out of sight of Phipps * land. The Phippses, according to one book, "own more of the Eastern land mass of the United States" from Long Island to Florida than any other private holder. Is it true? When I wrote the author for documentation, I received no answer. The Gerrys of Long Island, the Bradys of New Jersey are both said to have large holdings.

---

* The original Henry Phipps was the accountant for his childhood friend, Andrew Carnegie, and, with an $800 investment in the fledgling Kloman Company in the mid-nineteenth century, which J. P. Morgan would later buy for $250 million and rename U.S. Steel, he made a fortune of $50 million.

He was, by all accounts, a miser, feeling none of Carnegie's sense of responsibility

The Rockefellers own 3,600 acres at Pocantico Hills in
Westchester County, in New York. This is one of the most
expensive real estate markets in the world. Nelson Rockefeller,
the former governor of New York, the former vice president of
the United States, who, in 1974, estimated his personal wealth
at $218 million, maintains, in addition, a Fifth Avenue duplex
in New York City, a ranch in Venezuela, a place in Washington, and a summer house in Seal Harbor, Maine. But these
are for his personal use only. Who knows the extent of the
Rockefeller family holdings? The family has established almost
a pattern of development, by which they will buy a thousand
acres in Jackson Hole, Wyoming, or on St. John, or in Arcadia
in Maine, or in Vermont, or Mauna Kea, Hawaii, build their
private houses to one side, a resort in the center, and surround
the place with a national forest. They are the fourth generation
of a family tied to land, inasmuch as they have created more
national parks than any other private individual.

Or we glimpse the holdings of Cornelius Vanderbilt
Whitney, "Sonny," who on his father's death inherited the
controlling interest in the Hudson Bay Mining and Smelting
Company, perhaps the largest silver, copper, and zinc producer
in the world. He has 100,000 acres of forest land in the

---

for the men who worked twelve hours a day, six days a week in the "little hells of
steel" that he and his partner developed; on his death he gave away $7 million in
charity, "to lighten the workingman's lot both at home and abroad," and gave to
each of his five children some $4 million, then set up a trust, the Phipps Trust,
which continues to this day under the name of Bessemer Securities and which has
mushroomed from its initial capitalization of less than $20 million to some $400
million today. There are about thirty-seven trust arrangements that form a nucleus
for seventy-six subsidiary investment enterprises.

As for the Phipps heirs, they lack for nothing, everything being paid for by their
trusts. Tradesmen, servants, and charities receive their checks, we are told, from the
Office, and it is said that even to this day some seventy Phippses have no need to
carry cash or credit cards, but merely send all bills to the Office.

Adirondacks, where the distance from the gate to the baronial lodges is ten or eleven miles. He has a summer place in Saratoga, stables at Belmont Park, a hacienda in Mexico and other lands in South America, a Disney-like Marine Studios in St. Augustine, Florida, and the C. V. Whitney Farms in Lexington, Kentucky, with an antebellum mansion, the racing stables constructed in a circular shape with panelled stalls, and 500 head of Black Angus cattle (raised for their manure, to fertilize the fields), cattle that are removed to the farthest reaches of the farm when Sonny's wife, Mary Lou, comes to visit, because their smell offends her nose.

Periodically, we hear of other landholders, rumors, impossible to verify. Someone—a single family or individual—owns "most" of Martha's Vineyard. A man is buying up land "up our way"—hundreds and thousands of acres. No one knows his name.

How much land are we talking about?

There are 2.3 billion acres of land in the United States. Thirty-four percent of it is held by the federal government and much of this is rented out and leased to private interests for timber, mining, or cattle-raising. These leases are not supposed to be inherited or deeded, father to son, but by the exigencies of the law, which forbids transit across someone's private property to reach the federal lands, the leases are for all intents and purposes hereditary, and should be counted, in a sense, as ownership.

The Bureau of Land Management owns 8 million acres in Colorado alone and much other land in the West. I have heard that the state of Wyoming is something like 90 percent government-owned.

Six percent of the land mass is held by state or local governments, but much of this is wasteland, desert and swamp.

Two percent of the land is held for Indian reservations.

The remaining 58 percent of the land—1.3 billion acres, or three-fifths of the land mass of the United States—rests in private hands.

The trend is toward increasingly large holdings. In the nation as a whole the number of farms has declined from 4 million in 1960 to 2.8 million in 1976. This is not principally because of the transfer of farmland to suburb, but rather because the size of farms is growing larger, while fewer men are required to run them. Farm population fell from 15.6 million in 1960 to 8.9 million in 1975, the year the last estimate was made.

But it is easy to drown in figures. What does it mean, for example, that in Illinois 35 to 40 percent of the land is owned by women? Or that the same percentage is owned by people over 65? More than half, 58 percent, of the Illinois cornbelt is worked by nonowners under lease from their absentee land-lords. In eastern and central Illinois—the area of the most productive land—this figure rises to a whopping 70 percent tenant-farmed. Here land is held in the thousands of acres.

Some people believe the trend relates to the price of farmland, which has soared in the last five years from five or six hundred dollars an acre to three and four thousand an acre. In the year ending February 1977, farmland prices jumped 36 percent in Illinois, 32 percent in Indiana, 31 percent in Ohio. When you consider that the operating unit of a one-man farm planted in grains in Iowa, Indiana, or Illinois would require 400 to 600 acres, you are talking immediately of land millionaires, or men mortgaged to the hilt. According to Franklin J. Reiss, professor of farm management and land economics at the University of Illinois, therefore, it is not possible to expect to find anything other than a high rate of tenancy in these farmlands. The trend is apparently on the rise.

Foreign investors on the prowl are buying up 500 acres here, 1,000 there, at $2,500 an acre. Investors from Europe. Japan. The oil nations. Further drift toward landlordism.

How hard it is to talk of patterns in general. Move 500 miles farther west, into Iowa, for example, and all statistics change. Here, 1,000 acres is considered an enormous place. And there are men who farm more than 1,000 acres personally, without professional managers. They are automatically worth $2.5 million.

Iowa is our favorite Middle American state. We like to think of Iowa, with its stable and unpretentious white Protestant population. It has no gas shortage, no unemployment to speak of, no economic depression, except when the evening news is piped in from New York City. Iowa leads all other states in farm produce (number one in pork and corn production, number two in soybeans after Illinois, number three in beef after Texas and Nebraska).

We like Nebraska, too, where one little town was cited by the *Saturday Evening Post* after World War II as having more millionaires per capita than any other place in the country. The population of the town was 350. The farmlands in Nebraska are also held in small-scale family units, except in the Sand Hills, where the land rises into high rolling hills and vast seas of grass support the big cattle ranches. Then you get (as also in the Dakotas and on west to Montana and Wyoming) ranches of thirty and forty sections in size, for it takes a lot of land to support cattle on grass. And you get an even more sparse population and curious social quirks and new levels of gentry and gregariousness.

But still: who owns the land?

Only one official federal study of land ownership has been made that I know of. It was undertaken by our single most

authoritative source on land ownership, Gene Wunderlich, in
the Economic Research Service of the Department of Agriculture, and it covers one small and unimportant Virginia county.
The report, aware of the political sensitivity of such a topic, is
so weighty, so replete with quaquaversal information, unsifted
and unleavened by viewpoint, as to be well-nigh indigestible.

Rappahanock County is seventy miles from Washington,
D.C. It is an area of pasture, woods, and farmlands that is
becoming increasingly popular for country places for Wash-
ingtonians. The county is not so lush, high-priced, and socially
oriented as Middleburg and not so rutted, scarred, and rocky as
West Virginia. Here, half the land is classified by the USDA as
farmland, but only 5 percent of the owners considered
themselves farmers. It is, prototypically, the weekender's retreat.

Land is concentrated into the hands of the few. Seventy-
seven percent is owned by only 16 percent of the owners. One
absentee owner holds 8,500 acres or (excluding public park-
land) 5 percent of the county and 10 percent of the farmland.

Though most of the landholding population are absentee
owners, most of the large holders are residents.

The question of resident vs. nonresident ownership is
significant. Absentee landlords tend to know and care less
about their community than do residents, to be less well
informed, and in some parts of the country (as you shall see
when we come to California) absentee corporate landlordism is
equated with a ruthless disregard for the rights of residents and
even with the interests of the land itself.

Owning land takes money. It is not surprising then to find
that most of the large holdings are owned by those in the
highest income brackets. Nor that these owners should have
the highest education, nor that they should be the absentee

landlords, nor that the distinction between rich and poor in this rural county should bring to mind Disraeli's remark that "there are two worlds, rich and poor."

A very few, owning not quite half the land, had annual incomes of $50,000 or more.* A great many more, holding only 13 percent of the land, had incomes below $10,000 a year. One-quarter of the residents belonged to the latter group.

In general the report demonstrates what we guessed: that high income is associated with large landholdings, not only because much land produces much income, but because it takes much money to buy land, and much money is needed to keep it.

And so we come circling back to the point we made before: that no one knows who owns the land—their names, I mean—or how much land they have. Are they corporations? Family holdings put in trust? Individual and small-scale farms? No one knows.

Would any purpose be served by knowing the names of those who own the land? Yes, as is shown in the one state where at least some records do exist—California.

California is divided into water districts. A water district may comprise an area larger than a single county, and as a political unit the water district is superior to a county, not by statute but because in this dry state no issue so affects all other factors of life as water—its cost, source, and distribution. In addition to vast holdings of land, a small percentage of the population also controls water rights.

This is not so hard as you might think, because in a water district votes are counted by acreage. You do not have "one

---

* This level of income puts most of these owners in the top 1 percent of our population, where 400,000 households make $60,000 or more and own one-quarter of the wealth in America.

man, one vote" for water. You receive one vote for every
hundred dollars of the assessed value of your property. As a
result, the large landowners control the water district and wield
immeasurable power. The ripples are felt right up into the
federal government in Washington, 3,000 miles away. In 1976,
an example of the abuse of power came to light when the
Westlands Water District, which lies midway between Sacramento and Los Angeles, began to amend its 1963 water service
contract with the federal Bureau of Reclamations of the
Department of the Interior.

The original Federal Reclamation Act was devised by
Theodore Roosevelt in 1902 with the purpose of redistributing
lands equitably, and this principle was reaffirmed in 1926 and
again in 1959 and yet again by the courts in 1972. The land was
to be held in 160-acre tracts by individual families—160 acres
being enough land for one family to support itself completely.
The express purpose of the act was to guard against monopoly.
It was "not to irrigate the lands which now belong to large
corporations . . .," as the first director of the U.S. Reclamation
Service, F.H. Newell, said in a speech; "it is not to make these
men wealthy; but it is to bring about a condition whereby that
land shall be put into the hands of the small owner. . . ."

You might as well try to fell a tree by shouting at it.
Though the Department of the Interior was obliged by law to
enforce residency requirements and to force owners to sell any
lands in excess of 160 acres, there were by 1959 only 1,050
farms in the water district and only 214 land units were being
billed for water—this in an area that could have supported
27,000 residents on 6,000 farms, and another 30,700 rural
nonfarm residents. Eighteen years later, in 1977, only 6,000
people lived on that land.

In 1976, the amended contract somehow came to the

attention of the California State Legislature. It was discovered then that the federal subsidies to the Westlands Water District would cost an estimated $2.5 *billion* in direct expenditures and in subsidized interest over the forty-four-year life of the contract, that water was being sold to owners at $7.50 per acre-foot when comparable prices ran between $16 and $26 per acre-foot, that the $304.7 million cost of building dams and maintaining them was to be paid with an interest-free loan to the landowners.

And who were the landowners? They included:
- Southern Pacific Land Company, with 109,000 acres
- Standard Oil of California, with 11,593 acres
- Anderson, Clayton and Company, with 10,924 acres
- Boston Ranch, with 23,980 acres.

It was discovered that the excess lands (when sold according to the law), far from passing to the hands of small farmers, were being sold to paper farmers, consortiums, and investment syndicates in New York and California, to other corporate farmers, to absentee landlords, and in three instances to foreign companies, who would receive our subsidized water. Two were registered in Curaçao. In some cases, the original owners of excess lands, divesting themselves of their property according to the law, would regain title several transactions later through dummy corporations.

More than 100,000 acres of excess lands were sold during the first decade of the reclamation policy. Three hundred to 600 new farms of 160 acres should have been created. By March of 1976, the number reached was two!

In this case, we have hopes of having a just ending, fortunate indeed for those citizens who resent building free dams for Standard Oil and foreign corporations. Because the state of California knew who owned the land, the Westlands

Water District amended contract was stopped, and, in May 1977, a federal auditing team was sent out from Washington to investigate the relationship between the Department of the Interior and the water district landholders.

What would have happened in another state—can you guess?—where no one knows who owns the land?

"There Is No Landed Gentry in America"

It is curious how many people deny a gentry exists.

"Oh, there isn't any," says George McGhee, the former ambassador to West Germany, swelling with pride. We were standing in the bare foyer of a Washington slum house, celebrating over a styrofoam cup of jug wine the birth of his daughter's radical newspaper, *Newsworks*. Ambassador McGhee owns a beautiful eighteenth-century pink brick house in Middleburg and an African art collection that he keeps in a small museum on his farm there, and he often entertains his weekend guests in the country.

"But there's no landed gentry in America," he exclaimed. "People just don't know how to *do* it here. In England now. There, when you go away for a weekend...."

Almost the same conversation took place at a party, where I fell into conversation with Paul Richards, art critic for the *Washington Post*, except that Richards exceeded the ambassador in his contempt for American ways. Richards, now in his thirties, grew up on the north side of Chicago as urban as you can get. He has a "place" in Scotland that he goes to every summer. He too informed me that no landed tradition exists in this country, whereas in Scotland, he said, you have miles and miles of land owned by a single individual, "and they aren't even considered gentry," he continued happily, "until they've lived there for four hundred years. I love it. They're so nice."

I stared bitterly into my glass on this occasion, for if he saw that world from the outside, I had been witness to its pain.

I asked him why, when they did nothing and had no ambition, this gentry should represent his ideal. Loftily, he explained.

"They don't feel they *have* to do anything. They live there. They have a higher sense, that they have to hand down their property to their heirs intact. And that's enough." Then he waxed ecstatic on the beauty of this life, its quiet pace, the sense of propriety, of place, where everybody knows—and accepts—his place, master or servant; this rootedness of which through the generosity of these Scotsmen he had been allowed the merest glimpse.

Nothing like that, he said, was found in America.

He was, of course, quite wrong. A landed class is found just on the other side of the Elizabeth, New Jersey, gasworks, forty miles from New York City. And outside of Chicago, or St. Louis, or Houston. Even the gentry, however, sometimes cannot see the space around them, as witness Millicent Fenwick, congresswoman from New Jersey.

A magnificent woman. She is nearly seventy, and with her finely chiselled bones, her gray hair pulled swiftly back in a bun on her neck, she is remarkably beautiful. She dresses with efficient simplicity. She lives to work.

Born in 1910, the daughter of Ogden Hammond, a banker who served under Calvin Coolidge as ambassador to Spain, she traces her family back to the finest Maryland families on her father's side, to a royal land grant in Hoboken on her mother's. This same land now belongs to the Stevens Institute of Technology. Her mother died on the *Lusitania*. She was on her way to set up hospitals for the wounded of World War I, a venture considered harebrained, anyway, by the family. Millicent was raised by a stepmother. An unhappy childhood was followed by an even more unhappy marriage. There was little to indicate what she would become, and certainly no training or expectation of achievement. For a time, she attended Foxcroft School but was pulled out at the age of fifteen to accompany her father to Spain. She never graduated from school, much less from college, though later she took some classes at Columbia University and the New School for Social Research in New York.

She is scrupulously honest. Passionate. Idealistic. When required by election law to list her assets, she computed her worth to the penny: $5,112,637.40. Yet her concern is for the poor.

"We've got to do something about unemployment! We've got to do something about poverty!" She was addressing a group of women gathered in one millionaire's house among the Oriental rugs and French antiques—and there was Mrs. Fenwick, standing between the two grand pianos that occupy one end of the room, pounding her right fist into her left hand: "And the people we send to Congress! Who do they think they are? Princes, with their limousines and padded expense accounts. They don't care about good government!"

The assembled women looked into their limoges coffee cups and nibbled their breakfast brioches in puzzlement.

This is an area where the lush green pastures roll for miles on estates of 1,000 or 4,500 acres, neatly fenced for grazing horses. Fifteen or twenty acres is considered a small holding here in the fox hunting country, where Jackie Kennedy Onassis bought another $200,000 "hideaway" after leaving Middleburg. This is an area where a court suit was recently instituted to contest five-acre zoning as discriminatory to the middle class.

Mrs. Fenwick has lived most of her life in a pretty chateau, where the French windows open onto green lawns and large deciduous trees. There are said to be more horses than people in the area: Bedminster, Far Hills, Peapak, Gladstone. Horse races are still held on the old Evander B. Schley farm.

Her district is well above average in income and education. It contains 478,000 people, and the median family income of $14,000 is listed in the 1970 census as eleventh in the country. Forty-six percent of the families in her district make over $15,000 a year. Sixty-five percent are white-collar workers. Three percent are black.

"We don't have a landed aristocracy," she said passionately during an interview. "That's the great beauty of this country—our middle class. Look at our history! In the South, yes. There's landed wealth there. But in the rest of the country, wealth is based on merchants, on trade. The Adamses. Cabots. Lodges. They're not based on land."

Then she told how in 1939, when she was working as a writer for *Vogue,* she was sent with the photographer Toni Frissell to Argentina. She remembered visiting an *estancia,* where the family drove in carriages on the dirt roads.

"They were *fortified,*" she continued. "We drove up to this place by night, in the middle of a storm. I remember lightning was flashing, and you could see the cattle huddled against the trees. They had planted the trees. Eucalyptus and peach trees.

We drove up to a solid, locked gate. A watchman peered out at us through the rain with a lantern and opened the door to us, and as soon as we were through he locked it immediately behind us.

"We drove into a compound, a kind of barracks for prize bulls, where the three-year-olds were able to walk up ramps to suckle on the udders of the cows.

"And through the compound, past the barracks for unmarried men, then the houses for the married men, past a chapel, past a school. The house was fortified, too. It was built on three sides of a square, with the fourth side barred by a gate. All the ground-floor windows were barred, and inside this courtyard there was a well, so they'd have water in case of attack. . . .

"Oh, we have nothing like that." She shook her head. "They have a landed aristocracy in England, yes, and in France. And Italy. And in Poland they have, or did, those palaces with twenty-four dining rooms and china for each season of the year. But we don't have anything like that."

I tell you this to illustrate how even members of the propertied class are unaware of the strength of their situation. It was only a few years ago that Congressman Robert Daniel, Jr., of Brandon Plantation—and he was then in his thirties—gave a seated dinner for forty with a liveried footman behind each chair. Yet he is the first to deny such an act, though I know someone who was there. Certainly few are so shocked, so ready to deny its articulation as those in our upper class. There are two reasons for denial. First, because the upper class can always compare their own lives with "real" aristocracy in other parts of the world, as Millicent Fenwick just did, concluding our own a poor substitute for the real aristocratic style. Second, because hardly a group in the country exists that is more dedicated to the ideal of democratic equality, at least in the abstract, than is the upper class. Just as it is this class, our educated and propertied class, the class of inherited wealth, which is most committed to the idea of the work ethic, an unflagging belief in the Horatio Alger tales that with hard work and imagination anyone can make a pile from nothing.

Ghosts

I have no intention of trying to prove the existence of a landed
class statistically, of naming landed families in every state. But
let us look at four regions of our country, beginning with
Virginia, though we have already seen some of that. Virginia,
because it is our oldest state and because, in spite of the
pressures of population, the Tidewater plantations are still
much in existence. Virginia, also, because the patterns indicative of Virginia are illustrative of an entire class. Virginia
spreads across the country from Alabama to Arizona, Tennessee
to Wisconsin, and even today you can go to a Kentucky horse
farm or a San Francisco townhouse and there, staring from the
panelled walls, will be a portrait of "the Judge," the Virginia
ancestor, or of "the Planter," the Virginia forebear, and in the
dining room you will sit at the table brought out from
Virginia, and people will speak of "my great-grandmother"

who was a Virginian, or "my grandfather" who came out from Virginia after the War (meaning the Late Unpleasantness). There is whole cult of Virginia society.

And Virginia, finally, because my own beginnings are rooted there. However, it is not Mt. Airy I shall tell about, but Brandon, which is even older and much richer.

Brandon Plantation consists of 4,478 acres, 2,000 of which are under cultivation, and it represents the oldest continual agricultural enterprise in the United States. Fourteen families live on the place; fifteen men are regularly employed.

Today there is the farm with dairy, hog, and field crops: 150 Holsteins in their automated milking parlor; the hog-raising facilities with farrowing barns, nursery, and finishing floor that produce 3,000 hogs a year; the fields of corn and wheat. There is the Federal brick house with its two wings that was designed by Thomas Jefferson for his college roommate, Nathaniel Harrison.

Beyond the house is an old blockhouse, and beyond that, near the swimming pool and tennis courts, a large pool house, the walls of which are hung with the trophies of young Bobby Daniel's African game hunting: elephant, rhino, gazelle. Go anywhere among the propertied class and chances are you'll find the men engaged in shooting duck and quail or planning their African or Iranian game hunts. Blood sport absorbs this group.

Brandon Plantation lies on a curve of the James River, its 25 acres of formal gardens abruptly stopped at two towering urns on a high bluff, where you can look down and out across the water, four miles wide at this point and so deep that tankers and cargo vessels thrust, screws throbbing, up against the current toward the chemical plants at Hopewell. It takes a minute or two for the wash of their bow waves to slap the brush-covered duck blinds by the shore.

Brandon was founded in 1616 with a patent granted to John

Martin, Esq., companion to Capt. John Smith on his first voyage to America; and it has remained almost intact, the proverbial Tidewater plantation, for over 350 years, probably by virtue of being in a position to be passed over; a backwater it lies in, where the cataclysmic events of history rarely occurred. For 200 years, from 1720 to 1926, it was held by the Harrisons. Today it is owned by Congressman Robert Daniel, Jr. It is not the only plantation in this area of Prince George County or in the adjacent Charles City County—181 square miles with a population of 6,158, 80 percent of which is black.

There is Berkeley, which was another Harrison plantation. Berkeley, where in 1619 the first Thanksgiving in America was celebrated; where "The Signer" and one president were born; where "Taps" is said to have been composed. The house and 1,400 acres were bought from the Harrison family in 1906 for $28,000, restored, and in 1938 opened to the public as a privately maintained "public shrine."

There is Westover, home of the Byrds for several hundred years and now the property of Mrs. Crane Fisher. There is the 800-acre Shirley Plantation, notable among others for having remained not only intact but in the same family for 300 years.

Brandon is not in that category, however. For one thing, Brandon is a showcase, created, as we find is so often the case, through a rich marriage and the sudden fortuitous influx of cash. In this case, the money arrived in 1926, when Brandon was bought, much down-at-heel, by Robert Williams Daniel.

The story of its acquisition was told me by several Virginians. It begins to pass into general lore. The version I liked the best was that of the octogenarian, Miss Mary Wingfield Scott of Richmond, who spent fifty years watching the events unfold. It was verified with tormented and savage reluctance in a prickly interview with the present owner, Bobby Daniel.

Robert Williams Daniel married three times.

"He met his first wife," said Miss Scott, spinning out a grand yarn, "when he saved her life, stark naked in a lifeboat." The truth is always undramatic. He was dressed in woolen pajamas.

The time was April 1912. The scene was the sinking *Titanic.* Robert Daniel, a Philadelphia banker, was a Virginian of good family and comparatively modest means (by the standards of his day), but he had enough to know the proper way to live. The cream of American society had booked for the maiden voyage of the *Titanic* in April 1912. It was the place to be. The "unsinkable," she was called, "the star" of the White Star Line. "God himself couldn't sink this ship," was the White Star boast. Forty-six thousand, three hundred twenty-eight tons with 66,000 tons of displacement, she was eleven stories high, four city blocks long, had three screws, two sets of four-cycle reciprocating engines, 50,000 horsepower. She had a double bottom with sixteen watertight compartments and could float with any two flooded, since no one could imagine a worse collision than at the juncture of two compartments.

The passengers were enchanted, you can imagine. Never again would the scions of established wealth so occupy the popular imagination. On the other hand, never again would established wealth be so blatantly displayed. One hundred and ninety families occupied first class, attended by twenty-three handmaids, eight valets, an assortment of nurses and nannies, and hundreds of ship's stewards. The personal servants had their own lounge on C Deck, lest a passenger be embarrassed at striking up a conversation with a handsome stranger, only to discover it was a passenger's valet–perhaps the personal dragoman whom Henry Sleeper Harper, owner of *Harper's Weekly,* had picked up on his trip to Egypt.

The passengers were worth $250 million collectively. In first class, where a deluxe, walnut-panelled suite with canopied bed cost $4,350 (in 1921!), it was one big party, this maiden voyage of the *Titanic* from Southampton, England, to New York City. It was, you understand, a prewar, pre-income-tax era of gallantry, courtesy, confidence. Many had their pets aboard. John Jacob Astor (who had paid $800 for a lace jacket displayed on board at Queenstown) had his Airedale, Kitty; Henry Harper had his Pekinese, Sun Yat-Sen; Clarence Moore had 50 couples of English foxhounds just bought for the Loudon County Hunt, of which he was MFH, but these, thank heavens, were returning on another boat. And Robert Daniel had his champion French bulldog, purchased in England. All in all, there were 2,207 people on board and lifeboats for 1,178.

Some people said that 1,635 lives were lost when the ship sank; the American inquiry put the figure at 1,517, and the British Board of Trade at 1,503. At least we know the number saved–651.

But then, who of the passengers could imagine such a disaster? Certainly not Bruce Ismay, the president of the line, or Thomas Andrew, the ship's builder, or Capt. Edward J. Smith, who was making his retirement voyage on the *Titanic,* after fifty-nine years of White Star service–who could imagine that the unsinkable *Titanic* would hit an iceberg at 11:40 P.M. on her fifth day at sea and three hours later, by 2:20 A.M., would have sunk? *

They were evacuated by class, women and children first.

---

* It was the *Titanic* that sent the first Morse code SOS in history. As Harold Brude, the $20-a-month wireless operator, sent message after message to save the beautiful vessel, he received only silence. The message was intercepted by the *Carpathia,* 150 miles away, which steamed to the rescue. The *California,* which was halted ten miles away by drifting ice, watched the other ship disappear, fascinated by her odd cant and the way eight white rockets altogether were fired before her lights disappeared over the horizon. The officers agreed that the rockets were surely "not being sent up for fun." They recorded having seen them in the log–and went to sleep.

In New York, the message of the loss of the *Titanic* was taken by a young

On the *Titanic,* of 143 first-class women, 4 remained with the ship (3 by choice, refusing to leave their husbands); of 93 second-class women, the number was 15; and of 174 women in steerage, 81. As for the children, all but one of the 29 first- and second-class children were saved, in comparison with 23 of 76 children in steerage. How disorganized they were. The lifeboats pulled away 50 to 60 percent full. One, with places for 40, had only 12 people in the boat. Only 13 survivors out of 1,600 who went down were picked up by the eighteen lifeboats in the area. The sinking would mark the end of class distinctions in filling lifeboats.

Never again would first class automatically be saved first. Nor, for that matter, would women and children. A year later one prominent socialite divorced her husband because he happened to have been saved. Robert Daniel, on the other hand, married.

"He met his first wife on an iceberg," said Miss Scott, "survivors of the *Titanic.* Then he married a second wife. She had a great deal of money. She was a Durant of the automobile fortune, * and he went up North. Her family made a settlement on him, and he was divorced from her. They had one child. Then he married Charlotte Bemis,† a Virginian, and had another daughter by her. And later little Bobby. Robert Daniel died when Bobby was just a young chap."

---

wireless operator, David Sarnoff—the man who would one day be chairman of the board of RCA Corporation.

Marconi stock, which had sold earlier at $2 a share, soared to $225 at the news.

* Margery Durant, whose father helped finance the capitalization of General Motors from a small company to a billion-dollar corporation.

† Or Bemiss. There are two spellings to this name.

I am told by Sally Chase Daniel, Bobby's wife, that Brandon was bought with the second wife's money. It was Bobby, son of the third wife, who inherited it.

When the Daniels bought it, Brandon was falling down. Unlike many places that fell prey to Yankee invasion, the house still stood, largely because (according to family tradition) "Miss Bella" Richie Harrison, who was the wife of the owner during the Civil War, happened to be the sister of Abraham Lincoln's doctor. The Yankees burned the outbuildings, therefore, but left the main house. Still, when the Daniels bought Brandon in the mid-1920s, there was no electricity and no plumbing. A pump stood in what is now the study, and the gardens were in abysmal decay. Charlotte Bemis loved the place. "The best fertilizer," she told Sally many years later, "is the footsteps of the owner."

In Virginia it is not enough to buy a great house and restore it. That does not make it yours, for Virginians have long memories. Ancestors form one's identity, and the lines of a child's ancestors are taught by rote, at the knees of mothers, uncles, aunts. Which explains why even the names of children in Virginia are ancestral poems, reversible as raincoats: Beverly Marshall, Marshall Beverly; Peyton Randolph or Randolph Peyton. One's name, one's house are flown like a ship's standard for all to see. To be forced to strike your colors—ah, there lies disgrace.

You can imagine, then, how hard it was for the Harrisons (how hard for anyone!) to give up their land, the house, inhabited by Harrisons alone for more than 200 years. Even today a strained relationship persists, I'm told, as Mr. Gordon Harrison of Richmond returns periodically to work on the Harrison graves in the Brandon cemetery. It helps that Robert Daniel was a Randolph and Charlotte a Bemis—both, therefore, of "good family." It helped that the Daniels belong to the

Society of the Cincinnati, that Peter V. Daniel was the last Supreme Court justice from Virginia before Lewis Powell. Even so, they weren't *Harrisons*.

Now Charlotte Bemis, being herself a Virginian, understood these things, how giving up one's house is giving up a part of oneself. How mere ownership of a place does not make it yours. Impossible in Virginia not to forge ancestral links.

One Harrison tells how one day Mrs. Daniel invited Dr. Lyon Gardiner Tyler, former president of William and Mary College, to Brandon, in order to trace lineage, "because the house was bought lock, stock, and barrel," it was explained, "with all the Harrison pictures and furniture in it; and she wanted to know what connection she had to the Harrisons."

Dr. Tyler lived upriver, and he took his rowboat and went with a friend and a big picnic basket downriver on the tide to Brandon, where right off he got in a fight with Mrs. Daniel, drew himself up, and announced:

"I don't need to look at your letters. I know perfectly well there is no connection whatsoever between your family and the Harrisons."

She threw him out. He went down to his boat, docked at the river landing underneath the large Grecian urns, and had to sit for two hours waiting for the tide to turn to go back upriver, during which time she left him there.

Years later, a young lady from another state married into the Tyler family and met Mrs. Daniel, who greeted the girl so coldly that she asked a Richmond relative:

"Whatever is the matter with Mrs. Daniel? She was so strange with me."

"My dear, she cannot forgive you for being a Tyler. She doesn't speak to any Tylers."

If it was hard on the Daniels to find no genealogical

legitimacy in Brandon's ownership, and hard on the Harrisons
to leave their ancestral roots, the phenomenon is not unusual.
Nine times out of ten the matter of graves will cause a fight.
Mrs. Richard Byrd, when I interviewed her, was vice president
of the Colonial Dames of America, chapter three, and a special
assistant to the president of the National Trust for Historic
Preservation. She arched her comely eyebrows at the tactless
behavior of the Cranes, who felt so proprietary when they
bought Westover that they buried their own people in the
ancient Byrd cemetery.

Even today Westover is considered a Byrd plantation.

"Have you been to the Byrd plantation, Westover?" asked
one woman. "Beautiful! Beautiful place," she added, oblivious
to the fact that Westover was sold by the Byrds soon after the
Civil War and has not been in that family for a hundred years.

Some twenty miles down the road from Brandon and on the
other side of the kepone-poisoned James River lies another
plantation, and surely this exemplifies the difficulty of keeping
land in one's family at a time when zoning regulations and
subsidies to industry encourage urban sprawl on our richest
farmlands, while tax laws create land millionaires who can
barely scratch a living from their place.

Nine generations of Carters, descendants of the plutocrat
"King" Carter, have lived in the big brick house of Shirley
Plantation, square as a block and unadorned. Anne Carter Lee
returned summers to visit her parents here; her son, Robert E.
Lee, went to school in one of the small blockhouses that guard
the main building. And the flat, rough land lies swelling under
the summer heat, giving off a rich, aromatic scent of hay and
grass.

What a responsibility it is to be raised in the shadow of

ancestors. To survive takes character: a stubborn malice, a willful selfishness that casts aside all that is important to others.

"Ancestors are no asset," I was told once by Mrs. J. Robert Massie, Jr., executive director of the Garden Club of Virginia. "They're a liability." At one Virginia school the portrait of Robert E. Lee was turned to the wall when the students were bad, so that the hero would not be offended by their sight.

In one house, portraits of Jefferson and Lee hung in the living room, Jackson and Washington in the dining room. They looked down on their descendants, a constant reminder of responsibility. Right there you trace the confidence and insecurity that commingles in this group, or the smug pomposity, as with—I was about to name one woman I know, not even thirty-five, and rigid with the self-discipline of fear. Do you know this fearfulness? This discipline found in the upper classes? It is a discipline of moderation, in which the primary rule is never to be noticed, never to make waves, never to make another uncomfortable with unseemly display of wit or knowledge, much less of breast or limb. The clothing is rigid with discipline—classic suits, a string of modest pearls. The carriage erect. Discipline explains why accomplishments can be so great, and fear of failing or of embarrassing another explains why just as often there are none at all.

Discipline. Fear. This sense of privacy translates also into dignity. No puking, whining, public airing of one's pain. No wail of Freudian blame. Of course there's pain! That's what life's about. Back straight, you bite the lower lip and keep quiet about your pitiful pain. As if no one had suffered pain before or would again. Good God! All one need do is look to his ancestors to know what suffering is! Pain is expiated in Episcopal dignity. Or drink.

Do you disagree? Or do you imagine, perhaps, the degenerate aristocracy decaying in their manor houses. The Tidewater planters, with "Massa" decked out in white suit, white shoes, a stogie clamped between his flash of teeth, an arrogant, unintellectual curl to his handsome lip, surveying lands, cattle, Negroes, chattel, tobacco.

Degenerate! You miss the point—the hold that the past can take even over a man who cannot claim a Virginia ancestor or a manor left by primogeniture.

Material things take on a value beyond the monetary: the *old* brooch, the silver service are filled with associations, memories, ghosts. The past becomes an obsession. When Mrs. Bruce Crane Fisher was married in 1937 at Westover, the newlyweds drove away from the wedding in a carriage, and they were dressed in nineteenth-century costume for their wedding night at Colonial Williamsburg.

I met one woman while researching this book who helped prove the incredible hold of the past. She was young and pretty, and though raised in a big Eastern city, she had married a landed man. She moved into the Big House that was run by her mother-in-law, the dowager queen, and where her husband's old nurse, now cantankerous with age, puttered through the halls, bursting in on the young wife with malicious jealousy. It was horrible. Worst of all was that the young bride had nothing to do. Her mother-in-law was firmly in control. The servants did their part. For years her only task was to be pretty. She took up needlepoint and to some degree saved her sanity with the birth of her son. Eventually the old nurse died, and after that the mother, and suddenly my friend found herself . . . free! The place was hers! How wonderful! She was still young, no more than thirty-one or two, and like a windstorm she swept through the dark, old house, gleefully cleaning things out, packing up boxes of her in-laws' possessions. It was hers! The house! She pulled back the heavy draperies that actress Katharine Cornell had so admired on her visit. She painted the harmonious hallways fresh, put up new curtains, papered the children's rooms. Forty paperweights on one table alone went to the basement. Silver bowls and platters, loving cups, riding cups, and coffee services with their heavy Georgian silver sugar tongs and gravy boats, all removed from the Hepplewhite sideboards.

Then, in place of the old photos that covered the piano, she set out ones of her own children. Her sisters. Her friends. She moved the pantry, redesigned the antique kitchen and added new lighting and a dishwasher and all the comforts of modern life.

Weeks went by, and months. Do you know what happened? Gradually, she found herself uneasy in the house. Almost unaware, she began to put things back: the silver service in the dining room, the bibelots in the living room, then the paperweights, and then the photos of dead generations. Her own children's pictures were removed to her bedroom walls. It is as if the angel of God touched certain people, marking them as guardians of our heritage, in order that the rest of us can visit (on open days), feed on memories, and take away the nutrients we need for modern lives.

Or look at Shirley Plantation. Nine generations it has remained in the Carter family and now belongs to C. Hill Carter, Jr., and his Scandinavian wife, Helle. The place is estimated at $1,500,000, but to convert the assets to spendable cash, Carter would have to do the one thing he is committed not to do: sell Shirley. Instead, he nets barely $15,000 a year, renting his land and giving personal tours to the 23,000 visitors a year who pay about two dollars each to wander through his place. His wife works in a store in a nearby town and opened a gift shop on his place, and when I visited was hoping to start a small restaurant enterprise.

Their entire lives are committed to Shirley, scrabbling for

money to pay taxes, to make repairs—an endless succession of cracking walls and leaking plumbing, with Carter himself in work clothes and heavy boots doing much of the cleaning, plastering, building, repairing, and wondering always how to pass the place on to his children, when inheritance taxes would come to $650,000.

The family eats on folding auditorium chairs in the kitchen, which is in the cellar, with bare pipes exposed on the ceiling; while on the elegant floors above rest eighteenth-century antiques.

"Most of the important things in the world can't be bought and sold," says Carter. "In our society, nobody has roots. Everybody's mobile."

So he gives his tours of his family roots, telling the family history in a swift, sharp, nasal drawl, pointing out the downstairs bedroom, with cradle and four-poster bed, the parlor, the dining room where Washington and Jefferson were entertained, the schoolhouse where Robert E. Lee took lessons. He is glad to remember that once, when he heard John D. Rockefeller was interested in buying Shirley, as an adjunct to Colonial Williamsburg, he told him to beat it: nothing would make him sell.

One last Virginia story. Bear with me, for, again, I cannot use a name, so sensitive are those souls, so vulnerable to mockery and jibes. One story more to show the significance of the past to old families.

One of the Founding Fathers gave a portrait of himself, upon his death, to each of his sons. Eventually, all the paintings were sold, save one, and this one was passed from son to son, through war and depression, always staying in the family even at considerable sacrifice. The family was not rich. Several times they were on the point of having to sell—and each time, somehow, at the last minute money would be scraped up to pay for taxes, or the college bills, without the portrait's sale.

Until a few years ago, when insurance costs on the painting grew so high that the owner could no longer afford payments on both the insurance and his house. What was he to do?

He sold his house and moved with the painting to a small apartment.

The Hudson River Landlords

When I was at school, one of my classmates was a Pell, one of the family which gave their name to the area just north of New York City–Pelham, Pelham Manor. The Pell lands were descended from a land grant from Charles II, and to this day, the town of New Rochelle presents the family with a fatted calf according to its ancient tribute. I think it's the only such tribute still paid an American family, though the town of Pelham is supposed to give a red rose every year to the Queen. Some people I know are shocked at the idea of calf tribute in our nuclear age, but the landed aristocracy invariably find it enchanting. Certainly no one in New Rochelle has ever disputed the claim. In fact, one year a mayoral candidate ran on an anti-fatted-calf-for-Pells platform–and lost. There may have been other issues in the campaign.

Eve Pell showed me photos of a fatted-calf dinner, with the men grouped around a large table in the historic Pell-Bartow

house under the portrait of a long-locked cavalier. The
presentation took place in the Town Hall. There was a boy
scout, and an American flag, and someone in Tudor-ish
costume with plumes in his hat, and a calf that was presented,
she thought, to the Reverend Walden Pell, who is a direct
descendant of the original Lord of the Manor, and who was for
many years headmaster of St. Andrew's School in Middletown,
Delaware (a school founded with a $30-million endowment by
Felix du Pont in 1927 for one hundred boys). It was the
Reverend Walden Pell, proprietor of a cattle farm in Delaware,
who in 1952 had revived the ancient tradition of calf-tribute,
after centuries of disuse. He had no special reason: it was
merely whim.

Eve turned the pages of her photo album. There was the
present Lord of the Manor, and there the Honorable Claiborne
Pell, who, as a senator from Rhode Island and often in the
public eye, induces a certain uneasiness among the lesser
members of the family, a caution natural to a man when he
doesn't know what a person is going to do or say next.
Grouped about were assorted cousins. And there was also John
H. G. Pell, who runs Fort Ticonderoga, "a kind of historical
thing," she said with disinterest, "that the Pells have restored."
The Fort Ticonderoga Association is a national foundation
composed only of Pells or people who married Pells, and
dedicated, as John H. G. Pell told me later, "to the preservation
of Fort Ticonderoga for the benefit of all people." The reason
the Pells are associated with Fort Ticonderoga is that, having
been loyal Tories during the Revolution, their lands were
confiscated. One William Ferris Pell then moved, around 1820,
to a beautiful house near the historic fort, landedness running
in the family. His direct descendants still live today for the
public good on that same 3,000 acres.

Usually, the town of New Rochelle turns Fatted Calf Day into a sort of charitable occasion, the proceeds going to a hospital. My friend went twice. One year the Pells were given a roast beef dinner and there was a huge hall, she remembered, and a dais upon which all the Pells sat and ate their beef, while the common people of New Rochelle sat below; and there was entertainment in the form of celebrities who sang and danced.

Eve was swept by a schizophrenia on the dais, feeling part of this lordly clan on the one hand and, on the other, a reeling disbelief: "What a laugh! This is crazy!"

To confuse things more, there was the man known to the family as "Fishmonger Pell." He had arrived unexpectedly from Greenpoint, Long Island, and to the family's consternation he turned out to be a genuine, pedigreed Pell. More! He was next in line to the title of Lord of the Manor, so that the Fishmonger was the most noble Pell of all. Families adjust to such things quickly. He is said to be "very, very nice."

Eve Pell has not been back for Fatted Calf Day in many years, but the tribute still goes on, a calf being given whenever the Pell Family Association remembers to demand one.

But it was not the Pells I wanted to talk about, for they are scattered wide. Turn instead about a hundred miles farther up the Hudson River to the landholders of Dutchess County, many descended from the Dutch patroons. Here you find such names as van Rensselaer, Schuyler, Van Cortlandt, Beekman, Stuyvesant, who once owned almost the entire area that was later to become New York State and whose influence in the Albany legislature, I am told, is still pervasive. They too were Lords of the Manor. The Livingstons owned the southern two-thirds of Columbia County. The Van Rensselaers, largest of the landholders, owned, through lands granted by the West India Company, all of Albany County "to the Western Ocean."

Philipses owned the southern part of Putnam County and
northern Westchester County. The Van Cortlandts and Pells
owned that area nearest New York City. Their style of life has
always engendered awe.

In 1794, soon after the Revolution, an Englishman, William
Strickland, visited Robert R. Livingston, the Chancellor of the
state of New York, at his country seat of Clermont. His eyes
popped at the life-style of this gentleman, which represented, he
said, "more the spirit of feudal aristocracy than might be
supposed to be harboured in the breast of one of the staunchest
republicans." * Four slave-boys waited on the guests at dinner
and hung idly around the doorways, wrestling amiably with
each other and waiting for orders, for there were no bells in the
house. The chancellor, playing the gentleman agronomist,
pointed out to his guest the wild, unexplored territory across
the river, filled with bear, elk, panthers, and wolves, and noted
idly that he owned 200,000 acres beginning at those woods,
which he was just beginning to settle. Of human settlers he
spoke to his English visitor about so many bushels a year, so
many fowls, of mining rights, and one day's labor a year for
landlord with horses and oxen—"until his guest hardly knew
what century he was in."

* The chancellor, chief justice of New York, one of the drafters of the
Constitution, the man who administered the oath of office to President Washington,
was renowned for two deeds: as Minister to France, he pressed for the Louisiana
Purchase, and as a private citizen, he backed Robert Fulton's steamship invention,
which culminated in Fulton's successful trip up the Hudson in the *Clermont*. It was
the chancellor who told Joseph Bonaparte that a gentleman of rank in America
would need $55,000 for a town house and a country seat, plus $15,000 in regular
income, which he could expect to receive at three percent from revenues from his
land.

Two hundred years later, when I interviewed Bobby Daniel, I was told that the
congressman received a two percent return on Brandon Plantation's farms.

Livingston lived, as do his descendants today, not far from the town of Rhinebeck, New York.

Rhinebeck, founded 1688, lies 110 miles from New York City. It is an area sixteen miles long and one mile wide, and contains today no fewer than thirty-seven great houses. The country is rough and hilly, the land covered with dense woods that end as crags and cliffs and jutting embankments overhanging the Hudson. The atmosphere of tangled glen and high points evoked the romantic names of the nineteenth-century country seats: Wildercliffe, 1799; Wilderstein, 1852; Ferncliffe, 1860. The earlier settlers called their places by such clement names as Sunning Hill, the Meadows, or, with startling practicality, Mill Hill.

According to the Rhinebeck Area Historic Survey of 1974, most of the great houses will not exist by the end of this century, among them Rokeby, which was once an Astor house.

Its inhabitants are connected to all the patrician names of the area: Beekman, Delano, Livingston, Aldrich, Chanler, Lewis. The land has descended in a direct line since 1715; the house, since it was built in 1811–1815, by General John Armstrong, who was secretary of war during the War of 1812 and served as minister to France. General Armstrong's daughter married William Backhouse Astor, son of the original John Jacob Astor, and a man who turned his inheritance of several millions into $20 million, to become "the richest man in America" at his time.

Today, to call the present occupants of Rokeby down-at-heel is to be polite. In 1975, the property tax on the 340-acre place with its forty-five-room mansion came to $13,000, and a welcome relief it was from the previous year's taxes of $20,000. A new roof installed several years ago at a cost of $12,000 "now leaks," according to the owner, "worse than it did before." It is easy to see how an estate with eight principal houses and lesser gatehouses, coachman's apartments, greenhouses, and apartments could run every year in debt.

The house is held by four co-owners, or tenants-in-common, who are the three grandchildren and the daughter-in-law of Margaret Chanler Aldrich, who died in 1963 at the age of ninety-three. Each of the four inherited, in addition to the estate, $50,000. A decade later they said they had about $30,000 left, enough to keep Rokeby going for only three more years.

One heir, Winthrop Aldrich, was rocketed between conflicting emotions—despair that his wonderful brother, a linguist, was wasting his intellectual talents working the farm—and panic, lest Rokeby not be saved.

I visited Rokeby one long, soft summer evening in 1975. A chill mist rising from the river obscured the beautiful one-and-a-half-mile-long dry stone wall that was constructed from 1880 to 1888 by an octogenarian Italian stonemason, a pensioner of the family, as a gesture of gratitude; up the long, curving driveway, lined by a variety of trees, to a large, ungainly house, where each wing, decoration, turret, and addition stand as testament to the changing tastes and pretensions, comfort and necessities of each succeeding generation.

The high front steps rise to a porch, where ten doric columns lift higher to the roof. I stood for a long time, groping in the darkness for a bell, pounding on the door, uneasy that the house should be dark when I was expected. After several minutes, the door opened to reveal Winthrop Aldrich, one of the owners. A nice-looking man in his early thirties, with a shock of dark hair hanging in his eyes and glasses slipping off his nose, he took me down the wide front hall, past massive Germanic chests and chairs, heavy Astor heirlooms dark with dragon carvings, then through a warren of back stairs and corridors, twisting, climbing, dropping, turning to the kitchen–where his dinner was cooking on the stove. Two suspicious pugs burst into loud yapping and snapping as they darted around the table legs. It was a large room, lined with cupboards, and every horizontal inch covered with china services, dishes, cups, plates, pots. Two enormous kitchen tables were stacked with boxes of food, saucers, condiments, and more dinner services, as if laid out for a church bazaar. At the far end of the kitchen, a horse blanket covered a great stone fireplace, shoulder-high to a man, to keep out drafts.

There was nothing modern about this kitchen, beyond its possession of a refrigerator and gas stove. But a comfortable lack of modernity is not unusual in great houses: they frequently display a total disregard either for the comfort of their servants or the efficiency of the working space.

On the dirty, stained, gas stove, Winthrop Aldrich (Winty to his friends) was cooking his dinner: a bowl of white rice. His wife and children were in Vermont at a horse show, where he would join them over the weekend. Meantime, he was on his own.

Now, everyone knows a kitchen is no place to entertain a guest, and I could feel his hunger struggling against his embarrassment, his sense of propriety, as he quickly made me a cup of instant coffee. Then, with a long, backward glance at his rice, so hurriedly and only half-consumed, he led me courteously back through the jumble of corridors to the front of the house: up and down stairs, thriftily turning lights on and off in passing. We moved in pools of light.

The tour of the main rooms was generously long. The dining room, where radiators had been installed at the end of the last century, monstrous black beasts squatting over their basement cauldrons and subject, in winter, to sudden attacks of knocking, pipe-clattering, coughing fits, like death throes, that would subside finally into an exhausted hiss. The ballroom, with its grand piano covered with a shawl and this, in turn, by silver-framed photos; more dark, carven chairs, with needlework seats, placed stiffly around the room. A tapestry on one wall.

Winthrop Aldrich, however, chose the library to sit in, and anyone who'd been there would understand why, though the room itself is testimonial to pretense: the plaster is treated to look like wood, the wood stained to simulate a grain God never grew. Nevertheless, it is beautiful, like sitting inside an acorn.

It is a circular room, lined floor to ceiling with ten thousand books, many of them the leather-bound Armstrong-Astor volumes of the 1840s. The walls rise to a swirling Gothic ceiling, and all about are scattered in careful disarray the bronzes and statuary, marble busts, the leather chairs and sofas. On the floor is an Aubusson rug so irreplaceable that—"Watch out for your coffee." I could hear the wince in Aldrich's voice, a gagging at the bitter necessity that forces such admonition on a guest.

But the room, round and exquisitely proportioned, released its own soothing effect. The doors closed on the world outside, and we sank into lovely, timeless Gothic aerialness in this space designed by Alexander Jackson Davis, who had also designed, I was informed, the Gould house, Lindhurst.

Winty Aldrich had catalogued the books himself as one of his first tasks on inheriting the house from his grandmother: a task of love. Travel, Ancient History, European History, Military History, French Literature, English Literature, Italian, German, Classical Literature, Reference Books, Landscape Architecture—the categories went on and on.

Later that night, he led me up the five-story tower (of which the library is the lower floor) to the roof to see the moonlit landscape of the Hudson River valley. We were catapulted forward to the present time. The beam of the flashlight glanced flickering across the decaying boards of the stairs, caught on cobwebs, danced down the bare plaster walls, gashed in places right to the exterior brick. We crushed plaster and brick dust underfoot, felt the shattered glass from the broken windows crunch under our shoes, and I remembered that Mr. Aldrich had said that merely to keep the house clean would cost a hundred dollars a month in materials and supplies. Each floor exhibited worse repair than the next until the top, stepping through the bat dung and pigeon droppings, we climbed a dark ladder, pushed open a hatch, and stepped onto the tin roof of the widow's walk. The wind struck vertiginously chill. Beneath us the valley spread out, romantic and feathery in the moonlight.

There was a time when Livingstons and Beekmans owned all the land in sight. It is said that the first Livingston, Robert of Clermont, a poor boy from Scotland, received his royal land grant in return for saving the manor households from Indians. The actual history (as recounted in George Dangerfield's biography of the chancellor) sounds more believable. Born in Scotland in 1654, Livingston arrived in the Albany frontier in 1674, just as the English were wresting control from the Dutch. He had one overwhelming characteristic: greed. He married, as poor boys always should, up, winning Alida Schuyler Van Rensselaer, the widow of his first patron and herself a Van Cortlandt as well, thus connecting himself to three of the most powerful families in the colony. Then he began to acquire land.

In 1683, he bought from the Indians 2,000 acres of land for 300 guilders of wampum, guns, and powder, and this was fully patented and confirmed. A year later, he bought another 600 acres of Indian land, "lying," he said, "upon the same Kill," or river, though it turned out to be over on the border of Massachusetts some 240 miles east and 157,000 acres away. On July 22, 1686, the two tracts were united by royal patent into one Lordship or Manor of Livingston "with full power and authority at all times for ever hereafter" to hold a court leet and a court baron.* Thus, with one imaginative stroke of the pen, he increased 2,600 acres to 160,000; he became a lord with power to hang a man if necessary on his own estates. Apparently, the deed was termed free of fraud, although 200 years later, an attorney general of New York would express astonishment at the manner of the acquisition.

In the early 1700s, Livingston Manor was awarded a seat in the assembly—a pocket borough, in effect, and thereafter fat ran to fatter, the slave houses and tenants increasing, the storehouses bulging with produce from a thriving West Indian trade. In the early 1700s, three-quarters of the colony of New York was in the hands of only a dozen men, and this despite the fact that in England the Lords of Trade, recognizing the inequities of land concentration in England, were vainly passing law after law to limit Colonial holdings to 1,000 acres a man. They didn't stand a chance. Despite a tenant uprising against the Livingston overlords in 1750, another in 1766, and still another on the eve of the Revolution in 1775, despite the passion of such radical reformers as Cadwallader Calder, who charged in 1765 that juries were in the pocket of a privileged

* This is the definition of a lord of a manor. The title is found in the New York area and Maryland alone.

aristocracy, an alliance formed of great landlords, merchants, judges, and attorneys (the charge being statistically upheld, if you look, for the majority of justices and surrogates bore landed names)—that is to say, despite laws and pressure for reform and even armed revolt, the system went right on.

Livingstons had a hammerlock on the area. The six daughters of Robert of Clermont settled with their husbands in the province, building their own separate dynastic houses and running the Livingston mills and properties. Landed, conservative, exhibiting that special talent of Established Wealth to sidle always to a winning side, they were Tories during the Revolution, yet gave three ambassadors to France under the new Republic. When, in 1776, Beekman lands (tracing back to the Dutch proprietorship) were joined to Livingston lands by a marriage from which Winthrop Aldrich traces direct descent, the combined force of family could overwhelm almost any opposition.

Margaret Beekman was known as one of the richest women in the American colonies. Her daughter, Alida Livingston, was one of ten children, and when she married the aforementioned General Armstrong, she brought 27,000 acres in dowry. It was *her* only daughter, Margaret, who married, in 1818, William Astor. I think the next fifty years represented a pinnacle of power. From then on things went downhill in a long, slow attrition that lasted for another hundred years, while the Astor name passed to the Chanlers, and through them to Winthrop Aldrich and his siblings.

I spoke in an earlier chapter of the continuity of established wealth. The continuity of land ownership in America is worth noting as well, especially since it too flies in the face of all our preconceptions.

The Rhinebeck Area Historic Survey shows that of the

thirty-seven great houses of Rhinebeck, many dating only from the mid-nineteenth century:

• Three are owned by state or federal governments and are open to the public as museums.

• Twelve are owned by institutions, such as the Catholic Church, military academies, and girls' boarding schools.

• Twenty-two—yes, twenty-two—are still in private hands. Of these more than half (twelve to be exact) are owned by the descendants of the men who built them.

Now it is true that some behemoths, like Wildercliffe, built in 1799, are now reduced to mere acreage lots, and eight are for sale to anyone who will come along to buy them. Likewise it is true, as the Rhinebeck Historical Survey claims, that most shall probably not exist in another twenty years. They stand as shells of another life, about to be taxed out of existence, thus giving credence to the warnings of Judge Livingston, the chancellor, who, propounding in the mid-eighteenth century his "Reasons Against a Land Tax," wrote bitterly:

If this project takes, then farewell to all the great Patents in government, and for the purpose of breaking them I suppose it is proposed.

A distinction should be made in the life-styles of the early settlers and those who came in the mid-nineteenth century to build their pleasure gardens. The Livingstons, the Beekmans held extensive lands, but they lived with relative simplicity, pious and hardworking people with no ready cash. It was the 1830s and '40s that saw a change in the area, with the arrival of the weekend country gentleman, and enormous fortunes based on city endeavors. There was, for example, a Squire Dinsmore, who employed fifty to a hundred men on his farm, raising two kinds of hogs, beef and dairy cattle, chickens, geese, and ducks, and evincing such intense interest in agriculture that he consistently won prizes at the county fairs. It was Dinsmore who installed the first golf course in the country—on his sheep pasture. He opened it to the townspeople on weekdays, if they wished to play among the sheep; weekends were reserved for the gentry, come up by train from New York City

The area was made fashionable by the infusion of the Astor funds, for to speak of Rhinebeck after a certain date.is to speak of Astors. Astor money created the fashion. Astor money protected the lesser gentry and Astor estates held the area stable right up to the present time. It has been the withdrawal of Astor money that has brought shuddering change to the area, the gentry sinking to that state of genteel decadence so frequently recorded in Southern literature and so rarely noticed in the North. Money was plentiful for years. In the 1960s, for example, when Winty Aldrich looked up the records of his grandmother's dairy farm, which still used the same equipment installed in 1901, he found that in only one year out of sixty did the dairy break even. Rokeby, like many places in Rhinebeck, was taxed not as a farm but as an estate. Grandmother Chanler, heir to the Astors, was said to have been proud of paying the highest taxes in the area.

And then, in the mid-sixties, Emily's aunt, Brooke Astor, third wife of Vincent (whose father, John Jacob, was one of the 1,600 passengers enjoying a cruise on the *Titanic* with Robert Daniel, Sr., the difference being that Astor was a lot richer and he drowned)—Brooke Astor sold her place, Ferncliffe, to the Catholic Church and moved, I am told, to a quarter-million-dollar house in Scarsdale. Both the residents of Rhinebeck and the local gentry were shaken by her move.

"Colonel Jack," who died on the *Titanic,* had bought up many farms in the neighborhood, 3,000 acres here, 3,500 there, spreading his lands back from the river until he owned an enormous area. He tore down all the buildings he could, to let the forest grow up again. His son, Vincent, then held that land with filial piety for fifty years, selling none, changing none (as befits one of his class, dedicated, as I mentioned earlier, to the cause of conservation and historic preservation, the jelling of time and place). And when he died in 1959, he left his wife a trust fund, two million dollars in cash, and land in Arizona, New York, and Maine.*

Winthrop Aldrich finds her selling the Rhinebeck property unforgiveable. "She chose not to remain," he explained easily that night I visited him. "It was too far from the city, I suppose, to have people out for the day, and to spend the night was a bore. So she gave Ferncliffe to the Catholic Church, which built a high-rise nursing home. . . . She never thought that it would open the door to developers. There are two lessons in that." He checked them off on his fingers, his analytical, cold calculation belied by the tremor in his voice.

"Lesson number one. We have no place today for private baronies. Their whole *raison d'être* is gone.

"Lesson number two. They did incalculable harm. The area, the community, relies on the big estates for income and for stability and to tell them what to do. Now we need zoning, planning, and we're unprepared. The wolf is at the door."

I suppose he is not far wrong. The people I spoke to in

---

* Vincent Astor inherited $85 million in 1912. When he died he left half his $120 million estate to the Astor Foundation and a life interest in the other half (except for some $800,000 in twenty-five other bequests) to his widow.

Rhinebeck found the whole matter ... confusing. On the one hand, they were proud of the big estates on which their fathers and grandfathers had worked, and, on the other, they hated the lordly arrogance of the owners who had exercised control.

"So what if she goes?" says one man. "She never showed a proper interest in the place." And he proceeded to tell–his voice trembling–how Brooke Astor would give a lace table-cloth to her tenants at Christmas while caring nothing for their children's schools or teeth.

You will find her name on the boards of the Metropolitan Museum of Art and the New York Public Library (which was once called the Astor-Tilden Library) and she donates annually to the preservation of Central Park. Yet she sold her land in Rhinebeck. The reverberations are felt by everyone around.

Several years passed between my visit to Rokeby and completion of my book. In late 1977 I telephoned Winthrop Aldrich to see what had happened to Rokeby. Had it been sold? Subdivided?

"Well, it's still there," he said. "More plaster's fallen maybe. ..."

And further activities threaten it–a nuclear energy plant envisioned by Con Edison on the banks of the Hudson; a new Amtrak service that would run trains from New York City to Rhinebeck in only one hour ten minutes, creating further pressure for development and even higher taxes.

But some moves have been made to save the area as well. The local Rhinebeck historical association nominated twenty miles of riverfront as "a critical historical area" suitable for preservation and conservation, and began maneuvering to get the area listed on the National Register of Historic Places of the National Park Service or recognized as a National Historic

Landmark. Once on that status, a property owner can apply for grant-in-aid for maintenance and repairs and being on that level can also help prevent encroachment, both private and state.

Meanwhile the National Trust for Historic Preservation has taken an interest in the area, establishing a three-year task force to study tax abatements, easements and adaptive uses of the great Rhinebeck houses, "because the problem," as Winty explained, "is bigger than any local owner can cope with singlehanded."

For any landowners the options are few. Under the present tax and zoning laws, an owner can tear down his house; subdivide, leaving the great house isolated, bereft of purpose; or he can struggle. The Hudson River landowners are denied the option of owners in other states, who can sell or give away easements, donating water or mineral or access rights to others. Neither can they give an easement to the National Trust in order to limit the pressure of development on their property. New York State law does not permit it. The Hudson River landowners are simply in a bind.

In Old New Orleans

When Emily Astor, daughter of Margaret Armstrong and William Backhouse Astor, the richest man in America, married Samuel Ward, Jr., in the 1830s, the family was not elated. Ward was the fourth generation of a prominent New York and Rhode Island family that counted two governors and numerous Revolutionary patriots among its members. The eldest son of a New York banker, a potential millionaire, Sam knew everyone—Longfellow, Liszt, Paganini. His personality was charming, carefree, ebullient. It could only grate on someone like William Backhouse Astor, who had been educated in Germany (a classmate of Schopenhauer) and whose idea of a good time was to pore over an encyclopedia of an evening in the unimaginative pursuit of facts. That Sam would lose his first fortune and win and lose two others during his lifetime was taken as a personal affront by Astor, himself pious, sombre, and austere.

As it happened, Emily Astor Ward died in childbirth in 1841, and Sam drifted down to New Orleans and married a

Creole, Madora Grymes. The Astors were so scandalized they severed all connections and threatened to cut off Sam's daughter, their grandchild, without her inheritance unless she was relinquished to their care. Faced with legal action, Sam Ward gave Maddie away to the richest man in America, her grandfather, and ever after had to sneak and plot to catch a glimpse of her, arranging a secret tryst at Rokeby or unexpectedly turning up at her Paris hotel when she went to Europe with an aunt. Child-selling is not unheard of even today. I know of an instance in the Midwest where a divorced mother sold her daughter to the father in return for his paying the mortgage on the family place. One sells children too, you see, for inheritance.

It was not only their son-in-law, however, who shocked the Astors. It was New Orleans itself, degenerate and French. By the time he arrived, some of the streets were covered with galleries in the Italian fashion, so that the fashionable young ladies no longer lifted their skirts and dashed barefoot through the puddles of a drenching monsoon to arrive out of breath and laughing (wiping muddy feet, slipping on their shoes) to dance the night away at a fancy ball. And neither were Mulatto Balls held in New Orleans any longer, as they had been a hundred years earlier, when beautiful "High Yaller" girls, dressed in the height of fashion, were brought by their free mothers to dance with the rich Louisiana planters in hopes that an attachment might be formed. Such attachments, it is said, often lasted a lifetime, being by custom as hard a knot to untie as marriage itself. To the girl, who was kept in a proper house and dressed and cared for, came financial security; to the man a degree of affection to compensate for a marriage arranged on the altar of Property. By New York standards New Orleans, with its .mix of French, Spanish, English, and black populations, all seething in Mardi Gras splendor, may have seemed debauched. Yet nowhere is property treated more seriously, I believe, than in New Orleans, among the French. For example, there is the family of my friend, Marguerite Lelong Kelly. In 1843, around the time that Sam Ward arrived, Marguerite's Tante Nini had just been born. At seventeen, she was granted a papal dispensation to marry her fifty-year-old uncle, Désiré Chaffraix, a sugar broker, whose main virtue was his ability to keep the family fortune in the family hands.

I once saw a photo of Tante Nini taken thirty years later, in the 1890s, on the portico of her large and imposing house on St. Charles Avenue. Tante Nini was then in her fifties. She was dressed in layers of hot, black silk from chin to toe, from neck to the knuckles of her hands (for she spent her life in mourning for one family member or another). Underneath, she was undoubtedly laced into what my grandmother called "tree-boxes," and her face peers grimly out of that photo, locked for eternity in a straight-browed scowl of discomfort. It was not due to the light. She was by all accounts unpleasant, though the family was careful to disguise their opinion to her face. Tante Nini was very rich.

Dozens of girls were named Marie-Virginie after her. Tante Nini promised to leave her money to each one. Late in life she changed her name to Melanie.

Tante Nini had her own Dominican priest who came to her house on St. Charles Avenue to give her Mass. The grounds were a quarter of a block wide and one block deep. The house itself was stuffed with heavy Victorian boulle breakfronts with ormulu, and desks inlaid with enamel or mother-of-pearl: suffocating atmosphere. Every spring Tante Nini went for six months to her chateau in France. This had been built by Napoleon III in Puy de Dôme and had gardens to equal those of Versailles. Every fall she returned to New Orleans.

After a time, everyone in the family started waiting for

Tante Nini to die. She grew older and older. The new century passed, and finally her nephew, Michel, could bear the suspense no longer. He up and left his wife and children to devote himself full-time to Tante Nini. He was in his forties then and Tante Nini well into her sixties. He thought she might kick the bucket any minute.

After that he followed her to France every summer, and every winter he served her in New Orleans. She gave him a plantation outside of Shreveport, said to be the biggest cotton-producing plantation in the state in its time, and later, one of the biggest gas producers, though such figures change from year to year. In return, she exacted a harsh servitude. Tante Nini could barely speak English, though again, no one mentioned it to her face.

"Vat iss ze weather today, Michel?" she would ask, and her devoté, drawing back the nine-foot petit-point curtains that covered the deep windows would answer with charming sycophancy:

"As you wish, Tante. As you wish."

As it happened, Michel guessed wrong. Tante Nini hung on for forty years. She was one hundred and two by then. The year was 1945 and Michel was over eighty. But eventually he inherited her property.

Several years later, in the 1950s, Cousin Michel decided to make contact with the family. It had been a long time since that had happened. He decided to give a Mardi Gras party in the St. Charles Avenue house. He called one relative (a gentleman who was adopted by his own grandmother, making himself his own uncle), and asked him to spread the word of a dinner later in that week. Michel had never spoken English well, and he was old. He refused to understand that the family had scattered, that one sister lived in Texas then and another in Pittsburgh, or that any of the more distant relatives might have already made plans for Mardi Gras, and moreover, that the cousin, Lelong, whom he talked to by phone was too busy to extend invitations to everyone in the family for Michel.

That afternoon, a table set for twenty-six was laid out with one complete set of Limoges. The butler, John, was standing at the door, the food ready for the table, candelabra glowing against the white tablecloth. At one end of the table sat Cousin Michel, at the other his old lady friend. In between sat an eighteen-year-old girl, Jacqueline, visiting from Paris. All afternoon they waited for the family. Only one person had got the news, a young woman named Jeanne Lelong, an *au pair* at the French Embassy. Everyone else was at Mardi Gras. Jeanne Lelong was the only person to arrive.

It is strange to think of Michel Lelong, hardly able to speak English in the 1950s. But New Orleans, the center of Louisiana society, is as strict and rigid as are all provincial societies; speaking French is considered courteous. Example.

The mother of Walter McIlhenny, present head of Avery Island, was a Creole, who moved when she married to Charlottesville, Virginia, and raised her family there, this French aristocrat in an Episcopalian English clan. She never forgot, however, to be correct. Politely she addressed her son only in French, and she expected the same from him.

Once, during World War II, Walter was wounded in the Pacific. With considerable difficulty he found access to a radio to call his mother in Virginia. The only problem was that a censor had to monitor the call, and the censors spoke only English. Halfway round the planet went the call, until it reached his mother's phone.

"Mrs. McIlhenny," said the operator. "We have a call from your son in the Pacific."

Then Walter spoke. "Anitá," he said (for he always addressed her by her first name). "It's me, Walter."

There was a pause.

"Operator," said Mrs. McIlhenny. "That is not my son. My son would never *dare* to address his mother in English." And she hung up.

French is not the only language heard in the United States. In northwestern Illinois and in Minneapolis, you will hear Swedish and Danish spoken in the streets. Bill Jones of the Jones Dairy Farm in Fort Atkinson, Wisconsin, went to a formal Milwaukee dinner not long ago where the older generation spoke with a German accent and the toasts were all in German. In Nebraska, a Homestead state, the towns stretch out along the railroad lines like beads on a necklace, and there you find a Polish town, a Greek town, a Danish town; our immigrant pools, each reflecting the fancy of those pied-piper railroad recruiters who swept through the Chicago neighborhoods, picking up entire families with their in-laws, cousins, and friends, and moving them west.

The Scully Prairie

To an Easterner, the Midwest is a vast, indeterminate expanse stretching 2,000 miles between the Appalachians and the Rocky Mountains, an immense, white space on the map of his mind, marked "Unexplored." Do you know the story of the Bostonian who was entertaining a Midwesterner at tea and politely asked her guest where she was from?

"Iowa," came the answer.

There was an embarrassed pause. Then the Boston lady corrected her gently. "Here," she said, "we pronounce it Ohio."

People in the Midwest will tell you that they breed no landed aristocracy there; and when you hear of the Midwestern aristocracy, you are told of Milwaukee beer barons, whose family longevity and honors come not from the land but from banking and business; or of the Tafts, three generations of powerful political figures in Cincinnati; or the Pillsburys and Peavys of Minneapolis, who made their fortunes by milling the Midwestern grains into flour; or the McCormicks and Stevensons of Illinois; or the Fords of Detroit; in St. Louis, the Busches, with their private zoos and Clydesdale horses and "The Old Country" amusement parks they have built in Florida and Virginia.

Midwestern fortunes were made in railroads and farm machinery and milling and commodities. They were one step removed from those endless, big-sky prairies that Willa Cather wrote of so lovingly. Here lies some of the finest grazing and growing land in the world. The Midwest, the conservative backbone of our country, is the real America, people will tell you, a vast landscape, checkered with 200- or 300-acre family farms. But throw a dart almost at random in the heart of central Illinois, the "Land of Lincoln," respectable and Republican farmland, and here in Lincoln (population 17,000) you find seventy-two square miles of private land owned for 125 years by three generations of the same family. It is the Scully Prairie.

The Scullys are not the only gentry family in Illinois: there is the Patee family, who own 8,000 or 10,000 acres at Monmouth, and the Drakes, who have 30,000 acres not far off in Elkhart and who are descended from John Gillett, "the cattle king of Illinois," who came west in 1838 at the age of nineteen and acquired 20,000 acres by 1869. Gillett was the first man to ship cattle on the hoof to the Chicago stockyards and to Europe. He was a friend of Lincoln and one of the forty men who escorted the new president to Washington in 1861. Further north you find the Oughtons, who pretty well own Dwight County and whose daughter, Diana, was blown up in a Greenwich Village townhouse in 1970, while making a bomb for the revolutionary Weathermen.

The Scully family own lands in Nebraska and Kansas, too, but I shall describe only one farm in Illinois, where Michael

Scully entertained me, opening to me his family history, feelings, and accounts with astonishing generosity, and a lack of suspicion encountered nowhere else in my travels. Did I want to know the value of the land? Bushels per acre? Profits and losses? He told it willingly. Why? I don't know. Perhaps because his mother had died the year before in France, died suddenly and silently, this vigorous septuagenarian, while sitting in her car at the railroad station near her house in Cannes. Her death was unexpected and with her passing, as Michael said, went "a way of life," of which he was justifiably proud. Perhaps he wanted to have it publicly recorded, set down, before it passed from memory. Perhaps because everyone likes to pose a little for the photographer, if for no other reason than to be certain he exists. Who knows the reason? Michael himself is a blue-eyed dreamer, a romantic idealist, tall and handsome with his mane of gray-black hair and his soft, gentle mouth, who runs his 1,000-acre "bio-dynamic" farm off the proceeds of his 10,000-acre "nonorganic" ones. Michael is a follower of Rudolph Steiner.

He is the older son of Thomas and Violet Scully, his younger brother, Peter, a modern "mechanical" agronomist, lives not on his Illinois lands but in the south of Spain, where he breeds white Lippizaner horses and runs a cattle farm with his partner, Pedro Domecq (of the renowned vineyards).

Irish by extraction, the brothers grew up summering in Scotland, under the care of nannies and governesses, and wintering in their apartment in London, or in Cannes at "La Bastide de la Roquette," the forty-room house set on forty-three acres that was built around 1926 by their father, Thomas. Every fall, Thomas came to Illinois to collect the rents; every Christmas, he returned home to France.

They had a typical upper-class European childhood. At seven,

Michael was sent to boarding school. He remembers sitting in the garden behind La Bastide and hugging his knees: "These have been the best years of my life," he thought with romantic melancholy. "Never again ..." and so forth. In 1939, around the age of twelve, he was sent to Harrow, the school his father had attended. (Thomas was a classmate of Winston Churchill, whom he rather disliked and with whom, unprejudiced, he maintained a correspondence anyway throughout his life.) Michael stayed at Harrow only one day, for war was breaking out, and the family moved permanently to Illinois that fall to live on the lands that the family had owned for almost 100 years. You see how typical is this Midwestern American family. Almost no one has heard of them, except locally. Their fame does not extend even so far as Chicago. But their land has been in the family since the first thirteen square miles were acquired by Michael's grandfather, William, in 1850.

William Scully (1820–1906) was the younger son of an Irish landowner. With the death of an older brother (in a tenants' uprising), William found himself with £1000 in cash and lands in Ireland that produced £1300 a year.

In 1849, at the age of twenty-nine, he went to America and bought his first thirteen square miles of land in Logan County, Illinois. Before William died, he owned 220,000 acres—340 square miles of fat farmland in four Midwestern states: Kansas, Missouri, Nebraska, and Illinois. More than 1,200 families farmed it for him, and though you may never have heard of William Scully, his name was a watchword in Ireland in 1865 and, especially, in 1868. He symbolized all that was evil in the Irish tenant system, both for his rent collection practices (a Winchester repeater in one hand, a revolver in the other, and his henchmen at his side), and for the cruel eviction of tenants in the name of modern economics. He turned people off his land whose families had worked there for 500 years. It was in protest against the practices of William Scully that Parliament passed the Irish land reform acts of the 1870s.*

William Scully demonstrated no such harshness toward his American tenants, but in the 1880s his lands had grown so large in the Midwest, his name so notorious, that Populist outcries rose against the "Irish alien," who was transplanting an "Irish system of tenant serfdom in the United States" and draining his country for the benefit of "absentee aristocrats."

Between 1885 and 1896, nine states and the federal government wrote laws forbidding aliens to hold land indefinitely, and three states (Illinois, Kansas, and Nebraska), where most of the Scully holdings lay, passed their laws all in the same year, 1887. We must assume one target, among others, was Mr. William Scully. His reaction was simple. He applied for citizenship.

Today, one Scully cousin still owns 91,000 acres in Kansas, and another owns 70,000 acres in Nebraska. One 42,000-acre tract in Missouri was sold by Thomas to the federal government. (It had always been unprofitable, I was told, and when the government later sold the land, it took a loss, which the Scullys did not.) In sum, the Scully name today can still lay claim to about 203,000 acres—300 square miles—of fine Midwestern land. And this is as William and Thomas would have had it. Neither liked to sell off land. It was not in their characters. Lean and strict, they didn't even like to give it away as inheritance to their sons.

In Illinois, no Scully land has been sold or even offered for

* The Irish land question constituted a major political issue throughout the nineteenth century. Economics demanded the conversion of land from tillage to pasture, and the system gave the tenant no rights at all—not to land or buildings or improvements to houses made by tenants. All belonged to the feudal landlord. William Scully lacked all sentimentality concerning finance, and when his parish priest spoke out in church against the ruthless evictions, he swept his family up the aisle, got in his wagon and trotted over to the Episcopal church; since that time the Scullys have been Episcopalian.

sale since the late 1860s, except for highways and school sites. There are two large exceptions: in 1911, one twenty-acre tract was donated by William's widow, Angela, in a fit of generosity, to the University of Illinois College of Agriculture to use as a soil and crop experiment station, a purpose for which it is still used today. And four acres were set aside in the last century as a cemetery, to bury the tenants. The cemetery commands a hill, or rather a gentle knoll, among these flats. James Stewart, the farm manager, drove me there, and like the temptations of Christ in parody he showed me, through the windows of his Buick, the Scully lands. All you see is Scully land. It forms a wide circle of some 27,000 acres, not counting the town of Emden two miles north (white houses, barns, and silos, all square and neat and solid) or New Holland, a similar town one mile away. In Emden, half the population are Scully tenants; and underneath these rich, flat fields, where the topsoil reaches twelve feet deep, lie 1,200 miles of drainage tiles, 95 percent of them hand-laid, and on the surface wind another fifteen miles of ditches and open drainage systems, the largest privately undertaken swamp drainage system in the country. It is hard to see from a car. From the air, it is marked by a fine tracery of ditches and gullies that twist through the fields, like capillaries, spilling into creeks that are instantly full in a momentous six-inch Illinois rain, and that in dry times are merely unplowed hollows in the fields.

"In England, the Scullys would own Emden and Hartswell too," commented Jim Stewart matter-of-factly, as he looked across the field. He has been their professional farm manager for twenty-six years and he probably knows more about the Scully estates than any living Scully, and maybe knows almost as much about the family. He was an admirer of Michael's mother, Violet Scully, who for fifteen years after her husband's death was chatelaine of these estates. Stewart helped her give her annual tenants' party for the 135 tenant families on the place, complete with striped marquee on the front lawn and dinner and music and games for the children and a square dance to finish things off. It was all very nice, though a bit patronizing in the English sense, and with her death, Michael felt it appropriate that the practice stop.

Stewart also helped her build her gardens, for being Scottish, Violet Scully took her aristocratic responsibilities seriously in this grim, treeless prairie, where the winds howl down across 1,000 prairie miles from Canada. She built her house in Kickapoo. When I visited, it was for sale for $323,750, together with 14 acres of land, an undistinguished four-bedroom yellow ranch house of wood and limestone. It was in the plantings that the house became of interest, at least for this area, for Mrs. Scully had planted pear, apple, and peach trees, and put in yew and hawthorne windbreaks, and Chinese elm and cypress trees. She put a pasture beyond the house to look through the windows at, and this was cut by post-and-rail fences and then planted with a profusion of wild flowers. Violet Scully spent her winters here in the company of a multiplicity of dogs and cats that wandered at will through the house, shedding on the furniture. She built, in other words, a patch of English landed life. She donated trees to the town of Lincoln and tried to encourage the planting of flowering bushes as windbreaks. The citizens of Lincoln, distrustful of birds, refused her offer to plant tall maples around the courthouse. They let her put in hawthorns. She also restored the Lincoln railroad station and kept a small zoo at one end of her property. That was how she tried to civilize this land, which, like the sea, stretches out, billowing, heaving, lifting, flattening out again in endless prairie waves. It will take another hundred years to dominate it in the English gardened sense. To the farmers who live there, though, it is already beautiful, especially in summer, when the prairie turns into a green ocean of corn, standing higher than a man's head and rippling in the hot, green winds.

The Scully Prairie is farmed by tenants in a cash-rent system imported from Ireland more than 125 years ago and found nowhere else in the United States.*

The landlord (Scully) owns the land; the tenant furnishes all the buildings, fences, and improvements, including wells, and these belong to him to buy or sell, though they establish no rights to the land on which they sit. Each lease runs for one year, renewable each March 1. The tenant pays a cash rent at eighty-three dollars an acre, and the landlord pays the taxes (a populist tax reform that resulted merely in Scully's raising the rent to cover taxes).

If a lease is terminated (as it may be at the end of any fiscal year), the tenant can sell his buildings to the next tenant, who must be approved by the Scullys. Moreover, the Scullys demand that the tenants maintain their buildings properly and fertilize their fields and use proper conservation methods and keep the drainage ditches clean; and if the tenants are industrious, abide by the terms of the lease, pay their rents when due, and maintain a good standing in the community as farmer and citizen, they can expect, according to time-honored Scully tradition automatic renewal of the lease.

You can see the tenant system is pretty far removed from the *patron* system of the South—of Avery Island, for example, where Mister Ned, the patriarch,† ran his island so paternalistically that he ordered a basket of fresh fruit and vegetables delivered each morning to the doorsteps of his workers; or who once

---

* James Stewart, the Scully farm manager, said that Del Monte in north central Illinois grows corn and peas on a cash-rent basis, though without some of the Scully provisions. There was one farm in northwestern Iowa which also used a cash-rent system, but has now discontinued the practice. The common system in the United States is sharecropping.

† Edward Avery McIlhenny—"Mister Ned"—was a genius, charming, ambitious, difficult, who even though he died in 1949 still casts a shadow over the family: his voyage with Peary to the North Pole, his Jungle Gardens, his snowy egrets that he

asked one of the Cajun women to suckle a bear cub he'd found in the swamp. On Avery Island, the family feel a commitment to the Community, as they call the people who have lived and worked on the island for generations; it is their responsibility, *noblesse oblige.*

Mister Ned's food baskets were delivered right up till the 1940s, at the very time when it was worth Michael Scully's father's life to go into Grundy and Livingston counties in Illinois, so angry were his tenants. Scully had reduced rents during the Depression, then forgiven them entirely, and when times improved, he demanded his back rent and attached the wheat crops of those who did not pay. Justly his: you can't deny him that. But the action is indicative of the strict and rigid unyielding principles by which he lived. He toted up his life like a business account. That was it. Those two counties were inspired by his act to switch from cash-rent to a sharecrop system, though his tenants elsewhere made no move to follow.

That the tenants are not unhappy with the Scully arrangement is indicated by the fact that 85 percent of such leases are sold father to son or to neighboring tenant, and only four or five leases change hands in any given year. In a sense, the phrase *independent farmer* might better describe the situation than *tenant,* and many, I am told, have no idea what their leases say and only the vaguest idea that it is renewable, year by year, so automatic is the renewal. Some of the tenants (the present Scullys point them out with pride) are fourth-generation descendants of the first tenants to break the virgin land: the

---

saved from extinction, the nutria (a South American animal he introduced to Louisiana and which promises to overrun the bayous), his book on the life of the alligator, his collected pre–Civil War Negro spirituals—a towering figure he was, whose one failing was that he was easily distracted from the business of making money, so that the family will murmur (in the kindest way) how fortunate they are to have "Mister Walter" as *parrain* now.

Klockingas, the Coorts, the Crosses, the Aldags, and many
others, who came in the 1870s and 1880s—Germans many of
them, for William Scully, like many Irishmen, had a low
opinion of his own countrymen and advertised for dependable,
thrifty, hardworking tenants in Germany. Within the last
twenty years, one tenant, Mr. Cross, raised eleven children and
put every one on a Scully lease. Working a 320-acre farm in
corn and soybeans with a seventy-five-dollar-an-acre return, he
can expect to bring in $20,000 to $24,000 a year, and when he
sells his lease, he can get (as one 160-acre lease near Emden sold
for recently) about $90,000 for a house, barn, two machine
sheds, and a hog barn.

Michael took me to visit one farm family, and then we
caught a glimpse of the subtle relationship, the fragile exercise
of unarticulated inequality, as he knocked on the door of the
neat, white farm house, where a kitten skittered behind the
sandbox on the lawn. Lee, a pretty woman with a long nose
and a wide smile, came out.

"Well, look who's here!" She was surprised, ducking her
head awkwardly between her shoulders and laughing a trace too
loudly as she welcomed her handsome landlord.

"I want to introduce you to a writer," he said suavely. "She's
doing a book on the landed aristocracy, so I naturally had to
bring her round to meet you." He laughed and Lee twisted
with pleased embarrassment. It was enough to set anyone's
heart aflutter to have Michael Scully, tall and rangy and self-
assured—Michael, the founder of one bank, on the board of
another, trustee of the local college, and so forth—to have him
sitting in your kitchen at the maple captain's chair at your
Early American maple table, teasing you lightly in his culti-
vated English accent.

She recounted with sweet pride how her son was going to

Europe with the all-state high school band. Her son was a tuba player, picked especially to go with the group; and she told how he had already gone all the way to Chicago and in June would travel in practically every country in Europe. We said what a good time he'd have. He, age seventeen, had wondered at first if he wanted to go off for twenty-three days—such a long time, and just when the county fair was coming and his father needed him most; but secretly he was excited (his mother said) because he'd never been on an airplane before. Her husband came in, wiping his hands, nodding and smiling amiably from a broad, weathered face. He sat down deliberately at the table with us, quite formally and cordially both at once, and swept into a panegyric on the beauty of the land. From his heart he spoke, hands spread wide on his knees, and we listened, stunned by the latent poetry of his outburst. There was a moment of quiet, then—"Well—" We rose to go to our luncheon up the road. They bowed and laughed and smiled affectionately on Michael, whom it was clear they admired, and who lives in a style far beyond their dreams, though his house is not five miles off, and, like them, he takes his income from the land. Beyond that, hardly anything is the same.

Michael took over his farm in 1955. The year before, his father, Thomas, had been persuaded to give each son 11,000 acres in order to dodge inheritance taxes, and Michael put aside 10,000 to be farmed by tenants in the Scully tradition and took 1,000 for Steiner. Here he built his lovely Mediterranean-style villa, with its warm mosaic tiles and brick floors and bright reds and oranges and yellows and easy aspect of angles and sun. Here he began his experiment that has occupied him for twenty-two years, planting woods, gardens, hedges of dogwood, pine, white oak, and walnut; creating a soil free of pesticides and chemical fertilizers; raising hogs and cattle (for their manure), chickens and tillage; and cultivating in central Illinois, according to the precepts of Dr. Pangloss, his garden.* His wife, Jean, daughter of a Racine, Wisconsin, farmer, is an artist, whose religious and mystical paintings demonstrate that "color is the revelation," as she explains, "of suffering and deeds, of light and darkness." I admit I understood the principle only dimly. She–also a Steinerite–teaches art to mentally retarded children in a Steiner slum school in Chicago, once a month. It is four hours away by car.

In Michael's office the bookcases are filled with volumes on literature, art, religion, yoga, agriculture, and anthropology. Michael came across the teachings of Rudolph Steiner when his tyrannical father banished him from his house. Michael wandered dolefully off to Mt. Kisco, New York, where his girlfriend, his beloved Didi Ladd, lived. She was then a senior at Foxcroft, and her mother took him in. Didi's mother believed she was the reincarnation of a famous French courtesan, and being herself a Steinerite, she sent Michael to work on the farm of D. Ehrenfried Pfeiffer, in Chester, New York, forty miles above Tarrytown, and there he was initiated into "biodynamic" agriculture, the principles of which go back, I understand, to Herodotus and are based not only upon organic, or nonchemical, nontoxic farming, but also on the sweep of the planets, gyre and fall, the rhythm and rays of astral energy.

"I get 110 bushels of corn per acre," said Michael, pulling down the efficiency charts that he has kept for twenty-two years to compare the costs of labor, machinery, and fertilizer for the organic and chemically-fertilized fields and the return on hogs, cattle, and corn.

* It is work he expects to stop in another eleven years, at the age of sixty-one. For him that will conclude one 33⅓-year biologic or rhythmic cycle: time for a new career.

Three men work the farm on salary. They are paid according to government minimum wage standards and receive Social Security and retirement benefits as well, just as in any corporation.

"We can do about as well as the Amish," he said. "If you can get along on two or three thousand dollars a year, you can get along very well as an organic farmer."

But Michael is not farming for profit. He is a driven man, burned pure by a vision of corn and soybeans grown with no carcinogenic herbicides, of cattle free of toxic grains. Yet he can find no outlets to market an organically pure Scully steer, people in the Midwest not being educated to demand "organic" meat: he loses money there, too.

"Listen, we degrade man to the state of an animal," he said fiercely. "We degrade animals to the state of plants and plants to that of minerals.... We pack cattle into feed lots and stuff them with hormones and chemicals. Then we eat this cancer-producing food. We shoot plants with salt solutions. ... Did you eat the grapefruit for breakfast? It was an organic grapefruit. Could you taste the difference? It's sweeter and without the coarse fibers of a commercial grapefruit."

Michael is now breeding horns back on his cattle, for a Steiner theory, he solemnly explains, holds that astral radiations enter cattle through their horns, and that without these radiations the animals are poor beasts that drop their heads in the low-set, glazed-eyed, hang-neck stare of the common polled steer.

The horns have use beyond aesthetics. When his cattle are slaughtered, he cuts off the horns, fills them with manure, and buries them for a year in the earth. The following year he mixes twenty ounces of solution to sixty gallons of pure rainwater in a special machine that he has imported from Australia, stirs for one hour in vortex fashion, reversing direction every five minutes. This sucks in the power of the planets, he explains simply, and "potentizes the solution." It is then spread thinly over his fields and "enlivens" the earth as much as three feet deep, increasing his organic matter from 2 to 8 percent.

"We are not dealing with physical matter here," he explained in response to my skepticism, "but with forces of nature that we do not understand. That does not mean they are any the less true.

"Look, this is the wave of the future," he continued, turning over his manure pile with a pitchfork, to show me the beautiful black, rich, worm-filled loam. "Someday people will understand. We're coming to this. More and more, you'll see. This is the way everyone will farm."

The Californians

California, land of sun and desert and splendid beaches and high stands of mountain timber lying quiet in the snow. California represents the myth, land of the future. Oh, not in California shall we find that psychology of deadening, passive, fearful rootedness I described earlier. No, California brings to mind an easy egalitarianism, a sunlit indolence of tanned, blond bodies, rippling with high-protein health, who surf down the waves to white sand shores; and here is San Francisco, quaint and varicolored with its steep hills plunging to the Bay; and here is Los Angeles with its classless, restless, rootless association of actors, dancers, satyrs, singers, starlets, dropouts, beggars, blacks, pederasts, and parasites—migrants from other lands, casting out their pasts; all push and shove and hardly any present, much less a past, to draw us from the scurry of the day.

Yet even in Los Angeles sound the chronicles of class; so that we find Mrs. Collis Huntington marrying her own nephew to keep the money in the family, and the California Club spreading its wings to the present day over the local business community.

There are a number of reasons why we should pause over California. First, land ownership has been studied and charted in California as in no other state. Second, California society is feudal in ways that stagger the imagination. Third, many California fortunes are based not on land alone, but on water rights. In this the state is representative of Alaska, Hawaii, and seventeen Western states—from Texas and Arizona to Montana—"appropriative rights," they are called, the euphemism meaning that anyone upstream can take your water, cut you dry.

Finally, there is a fourth reason for studying California, and that is because this state may represent in its landholding patterns the direction of the future, as California culture, like a phagedena, spreads slowly eastward, rhythm, dress, music swimming west to east.

Look, then, at California. There are two great urban states in our country, two that have the highest concentration of people living in cities of 50,000 or more. The first is California—which is 90.9 percent urban. The second is New Jersey with 88.9 percent. In California you have land privately held in fantastic amounts: the Chandler's Tejón Ranch of 348,000 acres, 40 percent of which is owned by the Chandler Family, publishers of the Los Angeles *Times;* Southern Pacific Company, with 2,411,000 acres, or 4.7 percent of the total private acreage; the Newhall Land and Farming Company, with 1,590,000 acres; Standard Oil of California with 306,000; Boise Cascade Corporation with 303,000; Sunkist Corporation, with 192,000; and Tenneco Incorporated, with 362,843 acres. In Virginia, land was broken up by economics, poverty, war, and inheritance. In California, the pattern of vast holdings that began when no more than fifty families ruled an unbroken territory was never successfully broken up.

I have a friend from the Midwest who once told me that in the East "nice people," even when they are very rich, try to live "down" to the democratic system, that in the Midwest they made a pretense of egalitarian ideals; that in the Far West they make no pretense: they live like Spanish dons.

Even though the intense concentration of land was broken to some degree early in the century, it is now on the increase. There are 100,185,000 land acres in California.* According to the Nader study, *Politics of Land,* by Richard C. Fellmuth, the federal and state governments controlled 48,765,765 acres in 1969. Of the rest, twenty-five landowners hold more than 16 percent of the private land, or 51,419,000 acres. Combining the two, the federal government and twenty-five private landholders own 58 percent of the total land area in California.

Two-hundred-fifty-seven corporations own at least 25 percent of the privately held land. Including government ownership, 250 holders own almost two-thirds of the state's total land.

This is an extraordinary figure for a state with a population of 20 million, where 2 million are Mexican-American and 1.4 million are black, where 16.6 percent of the population, or 3.3 million people, are characterized as poor, meaning that their incomes fall below $3,000 a year, and another 2.2 million, or 11.1 percent, earn no more than $5,000 a year.

In rural counties, Nader found that, in general, the top twenty landowners control from 25 percent to 50 percent of the private land, and, if the government ownership is included, *the top twenty landholders are found to control from 50 to 90 percent of the land!*

* All figures from Nader's study, "Who Owns California," in *Politics of Land,* Grossman, 1973.

In the urban countries, the top twenty landowners of any county own 15 to 30 percent of the private land.

You can see the pattern for yourself. Drive down the coastal highway from San Francisco toward Los Angeles, and for miles from Carmel almost to San Simeon, you are driving on public land in the Ventana wilderness. This area is so rough, the mountains so sheer, rugged, barren, and dry, that the land is essentially useless for agriculture. Farther along, the cliffs dip down to luscious green valleys, where the mountains roll into high hills, less stubborn than those in the public domain. Barbed-wire fencing—or none at all—marks this open grazing land, and the place looks like a little piece of Scotland, all covered with soft mists and filled with water and thick grass. And all of this land for twenty-five miles along the highway belongs to the Hearst Corporation, owned by the Hearsts. After nineteen miles of driving across their land, you come to the town of San Simeon, where you can stop to see the Hearst Castle, constructed by the late William Randolph Hearst of the publishing and communications empire and left to the state as a state museum, state maintained, state controlled. All the surrounding land, including the town of San Simeon with the exception of one grocery store, still belongs to the Hearsts: twenty-five miles north to south and eight miles wide from the high-tide line at the ocean to a point beyond the Santa Lucia Mountain range. In that area, everything belongs to the Hearst Corporation except the castle with its fantastical art collection, the road leading to the castle, and the state concession at the foot of the hill. If you step off the tour bus and walk a hundred feet, you are again on Hearst land. One hundred and fifty square miles is held by that one family, and the Hearsts are not even listed among the top twenty-five private landholders in California.

Baronies, these are, yet they represent merely a continuation of California history. When the Spanish established their mission system in the sixteenth century, they were establishing the first corporate agribusinesses. The church gathered workers—in this case the Indians, who were the only proletariat available—and created the first industrial system of agriculture, a system in existence in California today.

Only a scattered few of these lands were Spanish land grants, though to hear most present owners, each is legally descended from royal investiture. When the Mexican government broke up the mission system in 1833, it granted 26,000,000 acres to some 800 families in reward for political, economic, and military favors. And still the population was so low, the area so remote that, in 1840, only nine years before the gold rush, there were only 3,000 non-Indian adult males in all of California. What was needed most were people. And so, in 1836, as the United States was winning the Mexican War, Governor Pico Pio, the last Mexican governor, was liberally bestowing land grants to family and friends. It was these grants that the Americans in later years would proceed quite systematically to plunder with the racial arrogance and arguments usually aroused in the breasts of the mighty. They did it by the simple expedient of the law courts, exerting continuous pressure on the recipients and heirs of these Mexican grants to demonstrate the legitimacy of their holdings, until, over the years, the original holders were simply impoverished, worn down by the expense of the suits, and forced, ultimately, to sell. It took a long time. The last such case was not settled until 1931.

In the 1870s, a federal commission approved some 588 of these grants, covering 8,000,000 acres. They form today the basis for many of the top twenty-five landholdings in California.

And such space! Such oceanic space!

No wonder a system of serfdom still exists today, institutionalized in the migrant worker system. No wonder the power of landlord, himself of a class with judges, businessmen, governors, and bankers, should combine with colleagues to rend powerless the attempts of the peasants to form unions, to form, in other words, a power block against the nobles. I use archaic terms, but have we really progressed beyond the sixteenth-century Mediterranean? The eighteenth-century Hudson River fiefs?

It is a matter of social complicity, the loyalty of class. The nobles go to school together, intermarry, eat and drink together at their clubs—the California Club in Los Angeles or the Burlingame Club in San Francisco, for no one should imagine that the owners all live in the baking heat of those flat, monotonous plains. No, like the rich of all ages, they live in cool villas by the sea. They spend their time escaping into physical activity—to the mountains to ski, to Africa to shoot on safari, to Mexico to sun and gamble and pick up bargains.

Nothing about our landed life-styles is new. Fernand Braudel, who spent twenty years writing his wonderful book *The Mediterranean World in the Age of Philip II*, shows how nobles have owned the great plains, and small farmers the rugged hillsides from the beginning of recorded time—in Sicily, in Andalusia, in Bulgaria, Turkey, and Thrace.* He explains the character of populations, where mountainous regions are populated by small farmers, fierce, tough, proud, independent, and poor, while the latifundia are the preserve of peasants. It is a function of terrain. A pick or an axe might be enough in the forests of medieval Europe (as it was later in America) to make the soil productive; but the malaria-infested southern plains,

---

* The Spanish enquiry of 1547 on property in Lombardy (which is now in Italy) indicates that peasants owned less than 3 percent of the land in the fertile lower region, while the poor hill land was mostly in their hands. In the 1930s, 38 percent of the land of the Campagna (another province of Italy) belonged to four landowners, while the mountains were "the reserve of smallholders."

with swamp and scrub, required vast investments in drainage and irrigation and long-term engineering projects before they could yield a crop. This requires money. It requires also a labor force organized into a strict social order—which on the flatlands can be easily maintained by armies, as it cannot be maintained in the mountains.

The character of a people, then, is influenced by terrain. Plains folk are conservative, attached to their environment, says Braudel. They are slow to contemplate social disorder or any change that might disrupt their land, and, since any change is disruptive, change at all is generally for the bad. In the plains, with its rigid traditionalism, we find the rich are very rich and the poor impoverished.

A great proportion of this inequality in California was created and perpetuated by the Southern Pacific Railroad, which received, pretty much as a gift, the 2,411,000 acres that make it today the largest private landholder in California.

All the Western railroads received land as an incentive to build the transcontinental system that would rake in billions of dollars over the years: it was a government bounty. Among those defending the system was one San Francisco attorney who asked that he not be quoted by name.

He was a gray, horse-faced gentleman, with that talent peculiar to lawyers (do they learn it in law school?) of taking any exciting tale and spinning it out with such long, reflective pauses, such phraseological caution (gumming each word like a toothless nonegenarian), that he bleeds the ideas dry.

"Now have in mind," he said, "that at that time this land was literally worthless.... Except for the railroad.... The railroad would sell the land, or trade it off, in order to help pay for the cost of building the railroad."

He leaned back, fashioning a steeple with his fingers, and examined the statement just made.

"Is that what the grant was for?" I asked.

"Right. To finance the railroads." He paused again. Minutes
dragged quietly by. "And in addition to that," he continued
when I made no move to interrupt, "the statute required the
railroads forever to give the government ... the federal
government ... a discount on freight rates. It's still in effect.
It's a substantial discount, applying to the movement of
government property ... and most important, to troops in
wartime. ... But that's what it is. ... And it's been an extraor-
dinarily good scheme," he pursued the thought, still rocking
meditatively in his big chair, still tapping his fingertips lightly
together, "because it's provided us fairly early on with a pretty
good railroad network in the western part of the country.
Southern Pacific, of course, is one of the best railroads, but it's
only one of several."

Apparently this gentleman did not know—had never ques-
tioned—that the Southern Pacific did not sell its lands, as
required by the act of July 1, 1862.

> And all such lands so granted ... which shall not be sold
> or disposed of by said company within three years after
> the entire road shall have been completed, shall be subject
> to ... preemption, like other lands, at a price not ex-
> ceeding one dollar and twenty-five cents per acre, to be
> paid to said company.

The act was never enforced, though to this day the present
use of the land in no way serves "in the construction of the
railroad." Rather, it is used for timber, mining, farms, and
grazing.

The Southern Pacific is still, as it has been from the
beginning, a major force in California land politics. If in its
history the railroad ruined many families, it made the fortunes
of its directors and associates; and none perhaps so dazzlingly as

those of Lloyd Tevis and James Ben Ali Haggin, partners and brothers-in-law, who were founders of the railroad and who ended up themselves with the largest empire in America— 500,000 continuous acres in California, almost 800 square miles in all, and one-and-a-half million acres if you count the land in other states. One-and-a-half million acres. Imagine. That comes to 2,343 square miles, an area more than fifty miles long and forty miles wide. It is hard to conceive of such a space in private hands.

Some properties in America are larger than that, but they are held in scattered parcels. This one was, in its time, the single largest holding in America, bigger than the King Ranch. The property was known as the Kern County Land Company, and it too lay in the rich, fat plains of California's Central Valley.

A feudal barony it was, and one heir was my father's friend, Gordon Tevis.

The Tevis Empire: 2,343 Square Miles

In the fall of 1976, I went to visit Gordon Tevis and his wife, Josephine, in San Francisco. They sent their chauffeured car to pick me up at the hotel and bring me to their Pacific Heights house. Gordon Tevis, heir to an empire, was, at eighty-three, paralyzed by a stroke. His moustache was white and thinning now, his bluish wrists hard as bird bones, jutting from the sleeve of his robe. He is confined now to his bedroom or one study at the head of the stairs.

Dressed in a camel bathrobe, a white silk ascot tied at his throat, he sat in a wheelchair, his knees covered by a cashmere plaid. On a tray before him stood a plate of cheese and crackers and a glass of white wine. The wine was served in a goblet so thin that it is a pleasure to feel the rim against one's lips, to twirl the long stem in one's fingers.

The study was painted a chocolate brown, and the walls were lined almost floor to ceiling with autographed photos of the friends and associates of a lifetime, for Gordon Tevis knew everyone. Will Rogers, Bernard Baruch, generals, movie stars, politicians, and presidents. To one side was a bridge table with four chairs, where we would eat dinner the following night with General Wedemeyer.

We ate with vermeil knives and forks, and we were served by Randy, who wore a white jacket and white gloves. The Tevises have two servants, Randy and Clarence, both of whom have been with them about twenty years, devotedly. When Clarence drives the car, he changes from his indoor white jacket to a discreet black.

I remember as a child when Mr. Tevis visited us at our house in Maryland. He was big and robust, filling the rooms with laughter. He and his wife took over the kitchen and cooked steaks with soy sauce, and tortillas—dishes as exotic to my provincial palate as squid or octopus. I didn't know that he was heir to a cattle empire. I wouldn't have cared. I adored his zest, his joyous buoyancy. I'd never seen anything like it.

Once, I remember asking my father what Gordon Tevis did for a living, and he answered: "Gordon has never worked in his life. But he's made it his life's work to entertain."

He knew a little about everything. He could converse on any subject. He cooked. He read. He farmed. He was the Rennaissance Man.

I remember one evening he set up in the living room a card table covered with a white cloth, on which he performed a series of magic tricks. My eyes bulged! I could not have been more than eleven or twelve at the time, and I knew that magic was no more than sleight of hand, but no matter how hard I watched, I couldn't see his move. One trick he did was the shell game. He called our two servants, Henry and Elizabeth, to the room (because we actually had someone in the house right then), put a quarter under under one of three shells on the table, switched them around, and asked them to find the coin. And when Elizabeth chose a shell—miraculous—it contained a five-dollar bill. It was a lot of money in those days. At least to me.

Twenty-five years later in San Francisco, he sipped his cold white wine and talked to me of the Kern County Land Company, founded by the partners Haggin and Tevis and incorporated in the 1890s, which controlled 500,000 acres in California's Central Valley and one-and-a-half million acres in all. The company is no longer held by his family, nor is the stock sold any longer on the New York Stock Exchange. But the land is still intact, having been bought in 1963 all in one piece by Tenneco. As the subsidiary of a giant corporation, it achieves today a singular anonymity in the sense that no single proprietor walks across its fields, no single man is responsible or can be held accountable for what happens on that land. As a corporate entity, its status is one step further removed from the public view. Have we, then, advanced? If it was once an unbroken private fiefdom, property of Gordon Tevis' grandfather and a great-uncle, it is today a barony of the brokerage houses.

Lloyd Tevis and James Ben Ali Haggin (his mother was Turkish) were brothers-in-law, having married two sisters back in Kentucky. They came West together, and it was in a natural familial association that they established a law practice in 1850 in Sacramento. Three years later, when they moved to San Francisco, their law practice was already declining, replaced by faster fortune hunting. In a short time they would belong to the group of Nob Hill magnates who dominated the development of the West. Many were associated with the railroads.

There was Leland Stanford (whence cometh Stanford University), Collis P. Huntington, Senator George Hearst (father of the William Randolph Hearst who founded a newspaper and motion picture empire, built the fantasmagorical St. Simeon castle, and fathered the man who would father Patty, gun moll by threat or volition for the Symbionese Liberation Army). There was George Crocker (whose name is preserved in the Crocker Bank of California). There was Darius O. Mills, who carried his wealth back to New York with him, married a Livingston, and saw one daughter, Gladys, marry Henry Carnegie Phipps, another become Countess of Granard; his son would later serve as secretary of the treasury under Herbert Hoover. There was also Henry Miller of the company Miller & Lux.

Miller, who acquired a million acres in five states, with a million head of livestock, and became the rival and archenemy of Haggin and Tevis in a running war over water that ended only after a lawsuit that changed California's water law and that still stands today as the longest opinion ever written by the California Supreme Court.

Before they finished, Haggin and Tevis held a monopoly, the conglomerate of their time. They had a hand in utilities, mining, and transportation.

Their close associations with the Central Pacific Railroad Company and with the Southern Pacific may explain the ease with which they acquired railroad lands in Kern County, for Lloyd Tevis was active in the formation of the Southern Pacific and later became a vice president of the company. In addition, he owned 1,300 miles of stage lines, for he founded the Pacific Express Company, a bus service in effect, which was to merge with Wells Fargo and Company (of which he was president from 1882 to 1893).

Finally comes the mining. Haggin and Tevis developed, together with George Hearst, the Homestake Mining Company—and again, Tevis was president. Homestake was the outstanding gold producer in the western hemisphere. To give you an idea of the size of the operation: In 1899, the net output of the mines in Nevada came to $15 million—all in an era before income taxes. In 1939, the heirs still held a major interest in the Homestake. For the three years ending 1938, which was the tail end of the Depression, net profits from the mine averaged more than $11 million, which was five times the average profits of an equivalent period ten years before.

Haggin and Tevis also founded Anaconda Copper Mines with Hearst and, also, the Comstock silver mines. They owned so many mines—gold, silver, copper—in California, Nevada, Utah, Idaho, and South Dakota that of Haggin it was said: "A list of the mines finally owned in whole or in part by Haggin in the course of his career would cover the whole Western Hemisphere, for his interests extended from Alaska to Chile."

Land investment in the Central Valley was a sideline to these men, a diversion almost, derived from that Kentucky background where the gentry owned land and lived graciously thereon. Eventually Haggin and Tevis, Midas-touched, acquired a monopoly of land as well.

Apparently their initial idea was to acquire some farms, irrigate them, and sell at a profit.* That was before they discovered profits in land could equal bonanza mines at far less risk. Silently they set out to get water and land rights on a large scale.

Their front man was the third in the partnership, Billy Carr, lobbyist and "political Napoleon" of the Southern Pacific Railroad. Word had it when he arrived in Kern County in 1874 that he was buying his retirement estates.

In the next few years, Haggin, Tevis, and Carr (as the

---

* For a detailed history, see "Land, Water and Settlement in Kern County California: 1850–1890," by Margaret Aseman Cooper; thesis for MA degree in Economics, University of California, Berkeley, 1954.

company was known until 1893) bought, for three or four dollars an acre, 59,000 acres of the most fertile Central Valley land, this being the odd-numbered railroad sections in six townships. In 1877 they bought another 66,000 acres from the railroad of which Tevis was a director, "including all in three townships of the choicest lands on the [Kern River] Island." They bought land wherever they could get it. They bought scrip for veterans' homestead grants. The scrip turned out to be fraudulent, but this did not come out until later and by then Congress was passing the Desert Land Act, so that just as 27,000 acres of scrip-land was declared invalid the trio relocated it as desert. No wonder some people claimed that H., T., and C. had pushed the legislation through Congress.

The Desert Land Act limited each entry to 640 acres. Carr claimed 70,000 acres through the use of "dummy" individuals and false claims. It was out-and-out fraud. But H., T., and C. were permitted to keep the land after explaining that they had indulged in the deception because they were the only ones big enough to irrigate and make the land useful. Which was perfectly true. They promised to sell it after the irrigation. Which was perfectly false.

Again and again in the 1800s Congress passed land reform acts. We're doing it still, to distribute homesteads to the "little man," the small farmer, backbone of our nation. Again and again it watched, baffled, as land monopolists snapped the offerings up. The same things had happened in the 1850s with the Swamp Land Act: explicit fraud. In that year Congress granted to the individual states all federally held "swamp and overflow lands," together with funds for their drainage. The lands were to be sold to individual farmers, at a dollar an acre, and a limitation of 350 acres per family.

By 1880, 51,000,000 acres had been patented to the states in a chaos of dummy entries and false titles. "There was never a cat rolled whiter in meal," wrote Horace Greeley, an advocate of the Swamp Lands Act, "and I for one was completely duped. ... The consequence was a reckless and fraudulent transfer to certain States of millions of acres of choice lands, whole sections of which had not muck enough on their surface to accommodate a single fair-sized frog; ... while never a shake of ague has any pioneer been spared by reason of the drainage done under that specious act."

Dry and balmy California sold more than 2,000,000 acres of "swamp." Two state surveyors, swampland designators, left office with 300,000 acres apiece and Henry Miller, of Miller & Lux, just downstream from H., T., and C. on the Kern River, ordered a team of horses hitched to a boat and had himself dragged over one tract in order to testify to the marsh. Miller held so much land that he boasted he could drive his cattle from the border of Mexico to the border of Oregon and sleep every night on his own property. Gordon Tevis in his San Francisco mansion put that one to rights.

"He didn't have much land," he commented scornfully. "He used to make that boast, but the reason was because his land was all cut up in little chunks. It wasn't *contiguous,* like Kern County's."

Gordon Tevis sipped his wine, remembering his upbringing. He was one of four brothers. His twin was Lansing. ("His photo is on the wall, up there, at the top. See him?" he said, pointing to a photo of four men, brown specks on a brown background, beside the dragonfly structure of an early plane. "He was an Early Bird," he explained proudly; he was so fond of him that he keeps returning to the theme, repeating: "He was an Early Bird, my brother Lansing, my twin.") *

* There were 588 Early Birds of Aviation when the group was formed in 1929. To qualify for membership an Early Bird must have made a solo flight before December 17, 1916, the thirteenth anniversary of the first powered flight.

None of the brothers went to school. They had tutors on the ranch. "I was the stupid one," proclaimed Gordon. "I graduated from Yale, and I was the stupidest of the lot. I graduated by giving them thirty-two tarantulas from the ranch. They were so grateful they gave me a diploma."

His mother's father was the governor of California in 1875, Ramauldo Pacheco, and, again, a magazine is pulled out for me, opened to a picture of the Spanish governor, a handsome young man with his long black hair and flashing eyes, roping a bear from horseback before a crowd of shouting friends. Pacheco left a Spanish land grant, which Gordon's father sold to William Randolph Hearst in later years. "It wasn't any great acreage," explained Gordon. "Sixty thousand acres or so. I stayed there many times."

Then he told me of the first time he really saw the ranch.

He sat in his wheelchair, stiffly, gesturing occasionally with his clenched right hand. His arm and wrist showed bluish white skin with a fine articulation of the veins. His wife had warned me softly, when showing me upstairs, that "he gets very emotional." And it was true that during his account he would suddenly stop, his jaw working. He would open and close his mouth—and he was so warm and emotional, greeting me, the daughter of his old friend, whose photo was with the others on the wall. "Call me Gordon," he said in his husky voice—mouth opening, closing, his jaw working against its ankylosis, while tears started in his eyes. I do not know if this was due to the depth of his emotion or to the reactions induced by his stroke: the tears poured down his cheeks.

"I remember the first time I really saw the land," he said, "We lived on a ranch called Stockdale. This was one of the ranches on Kern County, but there were also outside ranches, because it was so big. We had Santo Medeo," he recalled. "The Poso Ranch, the Bear Mountain Ranch, Bellevue, where the slaughterhouse was, and where the cattle were killed every day for the Bakersfield population–that was the nearest town.

"We had our own car," he continued, meaning his private Pullman, "called the Santo Medeo. It was built by Waggoner and reconditioned in New York by Pullman. I crossed the continent many times in it, and every summer I rode in it when we went to Lake Tahoe, and then we'd leave it and drive up to the lake." His family went to Lake Tahoe every summer for fifteen or sixteen years. And here he digressed to tell that there were four boys in the family, and pointing out the picture of Lansing on the wall, told how he had flown in 1912. Gordon himself was a pilot for a year and a half in World War I, being then about fifteen or sixteen years old.

"Anyway, the story I wanted to tell ... Alice Tevis, this girl, was my first cousin, the child of my father's elder brother, Hugh Tevis. He died, and my mother took Alice to live with us more than six month before ... before...." ·

And here, his jaw working, opening, closing, he burst into tears. After a moment, he wiped the tears from his cheeks, smiling toward me.

"The doctor recommended altitude to help her, and I was also sick," he continued, "with something wrong with my glands. He suggested Alice and I go up to the Santo Medeo Ranch, up in the Sierra Nevadas. It was my first, really–" Again he stopped. "My first remembrance of the ranch is out the car window when we came into Sunset. We were met by my father's foreman on a coach with four magnificent gray horses. The coach was built on the place, and it had gun racks inside and places for ammunition ... The foreman was Portuguese. Anton. He met us at Sunset, and I remember something, I don't know why.

"We, Alice and I, were in the room in the private car. I was sicker than she and lying in the lower bunk. We had to drive from Sunset about twenty-eight miles to Santo Medeo. She died within ten days of that." His voice broke. His jaws again began to work, and tears were pouring down his cheeks. "Rushed back to San Francisco. . . ." His voice broke. With an effort, he controlled himself.

"It was an early morning and on the oil fields in Sunset there were men standing about, workmen. They'd never seen a private railroad car before. I thought nothing of it. I'd been to New York, travelling all over in it. I was about twelve years old, I guess. And looking out the window, I could see they were looking at us in amazement, these big, hard-boiled fellas that worked. And then alongside the car came the four horses, and Anton, and this coach, waiting for us to emerge. We got in the coach and drove away. They thought us freaks," he laughed up at me. "Like a travelling circus.

"But it was so beautiful. That's what I remember. Wild-flowers in abundance. Lupin. California poppy and that lily—what is it, Josephine?—the mariposa lily, an absolute mass of them. We drove up to Santo Medeo. It was the first time I'd been there. There was a small orange grove my father had planted. . . . And we were there three nights when the doctors came to visit and said Alice had to go to San Francisco to be operated on. . . .

"And then . . . and then . . ." He tried to continue, working to hold back his tears. "Then she . . . died. . . . We . . . loved her so."

The Kern County Land Company was run by Gordon Tevis' father after Lloyd Tevis' death, "and not too well, I'm afraid to say," commented Gordon, for the son of the acquisitor is not always a fit manager of estates acquired. Later, when oil was discovered on the land, the property was turned over to corporate managers, professionals, who saw to it in the 1930s that the company was listed on the New York Stock Exchange and that holdings were diversified by picking up a few extras on the side: the J. I. Case Company of Wisconsin, which makes farm tractors and equipment; Walker Manufacturing Company, also of Wisconsin, which makes auto mufflers. No Tevises were on the board of the company for years, and when the corporate managers sold the company to Tenneco, no Tevises sat on that board either, although Louis Lee Haggin, who has a horse farm in Lexington, Kentucky, sits on the Tenneco board, as did John B. Fermor-Hesketh in the 1950s, the Heskeths, barons in England, being distant Tevis relations.

In 1963, Tenneco bought the Kern County Land Company. One source, who worked both sides of the fence as a lawyer, said that Tenneco was interested in the mineral and oil rights and in the two Wisconsin companies, and had little interest in the agricultural lands; and, indeed, Tenneco did proceed to sell some of the 400,000 California acres—626 square miles, in thirty-acre lots, retaining the mineral rights. It reorganized the company right out of existence, dissolving the name and merging the operations into a new corporate entity that it called Tenneco West. I was told with insistent sharpness by several people that the Kern County Land Company was not thereby liquidated. Tenneco West still owns some 300,000 acres—almost 500 square miles. But no one will step on the land now and feel his heart swell with its beauty, for no one owns it anymore. No one is responsible. It is now the domain of the corporate gentry.

The Running ᴍ

Well, this book is supposed to be about the landed gentry, and here we are discussing people who once owned land. Or people who can barely hold onto it, or who have turned their land into corporations and are as landed in a literal sense, therefore, as anyone else who owns stock on the New York Stock Exchange.

And what about fantastic wealth? Princes and kings and feudal peonage?

What about the largest place of all, the King Ranch in Texas, which owns and leases (sometimes with partners) 11,500,000 million acres around the world, more land than is at the disposal of any family on the face of the world? The King Ranch owns land in Pennsylvania, Florida, Kentucky, Venezuela, Brazil, Argentina, Australia, Morocco, and Spain; a kingdom it is, comprising an area almost 18,000 square miles in size, an area larger than Denmark, larger than Holland, much larger than Belgium, and eighteen times larger than the state of

Rhode Island. The Texas ranch alone, held in four divisions, is so large that between the north and south boundaries there is a month's difference in seasons.* And on it work the kiñenos, vaqueros, whose families have worked for generations for the ranch, father and son, until their names are associated with the place: the Mindiettas, Silvas, Quintenillas. There are said to be people on the King Ranch who have never in all their lives been off the Kleberg land, so large are the ranch horizons, so narrow the lives of the staff. But then the myths of the King Ranch are Brobdingnagian, even by Texas standards.

The writer Larry McMurtry tells how he once tried to write an article about the King Ranch thoroughbred stables for *Sports Illustrated* and was turned away at the gate—which is to say at the airfield. The family had changed their mind. He never learned why. He was not surprised. Almost no one can "get to" the King Ranch, he says, so private are the owners.†

---

* And even this is not the largest landholding in one place. That distinction belongs to the Gang Ranch in Canada, which owns, I hear, a province in British Columbia of approximately four million acres, all in a block. It is seventy-five miles across. The King Ranch, by contrast, a private corporation, has only some 860,000 acres in Texas, according to the brochure printed by the company. This does not include other lands held by family members, and you will find other figures quoted. *Time* magazine, in 1974, reported the Texas lands at 976,000 acres, and *Fortune*, in 1969, brought the Texas holdings to 1,200,000 acres. Whatever the case, the scale is so big that the distance cannot be comprehended anyway.

† I believe him. When I called John Cypher of the ranch public relations office after this chapter was written, to check my facts, I was told that the ranch would have to read the whole chapter first. "All writers," he said in a soft voice, "agree to an opportunity for us to read the manuscript . . . *Time* . . . *Fortune*. . . . I cannot see how we could cooperate to offer you quotes, unless you could conform to our long-term policy on King Ranch."

I explained it was my policy never to show a manuscript in advance of publication, but that I would check, sentence by sentence, any facts about the ranch. Since I refused the opportunity offered by him, he refused to tell me if any facts had changed. "Since it has worked so well for us in the past, I don't see how I could recommend to our board that it should deviate from it in the future. We have no commodity to sell to the public," he explained. "No reason to get our name before

The boundaries of the ranch are fenced and guarded, he says, like a private preserve. Once, a hunter shot and wounded a buck near the King Ranch. The deer, fleeing, jumped the wire fence onto King Ranch land. The hunter followed—a furtive look—and crept through the five-strand 59-inch wire fence (5,000 miles of fencing, specially made for the Running W by the Keystone Wire Company of Peoria, Illinois), and was just bending over his kill when a Mexican cowboy on horseback appeared with a rifle in his saddle and a holster at his hip. The hunter, frightened, leveled his rifle at the outrider, who turned without a word and disappeared over the hill. Then the hunter lost no time. Abandoning his deer, he scrambled back over the fence and hid in the brush on the other side. Minutes later, he saw the rider return, accompanied by six other vaqueros, who fanned out, shotguns over their arms, riding along the fence line. He did not wait for their return.

The myths gather and grow. In the 1930s, Luther Blanton and his son John were said to have jumped the fence onto the King Ranch property. They were never seen again. It made a lot of trouble. Rangers arrived to put down the threats of violence, and rumors flew about what had happened to the men, lost or killed in that "walled kingdom," though people on the ranch will tell you that they *know* whatever happened to them was no fault of the King Ranch ... because they know the people involved.

---

the public. We do deviate [from our position of silence] when we feel we have something to say—about once a decade. There was *Time* magazine in 1949 ... the Tom Lea biography in 1957, on which we own the copyright ... the *Fortune* magazine articles in 1969. We've had some bad experiences with the press, though, and don't want more."

The facts in this chapter are drawn from these three publications, especially the latter two, and a public *Legend,* published by the ranch for tourists. They are drawn, in addition, from the interviews conducted at the King Ranch during my short visit with a member of the family.

They are right to be afraid of publicity, the King Ranch heirs; they rear back from the light because when they are considered by their size alone (and how to separate them from the ranch?) they are ... what? Freaks in a sideshow. *Here they are, ladies and gentlemen, the largest landholders of them all. Step right up and ogle the leviathans of land.* Americans are preoccupied with size. We respond to their gigantism as we do to the beached baby whale that was found suffering on the hot Long Island sand a few years ago, its tender skin bursting, blistering in the sun. It was surrounded by a gawping crowd of humans (for some reason the term is an encomium in common parlance), who patted the frightened creature and tossed sand on that delicate skin, which nothing harder than water had ever touched; and then one man took his cigarette and burned small, round holes in the skin; and then another carved his initials in the animal with his pocketknife; and, finally, the terrified creature was left mutilated, gasping, and eventually dead, its blowhole stuffed with a lighted cigar, while the humans stalked off, laughing at their superiority over the behemoth stretched helpless on the beach.

There's some of that in our attitude toward the largest landholders in the world. No wonder the inheritors of the King Ranch shy off, fearful, a little cautious of being burned, playing down their place (though, at the same time, proud of their history, if it not be misunderstood). It was a young woman whom I met at the Ranch. Julie. She had short blond hair that bounced on her neck at each step. An upturned, freckled nose. Lips that lifted in a wide, flashing smile. She was in her twenties and bubbling with high spirits, but she too was wary of my book. Before she agreed to see me, she had to be sure who else I was seeing, and what I wanted to say ... and that I would check each fact about the ranch with the King Ranch Corporation, because each member of the family is aware that he (or she) is individually less significant than the ranch as a whole, that he (or she) can cause trouble to the ranch. . . .

I told of other families interviewed, and when I mentioned Haggin and Tevis lands, which had once been larger than the King Ranch, she burst out gratefully: "Oh, yes! People think we're the biggest, but there are lots of people with places bigger than this."

The freak syndrome, you see.

And that explains also why she would not let me use her name. Keep in mind that there are seventy or eighty members of the family now, as the descendants of Richard King have grown and multiplied, seventy or eighty stockholders, with names like Larkin, Johnston, Meyer, Armstrong, Mack, Clement, Shelton, Finger, Campbell. For the sake of simplicity, I shall refer to them all generically as Kleberg, that being the name most often associated with the ranch. Including Julie. Call her Julie Kleberg.

There was another reason for not divulging her name though, besides the invasion of her privacy. That was fear of kidnapping. We were having breakfast at the King Ranch headquarters, in the spacious tiled room with double fireplaces, stone floors, and three huge refectory tables. From shelves and mantles around the walls gleamed the highly polished bowls of the King Ranch racehorses: the "Westchester," won by Assault in 1946, the "Suburban" won in 1947.

"You're the first family I've spoken to that's mentioned kidnapping."

"It happens all the time," said Julie's cousin, who was eating with us—a pretty young woman with shoulder-length straight brown hair. She wore a slim skirt and espadrilles, and at her knee clung her little boy.

"Do you mean Patty Hearst?" I asked, racking my brain for a recent kidnapping.

"No. Well, there was the Lindbergh kidnapping," she

answered, leaning forward intently. "That was awful!" I stared at her, amazed. The Lindbergh kidnapping took place in 1932, a quarter-century before this woman's birth—and that memory lurks at the fringes of each Kleberg mind.

Yet consider. You can understand the problem. It was in 1935 that George Weyerhauser, of the timber family, was kidnapped, a little boy of nine, running home from school one day, intercepted by highwaymen in a car. They drove him deep into the woods and handcuffed him to a post in a pit, together with some blankets and a kerosene lantern for warmth. He stayed there two nights and a day and then, locked in the trunk of a car, was carried 300 miles across the state to Spokane, where he was again chained to a tree all day. That night his captors put him in a big Uneeda Cracker carton and took him to their apartment, where they locked him in a closet. . . . Days passed. Finally, the $200,000 ransom was paid, and the boy was repacked in the cracker carton, locked again in the trunk of a car, and driven back across the state, to be loosed, alone and lost, in the middle of the night by the side of a woods road.

You see, then, the threat, and since so many family members live abroad, many in South American or African countries that are racked with revolutionaries, insurgents, purges, bloodletting, and political kidnapping, what good would lack of caution serve?

Their privacy is further invaded by the sheer renown of their names. When Julie went to Foxcroft (her cousin attended Ethel Walker's; the Kleberg boys are sent to Dartmouth), she told no one who she was. "I come from Texas," she smiled gaily.

"Oh, the King Ranch?"

"Oh, sure." The girls laughed and that was all. No one pried or cared to know, and for that period of time, as later, when

she took a job as a guide at the United Nations, no one knew
of her association with one of the richest families in the world.
How else could she be free?

Often at a dinner party someone will ask where she's from,
and when she answers, "Texas," they will say:

"Oh, I know the King Ranch people."

"Oh?" she'll say.

"I'm real good friends with them," her dinner partner will
say enthusiastically, and then, if he is particularly tactless, he'll
start to drop names and tell about the ranch. Once Julie got so
annoyed that she pinned the offender down on place names,
properties, furnishings, houses, families, until his forehead
broke out in sweat and he backpedalled from the brink. Julie
greets such conduct with contempt. The social climbing. The
lies that are forced upon her (on all the Klebergs) by the
position of the ranch. Her real interests lie in her work. Her
office, where she goes every day.

Julie was given a small place by her father not long ago. She
owns it, together with her brother, and they run 600 head of
cattle there and keep the rest in farmland. Figures spill from her
pretty, upturned lips. A truck farm nets seventy dollars an acre,
except for tomatoes, which. . . . She's pleased with that, her very
own place; and a couple of times a month she and her brother
take the bus seventy-five miles from Kingsville down to
Raymondville "in the valley," south of Laredo, to conduct their
business. And that she thinks is fun, scrunching down in the
big bus seats and watching the ordinary people and knowing
that she is ordinary too. She has a pilot's license but rarely flies
a plane anymore, because unless one keeps up one's skills and
flies all the time, it really isn't safe; and anyway, the bus is
terrific because you can get so much work done on the way.

She and her brother lease the place to independent farmers,
she says, in return for a percentage of the crop. The custom is

called sharecropping, though when I mentioned the term, she looked surprised and knit her brow....

I don't know how large her farm is. She stopped when I asked her, cocked her head and thought a moment.

"That's like asking how much money a person has, isn't it?" She shook her head. "I don't want to tell that." And smiled. She is so pretty. So *alive.*

But we can figure that if she and her brother have 600 head of cattle, and each steer requires 10 acres of pasture and sometimes 15, then they have at least 6,000 to 9,000 acres. This is her own place, not part of the King Ranch Corporation.

For a history of the King Ranch, you should probably refer to the authorized two-volume centennial biography written under contract by Tom Lea and published in 1957 by Little, Brown and Company and the King Ranch Corporation. You couldn't find a more beautiful book, each page adorned with the Running W brand. The heavy paper, the print and margins, the heft of the volumes attest to its expense; and then the text, interspersed with Lea's illustrations that are so romantic and heroic that they make the heart sing with the clank of silver spurs; the nostrils fill with the smell of leather and rawhide and sweaty horses, and the burning flesh of bawling, branded calves. The book itself, like all authorized biographies, is frustrating in its toneless caution, its attention to bills of lading, accounts and records, cash receipts and debtor's transactions, each carefully recorded for posterity. It is full of facts.

What you lose is the sense of blood and guts, the sheer lust that must have driven Richard King, founder of the ranch. An Irish slum kid, raised on the streets of New York, he was apprenticed at the age of nine (it was 1833) to a jeweler. At eleven, he stowed away on the ship *Desdemona,* bound for

Alabama. For the next twenty years he was a riverboatman (with time out once when one kindly captain sent him to school in Connecticut to learn to read, write, and figure). He led a charmed life. In 1847, he wandered west with his friend, the steamboat captain Mifflin Kenedy,* to run U.S. Army steamboats up the Rio Grande during the Mexican War. In 1852, he bought 15,500 acres up near Corpus Christi. He paid $300, or two cents an acre, for the land and brought in as partner his friend Legs Lewis, who paid $2,000 for the privilege. This was followed two years later by the Santa Gertrudis tract of 53,000 acres, or 12 square leagues, that King bought for $1,800, or $150 a league. It was rough prairie with none of the mesquite that would invade the country by 1890 and cause the King Ranch later to invent mesquite treedozers, specially built for them in Peoria, Illinois. The land in the 1850s was occupied by Indians, thieves, mustangers, and outlaws. But the grass grew stirrup-high, and, best of all, on the banks of the Santa Gertrudis River grew scrawny, twisted live oaks—real shade

---

* Kenedy was a lifelong friend of King, and their two families were further joined by marriage later on. Captain Kenedy began his own land-buying operations in the 1860s, when he bought twenty-six leagues of Los Laureles. Sold twenty years later for a handsome $1.1 million to a Scottish syndicate, Kenedy invested in another speculation of about 400,000 acres south of Santa Gertrudis. Kenedy was never interested, like King, in living off the land. For him, the land was a means of making money, but he gave his name to the county, the Kenedys being one of the five ranchers (Armstrongs, Klebergs, Kenedys, Yturrias, and McGills) who owned 90 percent of Kenedy County land in the 1930s and controlled its politics and tax rate. The Kenedy ranch is unusual today in still being run in the old style, unfenced and with a gang of cowboys herding cattle, I have heard, on horseback. You still find such things in Texas. The 500,000-acre property is run by Tom East (his mother was a Kleberg), the nephew of Sarita Kenedy, who, when she died, left all the ranch and oil to the Catholic Church. A dispute immediately broke out between two Church factions over which one owned the land, but, to the Klebergs' amusement, Brother Leo and his monks are ensconced in the ranch at the Main House, and, as Julie said: "They all sort of hike up their hassocks and run out and shoot deer and stuff."

trees—and within its banks ran that liquid more precious than
oil—living water.

Water is the key to this droughty country of south Texas,
and today when you (the tourist) take the twelve-mile public
road into the Santa Gertrudis Ranch, the things you're shown
are the Dairy Dam and the Liberated Windmill and reservoirs
and watering troughs filled by artesian wells, for there is no
year-round surface water on the property; and you also see more
subtle signs of the presence of water—flowering trees and
bushes, their roots feeding on water drawn from more than 300
artesian wells that the oil and gas have helped to dig.*

In 1839, the map in the general land office of Texas had such
headings as—"Of this section of country little is known" or
"Immense herds of wild horses." Or "Wild Horse Desert."
Karankawa Indians (Cronks) inhabited the place. They were
said to be cannibals, seven feet tall. Thirteen years later, when
King began buying up scrip from Mexican War soldiers, the
land was still wild and empty. But King, financing his
speculations in sheep, cattle, horses, mules, and goats from his
steamboat company, drove himself into debt for land. He was
another of the prototypical acquisitors, the kind of man who
took his friend Lt. Col. Robert E. Lee seriously when the
Virginian told him: "Buy land; and never sell."

He didn't need the advice. His lawyers were occupied with
deeds and bills of sale and sometimes with buying the same

---

* Oil was discovered on the ranch in 1945; by 1969, Humble had 504 producing
oil wells and 138 gas wells, which spun off $18 to $20 million a year in income to
the ranch. Royalties came to $1.5 million a month in comparison to $5 million
annually in livestock revenues and $4 million from foreign operations on a $3.4
million capital investment abroad. The figures are from *Fortune* magazine, June 1969,
p. 166. *Fortune* also estimated the worth of the King Ranch Corporation at that
time, allowing $300 million as the one-sixth royalty for the ranch on oil and gas in
the ground and another $35 million in grazing land.

property over and over again from the multiple owners of undivided interests, these being the descendants of those who had first received Mexican land grants in the 1790s. It took him thirty years to settle the claims on the first piece of property he'd bought in 1852 at two cents an acre; and when he finished, he'd spent much more than that. Once, a new young lawyer asked when he should get in touch with him. King answered: "Young man, the only thing I want to hear from you is when I can move my fences."

King, you see, was no mythic pauper cowboy, but a river rat, who acquired, before he died, 614,140 acres of hot, dry, dusty Texas land; a man who kept careful, cautious records, who travelled to St. Louis and Chicago and sent his daughters to school in Kentucky and Missouri and understood that the rancher's best friend is his banker.* He was a businessman. He was a partner in three beef contracting livestock brokerage firms, owned an interest in the *Corpus Christi Free Press,* built one ice plant at Brownsville and another in Corpus Christi, owned the mail and stage lines from Corpus Christi to Laredo and from Brownsville to San Antonio (dependable lines but unable to turn a profit). King was director of the Corpus Christi Navigation Company, which was trying to dredge a deep-water channel for ocean shipping. Then he backed and helped to finance the railroad from Corpus Christi to Laredo,

* The same holds true today. The King Ranch is run by family and corporate executives well grounded in business school, banks, partnerships, public relations, the laws of leaseholding and income tax carry-overs. I won't waste your time on this, but direct you for more detail to a wonderful two-part series by Jane Kramer that appeared in *The New Yorker* on May 30 and June 4, 1977, about a Panhandle cowboy, several days' journey from the King Ranch. Its information on present-day land ownership and the economics of cow raising and feedlots, bank loans and European speculators is worth reading about, and, also, the need to have money before you can make it or keep it, despite our American dreams to the contrary.

what would later become the Texas Mexican Railway, the little "Tex-Mex."

King established his headquarters on its present site on the bank of the Santa Gertrudis, and he brought with him the Mexicans who had worked on the steamboats with him—Vicente Patino, Faustino Villa—the foundation stock, as Tom Lea calls them, for the ranch labor straw bosses. To King they were "my friends." Also, his guards.

No one went through the country without guards. When King brought his twenty-two-year-old bride, Henrietta Chamberlain, to the ranch in 1854, they traveled the 120 miles from Brownsville in a "large, closed carriage," a stagecoach. It took four days. Armed outriders flanked the dusty coach.

Later, King's hard-drinking toughness turned to drunkenness as he tried to deaden the pain of a stomach cancer, the courage and optimism that permitted him to disarm an outlaw and send the man off into the brush—"Get out!"—that fecklessness turned to bellicosity. You can read of it in the King Ranch book.

Once, "Old Cap" was to meet his family at a hotel in Galveston. He found his wife in the dining room entertaining a lady friend for dinner, and King, noticing that her meat was tough, first complained to the disdainful hotel staff, and then got up, marched to another restaurant across the street, and ordered a new meal to be served in the hotel dining room. When the waiters arrived with their trays, King pulled the tablecloth from the table, scattering hotel food, plates, drinks, and glasses to the floor, respread the tablecloth, and stood back. "Now," he said. "Serve that one."

You can imagine the conflicting emotions of his wife and her friend at this drunken, generous husband.

When King died in 1885, he left half a million dollars in

land and half a million dollars in debts. It took his son-in-law, Robert Justus Kleberg, to consolidate the property (a heavy, Teutonic effort, and solid hard work and pretty humorless from the sound of things, but ticking up the profits with mechanical regularity). Kleberg was a lawyer whom King had hired when the young man beat him in a lawsuit. Kleberg married King's youngest daughter, Alice. It was Kleberg who, in 1893, drilled artesian wells, built concrete water troughs, imported English shorthorns and Herefords, founded Kingsville (still a "dry" town in a "dry" county, according to the teetotaling covenant of the original deed), and constructed the massive Santa Gertrudis house, which now serves as the main headquarters for the ranch. It burned in 1911, was rebuilt in 1916. The cannons from the King-Kenedy Civil War gunboats were put out on the front lawn.

King's widow, Henrietta, died in 1925 at the age of ninety-two. By then the ranch had grown to 1,250,000 acres, which was left by a complex will in a ten-year trust, after which the property was divided among the heirs. Robert Kleberg II, son of the first Kleberg, received 431,000 acres and formed the King Ranch Corporation with himself as president and manager and his brother Richard (the congressman, 1932-44) as chairman. It is this corporation that has now grown to 860,000 acres.

The public can tour some portions of the ranch, can drive around the 120-mile loop road (speed limit 40 to 45 m.p.h.) that begins at the simple white gate one mile beyond the town of Kingsville. Two white pillars. The sun bakes down on the white gatehouse with its little wooden porch. A cowboy gateman tips his chair back against the gatehouse wall, hat low over his eyes and sunglasses shielding them further from the white glare as he reads intently a Baptist tract—or tries to,

between the interruptions of a stream of visitors who pull up in
their air-conditioned cars and, winding down the window, are
hit by a wave of Texan air. Then he rocks forward, ambles
bowlegged and cowboy-booted to the car, delivers his tour
pamphlets, waves amiably, and returns to his religious reading.
The road winds past green pastures of Kleberg grass (discovered by Nick Dias, the ranch agronomist, in 1946), past the
alternating ebony and date palm trees, past tamarisk imported
from Africa via Australia. Here are the one-and-a-half-mile race
track, the veterinary building, the quarter horse training stables,
and the open ring with its bleachers, where the cowboys school
the horses every weekday morning for their rodeo work. And
here also are pens where the magnificent bronze Santa
Gertrudis cattle, big as buffalo, swing their horned heads lazily
or lie down, disposing their hulks placidly on the brown earth.

Perhaps one in a halter is being groomed by a Mexican
cowherd. Don't be fooled. These cattle are dangerous. The
Santa Gertrudis are a distinctive breed developed by the King
Ranch from Brahman and shorthorn stock and recognized
officially by the U.S. Department of Agriculture in 1940 as a
pure American breed of beef cattle.

Most of the ranch, however, is closed to public view,
including the wildlife preserve of Escondido Trap, where not
even members of the family are allowed to shoot. This private
land is equally interesting. The fields stretch out endlessly, not
in the hypnotic plowed lines of cotton and sugar fields that
blink past the roads of the black-loam delta, but pastureland
that dips, curves, rises into embankments, ridges, and arroyos.
It is filled with variety. But the main impression, coming from
the East, is of emptiness. It is frightening, awe-inspiring. You
look out and see ... nothing. No cars, no domesticity. No
people inhabit this space where deer, quail, and javelina, or the

collared peccary, graze and grub right up to the edges of the oil wells. You drive at forty or fifty m.p.h. on hard dirt roads, passing through gates that open with a bump from the car and automatically swing closed behind, until you come to the plant, where wet gas is processed into dry. It is the largest gas plant of its type in the world. A sign on the chain fence proclaims its name: Exxon Corp., King Ranch Gas Plant, District Office. The massive gray planes, the tubes, cubes, and blocks rise against the empty sky. And, still, only a hot wind breaks the silence. White cattle egrets blown across from Africa flap across the pastures. There are no signs of human life. The main business of the ranch takes place around the headquarters or in international offices in other cities around the world, or in the King Ranch offices on the top floor of the Kleberg Bank in Kingsville.

Near the ranch headquarters, there is a small, rectangular one-story bungalow. Here, in a dim, cool interior, two Mexicans–sometimes three–spend their days, one carding and spinning wool from King Ranch sheep, another weaving the yarn on a huge wooden loom into saddle blankets for the King Ranch cowboys. The saddle blankets are unbleached wool, striped in white and gray (depending on the color of the sheep). Each has the Running W design woven in one corner. The Mexicans make two or three blankets a week. The lifespan of each saddle blanket is about three years.

Other things that are not shown on the public tour are the houses of the kiñenos. They are neat, white bungalows, some with air-conditioning and some with roses and crepe myrtle blooming at the entrances. The houses sit in one area of the ranch, not far from the headquarters: a pretty suburban plot, with green grass around them and family cars parked in the driveways. The children–short, sturdy bodies and stiff black hair—run across the lawns coming home from school for lunch. The ranch, you understand, is operated by the old *patrón* system, whereby the Mexicans are taken care of in every detail of their lives. It is a matter of seigneurial pride, a Kleberg privilege and responsibility, similar to that of a father for his children. The Mexicans get a free house, utilities, food, and insurance for medicine and drugs. Their clothes and equipment can be bought at the King Ranch commissary at prices that are cheaper than in the retail stores; and everyone agrees that this system works best for the Mexicans, who otherwise lose everything to loan sharks. But the kiñeno community is not shown on the tour, and neither are the Kleberg family houses. People in town talk of these with awe. The house of Bobby Shelton, vice president and general manager, was only recently constructed—a long, low, white ranch house, hidden behind bushes and landscaping; and if you believe the girlfriend of the plumber's brother (she works at the Corpus Christi Hertz counter), the house cost $1.4 million and goes four stories underground, with tennis courts and swimming pools. It fills you with admiration just to imagine it.

Finally, the tour excludes the main headquarters, where members of the family can throw a party or put up overnight guests, and where each quarter they are allowed to stay themselves for a certain amount of time if they make a proper reservation.

It is a large, white, three-story building, topped by a square Moorish tower, like the conning tower of a battleship. The house is set around an interior court, in the center of which grow huge potted palms and trees in tubs, which are cooled by the spray of the gardener's hose. Indoors the house is dim and cool; the stone or tiled floors are covered with oriental rugs or homespun King Ranch blankets, the windows with tapestry curtains. The white walls are hung with the original drawings and paintings from Tom Lea's book on the King Ranch (you can see them there) – wranglers, ancestors, horses, and range life. The King Ranch Corporation has no interest in European paintings, in Picassos or Calders or old masters; no, but in the commemoration of those heroic beginnings, and just as the Renaissance princes commissioned paintings by a Pintoricchio or a Mantegna to display and increase their splendor, so the King Ranch Corporation adorns its walls with its cowboy past. Their Texas pride is represented further by the oversize scale of the place–a St. Peter's, where the balustrade to the stairway is as thick as a man's arm and adorned with gleaming brass knobs set every twenty feet or so. The bedrooms on the second floor open onto a large central hall. The mounted heads of buffalo, deer, and other game gaze, unseeing, from the walls. The bedrooms were decorated in the time of Henrietta King and of her daughter, Alice Kleberg, with a Presbyterian restraint that favored a plain white bedspread, a chair, a chest of drawers.... Now the ranch is modernizing the rooms with striped wallpapers and color-coordinated curtains that give the rooms some of the sterile feel of a Holiday Inn. The open porches that once ran the entire length of the house have been enclosed and sealed into individual dressing rooms, and their plain floorboards covered with wall-to-wall carpeting.

Another flight of stairs climbs to the attic (where Julie played haunted house as a little girl); through a copper door to the tower balcony, and from there all one can see is King Ranch land right over to the water towers of Kingsville (population 28,141), where Texas A & I is located and where the largest employer is the U.S. naval base. The ranch owns a good piece of Kingsville, too, either directly, as with Raglands Department Store, the Kingsville Lumber Company, and the Kingsville Saddle Shop, or indirectly, as with more. It is a wonderful idea to stand on that balcony and survey those lands.

On the ground floor of the house there are two main living or reception rooms. In one, where the stockholders meet, a mural by Tilford Collins illustrates the family tree. It is painted quite literally as a tree, with Richard King and Henrietta at the roots and trunk, from which stretch upward the branches of Kleberg, Meyer, Larkin ... each name coded by dots to represent marriage, divorce, death, and children. On the grand piano in the next salon are five or six photo albums of the annual gathering of the clans. Open the books. Here are the handsome, strong women with their fearless eyes, their flashing smiles, and the huge tall men—giants, by any standards—also handsome with the vitality of life. They sport at barbecues and picnics, tennis and swimming. The women work their needlepoint by the pool and watch the peacocks strut and spread their tails and fly, screeching, into the trees, while the children, screaming with high-pitched joy, organize into sack races, horse shows (the children being the horses), and swimming competitions.

All the energy of Richard and Henrietta King have come down to these heirs, the stockholders, who expend it in Acapulco, Morocco, Rio, New York, Majorca. There is no place on earth they cannot go if they wish. But they all work, as Julie told me seriously. They are "taught to be doers," and so they're all on the boards of hospitals and universities. They are leaders.

Julie herself has an office to which she goes most days. Mainly she works for her dad. Then she has her farm that I spoke of earlier. Then there are her various interests and projects, one of which is coastal development, especially with regard to long-term water sources and quality. That is a problem in coastal south Texas, where all irrigation water comes from the Rio Grande. There is no other source of water, and as cities grow, competing with farmers for water that is already in limited supply, the problem will increase in size. The question is how to divide the water fairly and not provide for its overuse. There has not been a drought in south Texas since the seven-year drought in the 1950s, and already people have forgotten their dependence on water. But as soon as another drought comes, the question will be urgent.

So Julie is not idle. Her husband works with the King Ranch Corporation. He is in international finance. Julie feels grateful and pleased that her husband wanted to come to the ranch (and she put one exquisitely manicured hand on his knee when she said this and melted into his eyes: she adores him so much that she doesn't want children who will change their lives together). She had always said that she wouldn't care what her husband did; she would follow him wherever he wanted to go, because that's the best way for a woman.... But she never in her wildest dreams imagined that he would want to come to the ranch and that she would end up living right here where she grew up most of her life....

She met her husband in New York. He is the son of a tennis pro, tall, lean, handsome, intelligent. His family were White Russian nobility who fled the Soviet revolution, wandered penniless around Europe–Czechoslovakia, Poland, Paris–and ended up in Texas, where his father taught tennis at a country club. Which shows her lack of snobbery. Her in-laws are wonderful people. Julie was especially fond of her mother-in-law, who was a real lady. "Slow down," she would say in a soft, gentle voice. "Softly, Julie. Don't push." She taught Julie a lot about getting along with people, about not running over them in her enthusiasm. It was a real loss to Julie when she died, but she gets along fine with her father-in-law, too.

Julie and her husband rent a modest house in town. You

couldn't say it is unpretentious, since it is decorated in
Exaggerated Hollywood, with blue tiles, and pink shag rugs,
and sunken bathtubs, and a Spanish Colonial walnut-stained
bar that dominates the living room and overshadows the tiny
galley in which to cook.

The house is merely a place to sleep in, however, because
most of their entertaining is done at the ranch headquarters,
and meals can be eaten there, or in restaurants when they like.
Indeed, you have the feeling, considering the King Ranch
headquarters, that the family members use it like a large hotel,
and their attitude toward the staff is as graciously sparing, as
condescending, deferential, and polite as if they were in . . . yes,
a large, first-class hotel.

What I am saying is so subtle—attitude—so ephemeral that it
loses shape in the mere act of nailing it into words. They are
the "masters" certainly, yet they live by the house rules, are
boxed by boundaries of social courtesy, propriety, and place. To
some extent their wishes come second to the well-ordered
discipline of the whole. The place is bigger than they.
Therefore the rules. For example, they must make a reservation
to go riding on the ranch, and these must be made at a
reasonably early hour.

The little boy, age three or four, twisted at the table, bored
and impatient by our grown-up talk. He pulled his mother's
skirt.

"Can I go riding?"

"No, dear," she answered. "We didn't make a reservation,
remember? You said you didn't want to?"

"Why not?"

"We didn't make a reservation. It's too late now. You want
to ride tomorrow? We can ride tomorrow, okay?"

"Why can't we ride today?" he repeated.

"We didn't tell them." And then—"Go find Miss Smith,"

she continued, referring to the nurse. "I think she's looking for you. Don't I hear her calling?"

The little boy toddled off with a faintly puzzled air, while his mother sighed and poured another cup of coffee from the silver pot.

The Chains of Class

So now we have viewed a gallery of the gentry, all people of established wealth. Do you see the dilemma of the man himself? He is owned by property.

If he has strong talents and drive in one direction, if he is born a poet, perhaps, an artist, he turns his property over to professional managers, and soon—as with the Tevises—he has only public stock in a publicly owned institution, and then, in a generation or two, that too may dwindle away. If, on the other hand, he devotes himself dutifully to the care and maintenance of the family property—as did Walter McIlhenny on Avery Island, for example, who renounced his military career because "in time of war a man serves his country, in time of peace his family"—then he risks abusing his God-given talent or losing it altogether. Either way the man can't win.

The double bind is corollary, I suppose, to Christ's injunction about the rich man and the needle's eye, where selfless duty to family and property ends by interfering with the growth of the soul.

The problem is rarely stated in these terms, of course, in one's growing up, but there it sits, looming over the possessor of inherited wealth. Has he enough money? Too much? Can he hold up his head in public? Does he embarrass others with the dimensions of his wealth? And either way, *can he himself be seen?* Even his closest friends may view him through the scrim of property, either its possession or the absence of the thing. Property becomes one more clue to how we judge a man.

Moreover, if his friends cannot see him through the veil of class and rank, then neither can he see out. This accounts for the curious absences in the perceptions of the very rich: Nelson Rockefeller, telling an audience that the tax burden falls "on the average person, like you and me."

George F. Will, the columnist, collects these examples of the failure, as he calls it, of the "imaginative sympathy." In the 1920s, a Beacon Hill dowager, learning that many Boston houses lacked indoor plumbing, exclaimed: "You would think the people who live in them would have found out before moving in." In the 1930s, an industrialist declared it didn't pay to run radio ads on Sundays "because everyone's playing polo." The remark is still the same: "Oh, you won't have any trouble parking on Saturday," says the East Side New Yorker. "Everyone will be out of town for the weekend."

They are not joking, these people. Nor callous. Neither do their remarks arise from affectation, but simply from the isolation of their rank.

In May 1977, the *Washington Post* ran a remarkable interview by Sally Quinn with C. Z. Guest, wife of Winston F. C. Guest, who is the grandson of Henry Phipps. Guest's father was first cousin to Winston Churchill, and Guest himself was once one of the top-ranking polo players in the world. His wife, C. Z., now fifty-seven, was promoting a book, *First Gardens,* and, for the first time in her life (a string of triumphs: competition riding at Madison Square Garden Horse Show, Best Dressed Woman in the World, the Fashion Hall of Fame), she ran into situations and people beyond the scope of her normal experience.

"I'm not ashamed of the way I live," she told Sally Quinn. "Look at the jobs I've given people. If you have money and servants, then you're helping somebody. If rich people didn't spend money, the country would be in much worse shape than it is today. If you have money, then you give people pleasure. I wish I had more money. I'd spend more."

Truman Capote described C. Z. as a pale vanilla blond. She was brought up in Boston of faultless background and breeding, was attracted to the stage (or was it to Victor Mature, her beau?), strayed down to Mexico, was painted in the nude by Diego Rivera, and married Winston Guest. She was under his thumb, she admits, for years, keeping her houses and gardens, horses and dogs. Then, quite by accident, she wrote a book on gardens and suddenly found herself giving talks to garden clubs and appearing on television and taking up the defense of the very rich.

"Perhaps," she told Sally Quinn, "more is expected of those of us who are better educated and come from more affluent families." Listen. Listen to what she is saying: it is the Gregorian chant of the propertied class, learned by rote and repeated at the nurse's knee. It is the justification and reaffirmation for all wealth. "More is expected of us," she said. "Because we have learned courage and learned what's right and what's wrong. Look at Nelson Rockefeller. He did the right thing at Attica. And he never would have been able to handle it so beautifully if he hadn't been brought up the way he was. It means so much. If there had been people of his background, people who had been brought up the way we were in Nixon's cabinet, if Nixon had had the proper breeding, Watergate would never have happened. And who is the one person who came out all right? Elliot Richardson, of course. Because he was from Boston, he had been raised properly, he knew what to do, knew what was right and what was wrong."

Sally Quinn did not ask her about Mr. Jaworski. Or Judge Sirica, or any of the hundreds of others who assisted in the untangling of the Watergate scandal without the advantage of breeding. Neither did she bring up the point that I have observed: that it is often impossible for those of breeding to take the reins of command, for the care and training of this class prevent it. No matter. The point is merely that the rich—no, all of us—are blind. We all see through screens of class.

"Poor Nelson," Mrs. Guest continued happily. "People are down on him because of Attica. But he did the right thing.

"Someone without his background would have done just the opposite. Look how he behaved before the Senate investigating committee, look how well he handled himself. That's because of the way he was brought up. The Rockefellers have changed the course of the world, and I never hear anyone say one nice thing about the Rockefeller Foundation. Well, Nelson is proud to be a Rockefeller. He's got nothing to be ashamed of. . . .

"Let's face it," she concluded. "I'm so happy we were brought up in these surroundings, being able to make these important decisions, to have the courage to do it. When people read this, they're going to say, 'Gosh, why haven't I thought about this?' "

Listen, Mrs. Guest has had the same cook for twenty-two years, and the same French mam'zelle for fifteen, and that is an accomplishment these days. Don't laugh because her views are not the same as yours: they represent her class.

In America, money and class are often confused. Not long

ago an ad in the *New York Times* made a claim that the readership of a certain magazine was "upper class." It based its determination on the "Two-Factor Index of Social Position Scale," developed by Dr. A. B. Hollingshead, chairman of the department of sociology at Yale. Dr. Hollingshead calls his index "two-factor" because one element is derived from income and a second from occupation and education. He places those people with the highest scores in both categories in the "upper class."

This is not a bad method of cataloguing something that is closer to an emotion, an attitude, than to a tangible fact. Yet the two-factor index of class still confuses money and a state of mind, and, concerning the former, makes no distinction between salaried income and wealth.

In part, our confusion over class may stem from our reluctance to recognize the existence of a class system in America at all. We are embarrassed by the term. We substitute democratic euphemisms, like "socioeconomic stratifications" or "upper-middle-income group," terms that churn the murky waters further. Then, too, our rationalism blocks our view, the necessity to systematize and categorize our lives: it is a national obsession, as if a thing does not exist unless we catalogue it. The question is: Who belongs to the upper class? We cannot find an answer, and we respond instead with who is rich.

That definition alone occupies a government of sociologists and bureaucrats. The Internal Revenue Service, the Census Bureau, Robert D. Plotnick and Felicity Skidmore, G. William Domhoff, Ferdinand Lundberg, Dr. James D. Smith, Joseph Peckman, Herbert Gans ... and countless others, all busy counting out the pieces of our population's wealth.

As it happens, they cannot even agree on which set of figures to use, much less the interpretation. Ferdinand Lundberg, examining the fact that the top 1 percent of the population have incomes of $60,000, that 13,457 households had such incomes though none of the members worked, that "since World War II, one-tenth of the population has owned two-thirds of our liquid assets," is left frothing at the mouth. We have a fortress of interlaced wealth, he concludes, an established, hereditary, propertied class such as exists in Europe. *At least* 40 percent of the men, he says, and 24 percent of all top "wealth-holders" are heirs: "There is no process of estate destruction taking place in the United States through taxation, as is commonly suggested by propagandists of the establishment." We are, he says passionately, a nation of employees in a Banana Republic.

Others view the material with deliberate caution. Five percent of the population, according to the records, hold 40 percent of the nation's wealth. But that 5 percent represents 3 million families, or anyone earning $30,000 a year or more. Can they really be called rich? Or is the rich that top 1 percent, 600,000 households who make $60,000 a year or above?

You can go a long way in America these days without property. They point that out. A man can rise to prominence and fame and never reach an income in six figures. The distinction between wealth and income is important. Income is taxed and taxable without deductions. It is not money that can be borrowed against at a bank or sold and reinvested for higher yield. "Everybody except the infirm or disabled have the capacity to derive income from labor," says Peter Barnes, formerly with the *New Republic,* "but to derive income from wealth you must first own something."

The 1970 census, based on incomes for 1969, was a long time ago. At that time, 390,708 of our 70 million households had incomes of $50,000 or more. But $50,000 in income includes many people with no property and no real wealth, salaried and professional people, executives who can be called "well off," perhaps, but hardly "rich." Only three-quarters of one percent of the households in America reach that level of income. On the other hand, to illustrate wealth, 13,457 households reported incomes over $50,000 though none of the members worked. It is only when you pass the mark of $200,000 a year in income that property becomes the major source of income.

On wealth itself, however, as on land ownership, no reliable information exists. Among our rights to privacy, this one—what we own—is paramount. Neither the Census Bureau nor the Internal Revenue Service has ever asked people to declare their holdings, and what you own is no one's business unless you run for public office or die.

The work of Professor James D. Smith of Pennsylvania State University is, therefore, of much interest, for he has analyzed estate records to determine, at the moment of death, how much property a certain segment of the population has. Even so, his method is filled with pitfalls, not the least of which is the fact that his figures date from 1969.

According to Smith, about 50,000 Americans held stock worth $1 million in 1969; 5,000 held stock worth more than $5 million. Together, these 55,000 people owned 18 percent of the country's personally held corporate stock. America's rich, he concludes, consist of 50,000 to 60,000 people, representing perhaps 20,000 households. Many are retired. The largest group are local property owners, the proprietors of the big department store in a small city, of the newspapers, banks, and brokerage houses, the real estate developers, and the landlords of agriculture.

Distribution of wealth in the United States has consistently been less equitable than the distribution of income. According to one economist in 1810, the top 1 percent of families owned 21 percent of the American wealth. A century later, in 1915, the U.S. Commission on Industrial Relations determined that "the Rich," 2 percent of the people, owned 35 percent of the wealth. Today, the Rich, the top 1 percent of the population, or some 600,000 households, control 25 percent of all personal and financial assets, according to Professor Smith. "Except during the Depression and World War II, the relative concentration of wealth has stayed the same or worsened."

The figures, however, are subject to more play than one might imagine possible, given the mathematical purity of numbers. Most scholars who concern themselves with these questions agree that the distribution of wealth and income among households in the U.S. has not significantly changed since World War II, that we have arrived at a period of relative stability. They find the phenomenon mystifying.

Frankly, I find the whole porridge mystifying. Again, quoting the U.S. Census Bureau, the top 20 percent of the American families (those with incomes over $20,445) held 41 percent of the income in 1974, only slightly less than the 42.5 percent of the 1948 figures, and no change at all since 1952. The stability, according to some statisticians, is only "apparent," masking a number of shifting trends, among them the fact that earnings of individuals (as distinct from households) have grown "more unequal" in the postwar period. Much of the inequality in individual earnings, they say, can be explained by the changing labor force, since more teenagers and women are working and more individuals setting up single households. Individual incomes have, then, declined, although this does not imply a drop in individual *well-being*, or more inequality in the *distribution* of well-being.

Our only point of agreement, it seems, about who is rich and poor is that we have no reliable information at all, and none can be obtained until the federal government begins to collect more comprehensive data. Basically we do not understand the trends. All we do is track them, a situation that lends itself to the well-being of numerous bureaucrats, sociologists, statisticians, and writers and their families, pediatricians, orthodontists, bankers, accountants, attorneys, and golf club pros.

It is important to recognize that the propertied class does not see itself as rich. I have never met any rich person who ever read or discussed the kinds of figures we have just looked at, or has even been much interested in them. I have never heard a dinner table conversation in this set turn to the serious discussion of the redistribution of wealth. Instead, you hear a different tune.

"Do you know what a *subway* driver gets today? A subway driver. I don't see how we can afford to live. A *subway* driver get $13,000 starting salary. I wish *I* got $13,000 a year."

"And a policeman in New York," breaks in another, "makes $15,000 starting slary. Only at the end of twenty years he retires on half-pay. Can you imagine? He goes in at the age of twenty with a high-school diploma, and at forty he can begin a whole new career, with a pension for life."

"What's the world coming to?"

"But how can we afford it? Who's going to pay for that?" The propertied class are not selfish exactly. Just that they think they have a monopoly on dividends. They do not stop to consider that $13,000 in income for a subway driver is just that—income, taxed and taxable without deductions. All they see is their taxes going for the redistribution of wealth.

You should not conclude, however, that the propertied class does not discuss property. The subject is endlessly fascinating, and it crops up all the time. In land prices. In stock market investments. In the necessity for a nonmaterialistic view of the world. There are games to play, like "Do You Know" and "Who Are You?" But property is at the root of it all, and the reinforcement of shared values.

Here is a conversation overheard on the Fisher's Island tennis

courts one lovely summer's day. Two women were playing side
by side on adjacent courts, each against her own partner. They
called to each other across their individual games. Pock ...
pock ... the tennis balls floated across the two nets. Nina was
tall and blond, and Jinx, short, stocky, and dark. It was hard to
know which won the game.

NINA: Are you here for Ladies Day? (pock ... pock)

JINX: We were. But the Symingtons came over, looking for
some children to play with their grandchildren. So we arrived
too late for that.

NINA: Who? (pock ... pock)

JINX: The Fife Symingtons. From Baltimore. They live up
the road from us.

NINA: Oh. Yes. (pock ... pock)

Jinx won this round. She has just established that she is on
speaking terms with the Symingtons. Mrs. Symington is a
granddaughter of Henry Frick, and the Symingtons are well
known in horse circles as well as in politics. Jinx next proceeds
to explain she doesn't care, while Nina tries to place her
physically on Fisher's Island.

NINA: But they don't live near you. Don't they have Barley
Field Cove?

JINX: Yes. They bought it about two years ago. (pock ...
pock) I don't know anything about them really. We've never
even seen them really.

NINA (persisting): Well, that's not near you. Don't you live
on XYZ Road?

JINX: We've just bought the old house on the point. You
know, that big one with gables ... (pock ...) and it seems that
they're always going out of their drive as we're going in or out
of ours, so we see them all the time.

NINA: Oh. (pock ... pock)
JINX: We don't know them. (pock ... pock) My serve.
We're friends of the Symingtons in Lexington, though. They're
real good friends of some friends of ours in the horse business
there. The Stanley Petters.
NINA (with interest): Hi Petter?
JINX: Oh, do you know him? My husband was at school
with him. Harry's going to Saratoga next week with them.
(pock ... pock)
NINA: The Saratoga Horse Sales? Freddy may be going to
that. I haven't heard yet. (pock ... pock)

A draw. Both ladies have established that their husbands are
attending the most fashionable and social horse sales in the
country, where an untried filly may bring $500,000. Jinx now
makes it clear that her husband does not go for financial
interests.

JINX: Harry's just interested in horses. (pock ...) He's a
foxhunter.

In other words, Harry is a gentleman of leisure, a fact to be
appreciated by Nina, whose husband is a renowned steeple-
chaser and foxhunter. They now brought the game to a close.

NINA: Oh. How nice. (pock ... pock) Where do you live in
winter?
JINX (naming a community): In the hunt country.
NINA: How nice.

None go without medical care among this class, and no one
starves, and if some live in a degree of shabby gentility, it is as
much by choice as need, being part of that rootedness that sees

their lands and property as inseparable from themselves—a psychic arm or leg, which is chopped off only in peril to the soul.

Their lives are active, physical, centering on outdoorsy things: on guns and skiis and fishing rods, with all the accoutrements that go therewith, the harness and buckles and clashing gear of that mystique. They lead a lifelong search for physical sensation—even pain—to offset the soft, good life. The men wear caps and tweed jackets, and some let their eyes drift out and off to the left in a farmer's gaze, horizon-scanning, while others clap you with the old eye contact, forthright and flattering as city folk. And some affect a red-neck twang and manly swagger, legs wide, like a common farmer's stance; others adapt to the tight, taut rhythms of the mannered urban throng. The women often exhibit the same manliness. They dress dowdily in classic, timeless styles that are hopelessly out of fashion and always the same. Attractive people they are, fun-loving, nonreflective, nonintellectual by nature, and when you add two other ingredients—compassion and an intellectual acuity—why, I don't think a finer friend can be found on earth. Paradoxically, though, life itself seems to militate against these qualities, the intellectual and the compassionate.

Oh, I have seen such mutilation of personality in this group as hardly seems possible, when all God-given bounty is bestowed thereon. Each class drags chains behind, and those of the aristocracy, though forged in silver, pull just as hard. Privilege (only now do I see it) exerts a psychological tug: the weight of fear, possessiveness, greed, all universal qualities, yes, but add one more. The essence of the propertied class is an avoidance of the outside world, a shying-off from pain. Therefore the necessity for privacy among the aristocracy, who build, with their private islands, private estates, private schools and servants and clubs, walls of privilege that serve as much to imprison as to protect them.

They are not free. We are not free. Free of material need and still we suffer. To be free, we must be free of behavioral tics, of material possessiveness, of the psychological monstrosities imposed in childhood. Free of anger, guilt, and fear. And we must be free of class.

I do not know if that last is possible. Class envelops us like an invertebrate shell, forms our patterns of thinking, our habits, our ideas, our images of ourselves. Can anyone break through that? Class determines our manners, whom we shall marry, and how we shall raise our children. Class insures how we think of money, how we spend it, what foods we eat, what jokes we like, what loyalties we hold.

Is there anything but class to our development? We think our pathetic psyches are formed by our parents' hands and hearts, and influenced by environment; yet how many times do we recognize (Freud never mentioned it) that our parents and friends and *their* parents and friends and back through generations were likewise being molded, shaped, cut, cubed on the assembly lines of class, helpless, all of us, to change.

Listen, I have a friend, a dear friend. I shall call her Anne and add that she is connected to the plutocracy. Is she a Rockefeller? A Whitney? A Phipps or Mills, perhaps? Or is she a McCormick of Chicago? It makes no difference. Enough that she is distantly connected, not poor, but not with extreme, great wealth. For years, she and her husband went every summer to the family's private island off the coast of Maine.

One night three years ago their son, Augustus, was flying up to join them. Anne and her husband, Gus, started in the Boston Whaler for the mainland to meet the midnight plane.

It was stormy. The seas were building up so high that just

before they set out Gus ran back to the house for two more life jackets, and Gus is an excellent sailor, cautious without being easily frightened.

They set out. Lightning crackled against a black sky, the waves built so steep that the motor sometimes came out of the water entirely, spinning wildly in the crests of the waves. They followed the markers and buoys by the sheets of lightning that played in the sky, lighting the entire heavens and curling down into the waves.

Anne was terrified. In atavistic fear that Gus might be hit by lightning, she huddled in the bow of the boat, as far from her husband as she could get; the waves poured over the bow, soaking through her oilskins. She prayed to God. She told me this story herself later, and this is what she prayed:

"Dear God," she said with Episcopal devotion, "I don't know if you intend for me to die tonight, and if you do, that's all right with me, and I understand. If you intend that. I really do understand. But if you're just having fun tonight and hadn't noticed that we're out here, I want to remind you that we're here and I don't want to die. Not yet. Dear God, I have so many things I want to do. I haven't begun to live my life. But if you know that too and if you realize that we're here, then it's all right with me, if you want us dead. But if I'm spared, dear Lord, I promise I'll begin to live. I have so much to do."

They arrived, wet and shaken, at the nearest mainland village to discover that their son's plane had been delayed in the same storm and would not arrive that night.

Do you know the Maine fishing villages? Tiny hamlets, barren of people during the rough, cold winters and bursting with tourists in summer. Sparkling white clapboard houses and decaying town halls and libraries. The churches are decorated with fine steeples and stained-glass windows, and the houses have handsome wooden cornices or latticework, rectilinear and plain against an azure sky.

Anne sat shivering on the steps of the Knights of Columbus building in the center of town, while Gus went to find a motel room. It was one o'clock in the morning; the storm had cleared; the moon was scudding behind windblown clouds. She sat there, an agamic figure, in her yellow slicker latched at her throat and her oilskin hat pulled over her head. Only her nose was visible under the streetlight, as she waited for her husband to return.

Suddenly, a limousine turned down the street. It cruised slowly past her. Imagine. A long, black limousine purring down the street at that ungodly hour, and inside were three men in full evening dress. The one in the back seat was leaning forward to talk to the two in front, and as the car glided by all three glanced over at her, on the steps. The car proceeded with brooding dignity around the corner and was gone.

"In a moment," she thought in panic, "that car will come back." She knew it in her heart, even as her mind denied it. What danger could she possibly be in?

But in a moment the limousine returned—this time from the opposite direction, so that she knew it had turned around, retraced its path to find her. It slowed down as it passed, cruising noiselessly, while all three tuxedoed gentlemen stared at her, the yellow-slickered figure on the steps.

Then she was really scared. "They're going to come for me," she panicked; and as soon as the car had disappeared, she leaped to her feet. At the end of the street, she saw her husband. She ran toward him, shouting: "Hurry! Hurry! We haven't a minute!" Such was the intensity of her fear that, without a word, he responded. Together, they raced to the motel, entered their room, locked it, and then gasping in urgency, they pushed the heavy chest of drawers against the door.

Not a moment too soon. The limousine was right behind. It parked outside their door, lights on, and there it sat for ten minutes, with the motor softly running and the three gentlemen inside, silent in their black ties, menacing. Finally, it pulled away.

Anne felt tears starting in her eyes. She had no doubts that it was God's warning.

"If you really meant what you said in the boat," it warned, "about changing your life, then go ahead. But if you were not serious, if you intend to continue living your rich and easy life, then know what waits for you. And be afraid."

It took Anne a long time to come to terms with her promise. Eventually she returned to college to get her BA and began a long and serious examination of her life and values.

She had to change her life. But change from what? And why?

Expectations

The first thing you notice about the gentry is a sense of assurance. Even the *children* have it, a fact that a foreign service officer once brought to my attention. He had repeatedly observed it at State Department gatherings. The children of the gentry had only to enter a room, and there was something in their manner, their carriage, the toss of their heads, their glance around the room (lilliputian imitations of their parents) that carried an expectation of success. With expectation, the prophecy is fulfilled. The other children, he noticed, were attracted to them as plants to light. They had that air of ease, that unambitious expectation of being well received.

"Why is it?" asked my foreign service officer about the little children. "Where do they learn it?"

But it is not learned. It is acquired by intangible transpiration, a part of inheritance that begins at birth. It begins at the moment that the private doctor places the newborn babe in the hands of a nurse, who carries him to his own special plastic crib

in the private hospital. It continues for the five or six days of
his mother's lying-in. Even in the baby ward, that infant will
receive a special attention, though no nurse would admit it.
Attendance is not due to personal attraction. Certainly, the
children of the gentry are no handsomer than others, and often
are marked by remarkable lack of looks, if you consider the
receding chin and pale pop eyes—no beauty except to his
mother, perhaps, who probably thinks him fine enough, just
like his Daddy. No, it is not for his personal charm that his cry
produces a glance just a trace quicker than that for the other
babies or a thump of his bottom at diaper-changing time, and a
satisfied "There." It is because of who he is.

Put the equation another way: watch his grandmother come
to visit, a handsome woman with great, hooded eyes and a beak
of a nose and a straight back, who will trounce down the hall
in her tweeds, a fine leather purse over one arm, her gloves, her
hat (properly dressed, that is to say, lest she be taken for
riffraff), and when she asks where the babies are kept, her voice
holds not a question, but an ineffable demand.

It is in response to this demand that people jump. The
expectation of success.

"Second window on your left."

And so the babe, with his first breath, is sucking in the
investiture of his power and privilege, the inheritance of
established wealth.

Who is he? How will he grow, marry, live, die? Already the
world is in a state of flux, and customs change. I don't know
anyone anymore who is brought down to tea at four o'clock to
sit formally in the living room with parents and make polite
conversation for half an hour before being excused again to the
nursery. People don't do that anymore (though the man who
told me of this, his upbringing, still suffered from that
memory, still choked with rage, thirty years later).

The baby today will be christened later than in former generations, though he will probably still be dressed in the long, white christening dress that has been in his family since the eighteenth century. The ceremony will take place in the local Episcopal church, which probably dates also to the eighteenth century, and has been restored recently with charitable donations from the community. His family contributed to the chapel, just as they contributed to the hospital in which he was born, so that never is he far from the influence of his forbears.

Chances are he will not be christened in the private chapel of his grandparent's house. That is hardly ever used anymore, dusty reminder of a previous age.

There is a chapel in one house I know. You open the door off the gallery (and all around is spooky silence). There it stands. Four rows of green velvet prayer benches face a modest altar, still covered with its fringed white cloth. It holds high candlesticks and a silver chalice. The walls are white. The room is simple, with a stark purity. Over the altar hangs a lithograph of da Vinci's *Last Supper* and, on another wall, the parchment signed by the bishop of the state when he consecrated the chapel in 1912. In one corner droops a fading U.S. flag. The Episcopal minister left in the late 1950s, when grandmother died. No longer do the children gather for services or stare at the three Gothic stained-glass windows—a memorial to grandfather's life—or try to work out the family arms and Latin motto.

And what of the mother? See her propped in bed against her pillows? (One is her own silk baby pillow that she takes everywhere with her; it looks very pretty in its lace-trimmed pillowcase.) She has on a new bed-jacket and no makeup. In a moment, the nurse will bring in her baby. She had the baby by natural childbirth (and would love to have had the water-immersion birth, but they don't do that at this hospital). She intends to breast-feed, though her mother says it's a waste of time and why wear yourself out getting up several times a night when a nurse can feed the baby for you. Her mother is scornful of most new ideas. Meanwhile, she is a little afraid of her child. She is afraid she will not raise him right, to be strong and firm and fine. She hopes he won't be spoiled and resolves when she gets home not to cuddle him too much, as she had seen other mothers do, nor to coo over his crib, nor to run to him when he cries. When she thinks about it, she gets scared.

What she knows about babies is this: he will go home, driven by his Daddy, carried by his Mummy. The new nurse will meet them at the door and take him from her arms. After that, he will have a schedule of feedings, baths, play, and walks in the high, black pram that grandmother bought for him. It has a wide, square hat and high, silver wheels that flash in the sun. Like a Rolls Royce, which requires a uniformed chauffeur, this pram requires a nanny, but she is determined to raise her child herself.

For a short time, though, the prince will have a nurse, as befits his position, and the nurse will wheel this silly pram out to the park (or if they are at grandmother's, out onto the lower terrace), and the baby will be encased in layers of white jump-suits, blankets, hats, and shawls. Then he will be wheeled back inside to supper in the nursery kitchen.

Beyond this point, the mother cannot think, because no woman can imagine any further than this when she has just had her first baby. What she is thinking about is writing her thank-you notes for the silver rattles, and the Beatrix Potter set of china baby dishes, and the plug-in hot plate, and the silver reproduction Revere porringer.

One day in 1976, my friend Marguerite Kelly, who had just

published a wonderful book on child-rearing, received a telephone call from an editor at *Harper's Bazaar* in New York. She wanted Marguerite to write an article for them.

"Something like, 'How to Pick a Nanny,' " said the cultured voice over the phone. "That's always hard."

"Well, the first thing is," Marguerite laughed, for she had raised four children without so much as an occasional maid, "you don't call them nanny anymore."

"You don't?" The editor was genuinely surprised.

"No. They're called *housekeeper* today. Or maybe *babysitter*."

"Oh. I should think that would be entirely different. I had nannies when I had my children," she chatted amiably along. "Once we had two nannies, one for each child."

"How could that be?"

"Oh, well, we had already one nanny for the three-year-old, and she couldn't be expected to take care of the baby as well; so we had to have another for him. That made two. My husband said to me: 'Now we have two houses and two nannies, I think you should have two jobs as well.' " She laughed.

Very, very occasionally you read about the upbringing of someone with money. C. Z. Guest, for example, who was raised and who raised her own children with nannies, mam'zells, and duennas. "I had a governess for my children," she told the *Washington Post*. "I think children are better brought up with a governess. Children need someone to discipline them. And after all, Winston didn't marry me to be a maid. Besides, I couldn't go around with Winston, travelling, doing all the things he wants me to do, if I'd had to stay home and take care of the children. . . . That doesn't mean I never saw them. Of course, I saw them. I went fox hunting with them. . . ."

Her daughter is thirteen now. "She can't go around by

herself. I have a young French girl who goes with her."

It is common for the very rich to employ tutors for their children, because often they live at great distances from the "good" schools. Julie Kleberg, for example, of the King Ranch, grew up on a plantation in Alabama. It was about 50,000 acres in size and so remote, she says, that she and her brother were tutored by the farmer's wife, using the Calvert School Home Instruction Course, until she reached the age of eleven, when she was sent away to boarding school. Not many mothers are willing, like Sally Chase Daniel, of Brandon, to carpool their children 150 miles a day to school.

Sally Daniel's husband, Bobby, the congressman, was brought up at Brandon. He lived a solitary life, for if you drive to Brandon you can see that the river itself and the country roads provided the only access for generations. Superhighways did not exist until the 1960s. Even the country roads are removed from the place, for the Brandon drive itself is five miles long, winding past ponds and marsh and barns.

Bobby Daniel, Jr., was born in 1936, only four years before his father died, so that he has almost no memory of the father who bought this place, who stabled his racehorses there and began the massive business of restoring and rebuilding Brandon.

Bobby grew up with nurses, walked the grounds with his private tutor, and lived a kind of eighteenth-century existence. How curious it must have been. Isolated and lonely. Brandon was not then as large in acreage as it is today, but large enough so that finding friends among one's social and intellectual peers would be different for a child. Impossible not to be touched by his surroundings. A certain pride attaches in connecting yourself through an estate with the power of former years. And what power there was! John Martin, who arrived in Virginia in 1607, was a member of the original Council. His patent, now in the Virginia State Library, bears the names of Pembroke, Francis Bacon, and John Smith, and it grants Martin 7,000 acres "with privileges ... never accorded before or after to any planter in Virginia," according to the Brandon brochure, for it gave him total authority over all persons on his place and exempted him from obligation to obey the laws of the Colony.

Charlotte Bemis is said to have kept Brandon in great style, according to the fashion of the 1930s. Think of the effect on a small boy, brought up with the spacious main rooms upstairs, and the dark, twisting kitchens and pantries in another wing. The servants, I am told, wore livery. Was it the gold and hunter green that the household staff still wears?

I know one girl who remembers receiving a letter from Bobby Daniel as a young man, signed "Robert Daniel of Brandon."

The congressman, on the other hand, was not amused to be asked about it. He shot back angrily: "Why would I do that?"

But now I am ahead of myself. Bobby has had a number of jobs in his life. He began as a stockbroker, taught economics for a time, then sold commercial real estate. For five years he lived in Georgetown, outside Washington, D.C., and worked for the CIA. Then, in 1972, at the age of 36, he won his seat in Congress, his district extending from the city of Richmond to that of Norfolk, and excluding both.

I went to see the congressman in his offices in Longworth Building a few years ago. It was a standard Representative's office, with its green rug and heavy, walnut government-issue desks. Two or three secretaries were busy on phones or at their typewriters behind the file cabinets and bookcases. On the walls hung a print of "Blooded Colt, 1853" and three framed quotations. One was by Helen Keller:

> Everything has its wonders,
> even darkness and silence.

Another was by Edmund Burke:

> All that is necessary for the forces of evil to win in the
> world is for enough good men to do nothing.

A third was by Albert Schweitzer:

> I don't know what your destiny will be, but one thing I
> know, the only ones among you who will be really happy
> are those who have sought out and found how to serve.

Congressman Daniel is a Southern Democrat, which makes
him more conservative than a Midwestern Republican. He
serves on the Armed Forces Committee and on the District
Committee, the latter being concerned with the administration
of our nation's capital, a city which is 61 percent black and
which, though recently granted home rule, is still a Congres-
sional Preserve.

According to Daniel's administrative assistant, he has introduced some 300 to 350 pieces of legislation. As is common
with most congressmen, most of his bills died in committee.
One was a prospective drug law requiring mandatory sentences
for drug pushers and allowing judges to keep repeaters in jail at
their discretion. He introduced no legislation concerning the
poisoning of the James River by the Allied Chemicals Kepone
plant in Hopewell, Virginia, though he did attend the hearings
that led to the closing of the river to fishing and to the
prosecution of the corporation.

The congressman himself is a thin, pale man, all sharp angles
of chin and nose and eyes and voice. His hands fiddled

nervously over the empty desk top, long fingers playing with a pencil on the shining walnut surface.

I had heard that Daniel was shy, solitary, intense, that he would sit for hours alone in a duck blind during the shooting season, that he frightens some people with his cold veneer. Certainly, he was unwilling to be interviewed, suspicious, unhappy at the journalistic invasion. It had taken considerable pushing merely to have a meeting. When I arrived, he was brusque.

"I'm sorry to have kept you waiting." His voice was cold. "But I'm very busy. I'm up to my ears in work."

His desk blotter, paperweights, his family photos, and pen sets were set with compulsive neatness on the empty desk. Not a paper was in sight. The interview stumbled on, clumsy, strained, and uneasy, until in a superhuman effort at courtesy, the congressman reached into a desk drawer and produced, one after another, a series of glossy 8-by-10s, extending them with the pleasure of a child. Then his face took on a glow of interest. The pictures were of himself, as a member of the Armed Forces Committee, flying the "most advanced military systems." There was Bobby Daniel in helmet, suit, and goggles on the runway before a phallic Air Force fighter; himself in the cockpit; himself criss-crossed with bandoliers of chutes and straps and buckles and gear; and himself before the smooth, sleek, unearthly projectiles faster than sound: the F-15, the F-14, the F-11, the F-4, the A-6, the A-7, until the desk was littered with these photos of himself and the deadliest planes the world has ever seen.

The women's magazines tell you nothing about raising a prince. That is one reason why it is hard. He is different. From the beginning, he is raised with one goal in mind: inheritance.

Inheritance is not only a question of property and money,

but of expectations and responsibility. An expectation of status, of polite deference extended by one's inferiors and of polite acceptance by one's peers. Occasionally, this politeness may warm to deep friendship. That is not the point.

The expectation demands responsibility, and therein lies the clue to the character of the gentry. Responsibility. The expectation of inheriting property demands that one retain it. One cannot lose it. That is the first requirement. But the other, often contradictory, requirement is that one must do nothing that is not commensurate with one's station. The obverse of the coin. A responsibility so grave as to be nearly paralyzing. Often it negates the very possibility of success, that expectation that I spoke of earlier. Then the expectation curls into an arrogant, cold sneer, a public mask that hides—can you see it in his eyes?—sheer terror.

I know a family that was destroyed by this contradictory responsibility. In the family there was: a mother, married to her second husband (who was her cousin), and her three children by her first marriage. Her first husband died in a horrible accident when the children were small.

Many years later, I sat with her son, Robert, over a bottle of wine in an empty restaurant and drank the afternoon away, as he told me what it was like for him growing up. His stepfather was a rigid man, he said, humorless, stern, and as uncompromisingly disciplined with himself as with the children. He had married Robert's mother for her money. She, on the other hand, was fascinated by him, to such an extent (Robert told me painfully that afternoon) that she loved him more than her own children. The boys, already half-orphaned, were further removed by the remoteness of their mother. Nurses cared for them. They saw their mother—does it sound like a grade-B movie?—when she leaned down to receive their goodnight kiss before going off to a dinner party.

"Just a little kiss. Don't muss Mummy's hair." Fingertips to her lips, waggling a dainty kiss. The children walked around their parents all their lives, careful not to make a noise. As for the stepfather, he never spoke to them at all, except in reprimand.

One boy in the family was five or six years old when he was stricken by tormenting headaches. They were so severe that he would beat his head against the wall in pain, and when he ran to his mother, clinging for relief in her cool, silk skirts, she would pull him off.

"Here," to the nanny. "Take him away. He's only pretending to have a headache to get attention. He's so *spoiled.*"

Years after that, when he was a grown man, it was found that he had a brain tumor. One story has it that he received it when a horse smashed him in the face with its head, breaking his nose and sending splinters to the brain. His old baby nurse dates the tumor to the time when he was just a little child.

No matter. The man was grown when his illness was found, and he had a wife and children of his own by then. He staggered to the club on crutches, a beautiful, wistful smile on his face. He could not work at a desk job, as one might expect of a man of his caste. But one day he found a job on a road gang, as a member of a surveying team. He loved the nonintellectual, outdoor work.

His mother made him quit. A laborer's job was beneath him, and he lived the remainder of his short life as befits a gentleman, on his income.

You may think this an isolated example of an outlandish provincial custom. But consider. Think what it means to be told that honorable idleness is better than labor, that to work with one's hands is demeaning. That too is part of the expectation of class.

Now, today, times are changing, as I said. I know one family where the oldest son is a truck driver, but the family is confused enough by it to pass it off as a joke, and wonder what he'll do when he "grows up." Also, I know of several men who have no salaried job (besides the care of their investment portfolios) and who, embarrassed at their position in our work-oriented society, go to make-believe offices and putter their days away doing God-knows-what until at 5:30 they can return home in the rush-hour traffic.

When I was growing up, I knew a wonderful man. I adored him. He had an acerbic, biting wit, a proud stance. He was so troubled and so arrogant that he managed to get kicked out of three boarding schools and never graduated from school at all. By the time he cared about having a degree, he was already in his mid-twenties, and who, then, a gentleman of means, can go back to high school, especially for a diploma? He could not go to college without a degree, and he could not get a job without college. One day he told the gang down at the club that he had a job with Pan Am, and we were all impressed, imagining his offices in this futuristic, dynamic industry so far removed from our own lives of hunts and horses. That continued for several weeks until a girl in our group returned from New York by plane, landed at Friendship Airport, and saw this boy wheel out the steps to her plane.

"Lou-iss!" she called, pointing her index finger and doubling over in exaggerated pantomime of ridicule, for she was young and stupid and hard. "Louis! Is this your great job? Just wait till I tell!"

He walked off his job and never held another in his life.

The cruelty of class. Dear God! You can't imagine how it tears a man to shreds.

You see this life everywhere, gentlemen living on their income, playing at various inventions or investments. Many of them have not even any land in order to maintain an existence as a gentleman farmer. Yet they are, by class demands, above a job. Or they have been writing—for twenty years—a book.

"Timmy's writing the most *wonderful* book," his mother will announce, and whether she is blindly proud or pretending to a social convention, I cannot say.

"Christopher just quit the State Department," you will hear. "He couldn't *bear* working with such mediocre people at such inconsequential jobs. And then, you know, he's always wanted to be an historian. He's writing a book."

Or: "No, Hamilton's in business for himself. Investments, you know."

No one expects certain people to work. They are born to command. "Jock" Whitney, who pulls in income from his newspapers, racing stables, investments, and interests at a rate, we are told, of $1,600 a day, has no need to take a salaried post at someone else's firm. It is the same with these others. They sit on the boards of their family foundations, and they take friends to shoot at the family plantation in Thomasville, Georgia, or at the duck camp in Canada, and they laugh because the federal government now demands that duck hunters use nonlead shot in their guns because of lead poisoning in our waters: "But who's going to know? It's private land, and Joe, who's been our overseer forever, says nonlead shot isn't good for the gun." So they do what they wish and shrug their shoulders if people call them arrogant. What do they care when they have their own definition of success?

Rules and Discipline

One's early childhood is always sheathed in mists, and these are pierced by an occasional shaft of sun, in which is set a frozen image: a dog, a horse, the immobile tableau of yourself and sister swimming in a laundry tub at the back door, or eating dinner on a winter's night beside the hissing, warm radiator in the kitchen.

The images appear isolated, unattached. They group, however, like atoms about a central form, and in a certain class the form is discipline, awesome and externally imposed. This seems to be the common theme among all the memories that were dredged up for me by those with whom I talked. Sometimes the discipline was imposed by a governess or nanny. Then that person's image is most frequently frozen in those early childhood mists. In our family, it was my mother who taught us discipline.

My earliest recollection of my mother is of her teeth, long and yellow and gritted in rage as she advanced across the

Oriental rug, eyes flashing, lips drawn back in a snarl. A terrifying sight. I steeled myself to show no fear.

Many years later, while laughing with my mother at the intense selectivity of childhood memory, she told me how *her* mother would mete out punishment. "Down on your knees," her mother, my grandmother, would command, one finger pointing at the floor at her feet. "Down on your knees, and pray to God for forgiveness for your sins."

And the poor little girl would fall, weeping with remorse, to beg God's mercy and her mother's for her awful crime.

This adequate, swift punishment comes to mind today when I see little children hauling on their mother's hands in the supermarket, whining for a sweet, while the mother gives a sickly smile and sings: "Now come along, Lisa, you know Mommy just bought you a big lollipop."

" 'Nother. Want 'nother," screams the monster child, until the mother, presumably fearful of inflicting long-lasting psychological damage (or is she simply lazy?) capitulates.

Among a certain class, such manipulation of an adult is not tolerated. If a child interrupts a conversation, the adults are quite likely to turn on him, necks craning like the creatures in *Alice in Wonderland,* all screaming: "Children should be seen and not heard!"

Our family was tolerant, easygoing by comparison to those I met in later years. At age three or four, one college classmate was dressed in velvet by her child-bride mother and made to sit on a high-backed throne for hours at a stretch, motionless, submissive as a doll, while the tears of pain seeped down her face. I know of another family (but they were urban, not your country gentry) whose two children, aged four and five, ate at the table with the grown-ups, suffering through four-course dinners, with impeccable manners. *They were not allowed to speak.* A word, an outburst, and their father would impose instantaneous authority: "Up! Up to your room!" he would command. During a conversational lull, they might ask quietly for the butter or the radishes, but otherwise they cleared their plates in monastic silence, while the adults chattered above their heads and cast vague, disapproving glances if they squirmed.

Things were easier in my own family. We children were allowed considerable latitude to grow. Once having graduated, at age six, from the kitchen to the dining room table, we were allowed to speak, to play. Merely that absolute obedience was demanded of us, as of dogs and horses. It was a hopeless ideal on our place, all three forms of animal life bringing constant disappointment. Children, like dogs, were enjoyed by grown-ups, laughed at, poked tolerant fun at, and used for playing with. They were not taken seriously. They were expected to be tough enough to withstand any physical or emotional demand, including the public humiliation of teasing, and to smile while taking it, too—a foolish, slack-lipped effort, perhaps, but bravely attempted, nonetheless. It was part of discipline. Had anyone suggested it might harm our psyches, the remark would have elicited peals of laughter, psychiatry being yet another urban artifice for which the country folk had little stomach. If a child disobeyed, or made others (which is to say, adults) uncomfortable with his poor manners, he was instantly punished by voice or hand or both.

Self-discipline, self-reliance was expected from birth, these being the foundation of the aristocratic code. In public, where beatings were looked at askance, a child would receive a low hiss: "Now hush! I expect you to behave like a lady!"

During an interminable church service, if the boy squirms or kicks the straight-backed Puritan pew biting in his back, he is shown an index finger warningly: it is enough. He's still.

My second memory of my mother is of watching her chop the head off a chicken.

Chop! and the head fell to the ground, and she tossed the

red-feathered creature with its bloody stump of a neck into a half-peck basket, where it flopped about and flapped its headless wings.

"How long is it alive?" I asked, with horrified delight. "Is it alive now? Is it still alive?"

And when she answered no, that it was dead as soon as the axe hit, I asked, "Well, are the legs still alive? Why does it kick?" To which she growled an incoherent answer and headed for the kitchen, to pluck and disembowel the fowl.

I suppose this happened during World War II, since earlier we'd had a yardman, Theodore, who killed the chickens. He blew off his fingers one day, using dynamite out at the woodpile, and then he left.

At night, my mother would appear in evening dress on my father's arm, to give us children a kiss goodnight in bed. Her perfume would rise around her, her long skirts would rustle sensuously, and my father would laugh and pop his top hat in and out at us, wind a white silk scarf round his neck, and off they would go to dinner or a dance, leaving my head swimming with the grace and enchantment of grown-up life.

My childhood was full of contradictions.

Discipline, order, begins at home. The authoritarian values are reinforced by school.

"Do they all go to St. Paul's and Yale?" asked my State Department friend one day. "Surely some–"

"I don't think so," I answered. From my observation, attendance at public school is rare. Most of the gentry send their children where the others go, or else, like Bobby Daniel, they are taught by tutors. Governesses and tutors are rarer today, however, than they were when I was growing up, and even in those days the practice was fading out. Mrs. Arthur Strubel and her cousins on Avery Island were taught by private tutors; they read the classics aloud by lamplight–Thackeray, Dickens, Longfellow–and took the train twice a year to town on the mainland to go to the dentist, and once a year for the circus. Tutors taught the Tevis boys on their remote ranch in California, and the Ferguson children on Cumberland Island, Georgia. I could name a dozen more.

William van Petten, scion of the Pauley Petroleum Company, lived in the family compound in Pasadena, California, vacationed at the ranch in Santa Maria, went every summer to the Royal Hotel in Hawaii (this was before the family bought Coconut Island), and grew up in the same sheltered, protected environment on the West Coast that we have seen on the East. At the age of eleven, he was sent alone to an English boarding school.

Q. But didn't you ever go to school in California?
A. No, never. No.
Q. But was this common or unusual among your peers?
A. More the common, more. Because there *were* no schools. Later on now, later on, my uncle's children did go. Because they moved on over to Beverley at a fairly early time, and they went to.... There was a school you went to, a private school. But there wasn't any in Pasadena. There was one that the girls went to, yes. Uh ... a Miss Somebody's Classes.

Going to boarding school at the age of twelve or thirteen is fairly common. Going at a younger age is unusual in our country, for Americans do not hold with the English system of banishing their children at the age of five or six. Yet, occasionally—rarely—you come across the single boy who was sent away to camp at six and to boarding school at ten. The parents, abdicating responsibility, toss the child from school to school, as he acts out his anger, is kicked out of one after another, and, in spite of himself, learns discipline. Distant, closed people, these boys become, but self-reliant, too.

Van Petten loathed his English boarding school, where in a

cold, rainy climate he ate bad food. After two years, he switched to the Swiss Ecole Rosé for two years, and ended up in 1938 at a Nazi military academy in Berlin. An eclectic education. It was not that his parents deliberately planned this exercise in autocratic European schools, culminating in a Nazi academy. What happened was the boy got sidetracked while travelling self-reliantly by himself from Switzerland to his new German boarding school and fell in with some boys who turned out to be members of the Hitler Youth, training for the SS. Van Petten had drunk much wine that day. He was sick all over the clean uniforms of his guides, who then led him, with some disgust, not to the old-fashioned Gymnasium where he was expected, but to a military school. There, he decided to enroll. He chose his own school, in effect. His parents were perfectly satisfied, once they were assured that his degree would be effective. He stayed with the Nazi academy for another two years, graduated, went for another year or so to St. Andrews School in Delaware, the du Pont school, to prepare himself for college, and finally arrived, around the age of twenty, at Yale.

For those subjected to private tutors, then, the introduction to school and one's peers can come relatively late in childhood. Today, with our new emphasis on kindergarten and preschool and nursery school and reading readiness (the logical solution to the lack of nannies), a child's schooling can begin at two-and-a-half or three. My own school began at five, with first grade. It was there, outside the shelter of my house, that I was first confronted by the contradictions of class.

I understood nothing. I was isolated by my puzzlement and awed by the other girls, who seemed completely adjusted to their place, manipulating teachers and peers with exquisite skill.

Do you know what game we played in first grade? A metaphor of life. We played Club.

Club was played under the sliding board, and the point of

Club was that two or three people belonged in the club. One other girl was needed to play. She would come up (all unawares) and say, "Can I join your club?" And we would turn on her: "No! This is a private club!"

I played it only once. I remember watching our victim reel sickeningly off. I refused to play again, and to that extent, not participating, was not accepted, really, in my school.

I understood nothing. History of Art, for example, where the Exalted Seniors memorized the names of black-and-white photos of Great Paintings that hung on the walls of the gym. At ten or twelve, I solemnly studied the pictures during sports, uncomprehending. Why did seniors seem to like art? The pictures affected me not at all. It was not until I went to Italy and France years later and saw the originals that I began to understand.

Or sports. Up and down the hockey field we ran, bare thighs goose-bumped with November cold. I was a wing. I ran sometimes for an entire period without getting the ball. I never understood why I was there, running up and down that field for forty minutes, while the centers hogged the ball. I was too stupid to rebel, too cowed to go on strike. "There must be some reason," I thought dully. "What is it I am supposed to be learning here?" For I never doubted that my teachers, being in authority, had prescient knowledge that it was my obligation to obtain.

I will talk about boarding school in another chapter. Suffice it for now to say that learning in these elementary private schools was—is—delivered to us, captive students, with a steady, unremitting lack of imagination that concentrated on drilling facts by rote and repetition—as if designed to dry up the challenge of learning. Looking back on it now, I realize there was no pattern to the education, no overview, besides a reverence for Christian Episcopalianism and an orthodoxy of thought. Especially, it evidenced a distaste for the dissident idea; this should not be unexpected, though it is sad, when we consider that only in the radical, the new and revolutionary, lies creative energy. Our schooling played it safe. We learned the proper thoughts.

They were tinged with romanticism. In history, we studied, for three years in a row, the European feudal system. Incredible. Three solid years? We learned the duties of a vassal to his lord, the inferiority of serfs, the gentleness of ladies, virtuous and chaste. We thrilled also to torture by burning, maiming, drawing, quartering, incarceration in foul dungeons, and death by Iron Maidens—our books being graphically illustrated with the punishments of traitors and outcasts. We heard little of the Children's Crusade, hygiene, the Courts of Love, the flagellantes, or the thievery, rape, and butchery of knights on the prowl. On the other hand, we spent considerable time learning the ceremonies and vows taken by a neophyte knight as he knelt in the cold, stone chapel, dedicating himself to God and a life of purity and good.

Only our own religious training and School Loyalty were more assiduously instructed in this place, where the motto was, "To Be and Not to Seem."

For all its romanticism, however, the educational system was predicated on fear and punishment. This was meted out by a strict system of demerits, suspension, or expulsion. There was no provision, that I remember, for reward.

The regulation, the regimentation of rules works like cookie molds, pressing out identical and pleasing schoolchild forms. Elementary school delivers the child's first instruction in the importance of institutions, where institutions become more important than the individuals that support them: the institution of marriage above the individual, of school above education, of the Church above God. Institutions are founded upon fidelity, first to one's family, then to friends, school, church, clubs, community. It is not all bad, you understand, for without such loyalty, society would cease to exist.

Rules governed our lives. The rules turned to regulation, and this to regimentation. And all of this exists almost unchanged today. Go to any proper Protestant private school, and you find this same regimentation. In behavior. In intellectual development. Yes, the children learn an assurance, a self-confidence that astounds us. Their manners are beautiful, their postures straight. On the other hand, they are taught one crippling lesson: that there is only one right way to resolve any problem, and this single way is hidden by one billion surrounding wrong choices. It is up to the child to find—on the first attempt—that single solution in a world of chaff. A terrible responsibility. I watch our children at times, almost paralyzed by the necessity of choosing right; I see them grow inflexible in their poignant desire to please.

This is called "having values," and those who learn best the conservative security of punitive regimentation, those who take it most to heart, become the backbone of the propertied class, for property and dissident thought or change or deviation are irreconcilable contradictions.

Going Through Gates

Contradictions. We moved through a thicket of contradictions. Rules governed our lives, and not only were there the basic physical rules of good health and exercise and the explicit structure of good manners and courtesy, all learned at home, but there was also a labyrinth of social and emotional regulations, made more difficult to explore by the absence of maps. Oh, the physical rules were simple: brush our hair before breakfast and our teeth afterwards, make our own beds, sit straining on the toilet until the accomplishment of "our duty." Move slowly around the horses. Stay out of doors at least six hours every day. The physical strictures were simple compared to the subtlety of social rules: the relationships of servants, of men to women, the even more complex rules on what was called "the race thing." They created the contradictions of class. We suffered if we did not follow the rules or inadvertently broke them, and we suffered also by adhering to them. Always there was the fear of misinterpreting a rule. Yet some were

almost Chinese in the fact that they were never articulated.
Merely to speak could lead you to disaster.

A friend of mine did once. She was twelve years old when
her mother gave her a lovely, tiny, pearl necklace with a
diamond clasp. She ran upstairs:

"Oh Nanny, look what Mummy's given me. It's worth at
least a thousand dollars."

The comment came right back to her. She had broken a rule.
"Never mention money or value." And do you know that my
friend carries that story with her to this day, pierced to the
heart by her blunder?

What a delicate line we had to tread. I don't see how we did
it. We *absorbed* our rules through a complex osmosis of adult
gesture, intonation. Our paths were made more difficult (our
fears more intense) because these rules, these shadowy areas of
social propriety, were sometimes actually misrepresented to us.
Why? To this day I do not know. I would study someone in
the Valley—a family acquaintance—and say later, "I can't stand
Mrs. So-and-So."

"Oh no!" My mother would leap to her defense. "Mrs. So-
and-So is a Great Lady."

My mother is over sixty-five today and her standards have
relaxed, so that she will confide in me today. "Do you know
I've never been able to stand Mrs. So-and-So?"

Oh, Mummy, why didn't you tell me before? Why did I
spend twenty years worrying about setting up my judgment
against yours? What was being shielded? Me? A way of life?
The result was to increase my confusion and produce, as I grew
older, an inchoate rage at the hypocrisy.

Listen, this is not an isolated example, though isolation was
one side effect. The same misrepresentation—perhaps uncon-
scious—was at work on all our peers and classmates. None of us

knew it, for none of us discussed such things. Class is more taboo than sex.

Years later I was talking to Eve Pell about this delicate line we learned to tread. She told of a similar misrepresentation, or blundering, with class.

"Once my sister was upset about something. She went upstairs and sobbed to our nurse about it. And, for some reason, I felt she should have discussed this with my mother and I scolded her. 'You must not discuss this sort of thing with the *servants*,' I said.

"Well. This got back to our old nurse. She was upset. My mother turned on me. 'Nurse is *not* a servant. She is as much a lady as there has ever been.'

"But, of course, that wasn't true," said Eve, all these years later. She leaned forward on the sofa, palms together in supplication, eyes searching my face. "Nurse wasn't a lady like my mother was a lady. Nurse sewed up her hems. She didn't sew up Nurse's hems. But I had said something that was not supposed to have been said. And every now and then, I would say the wrong thing along that line, no matter how I tried."

No wonder caution so often replaces the exuberance of youth, a close-lipped tautness even in the very young. It is easily misinterpreted as arrogance. Early on, you learn whom you may invite to play tennis at the club, and it is usually not a Jew (if somehow you manage to meet one). To invite a black may be easier. If you prefer a "townie" in your summer resort, you play on the town-supported macadam courts and lay yourself open to shameless teasing.

In a most subtle way, we suffer. By going along with the rules, we acquiesce, actively or passively, in racist slurs and snobbery. By refusing the role, we suffer equally, for refusal constitutes betrayal of those we love, and also (perhaps the worst offense), a breach of manners. Manners alone require that we never point ourselves out or make our peers uncomfortable by a dissenting view.

"When I was in England," said one woman I interviewed, "I had a very brief and superficial romance with an Indian Maharaja, who was a little older than me. I had this wonderful week of being squired around London in Jaguars and going to the theatre as the . . . what would you say? The escort? of this prince. I had a wonderful time. It couldn't have been sweller. And then I came home and my father said: 'How'd ye like thet Black Sambo over there?' " She paused. "I mean, there were all these hideous racial things about the Indian, and I'd thought that, class-wise, I wasn't doing badly. A genuine prince, with palaces and polo ponies and jewels. But I was kidded as if I were going out with a black laborer."

You think this doesn't happen anymore? That was years ago, you argue, long before the open 1960s changed our views; such behavior could not happen now, you say, and you point to your friend who dates an Iranian—just the same thing—and no one says a word.

Oh, but the parochialism is there, just under the surface, and sometimes bubbling up, ugly, sad, and bitter fruit of human souls, as when Billy Zantzinger hit Hattie Carroll with his cane—though his going to jail for it indicates a change.

It happened in Baltimore in the mid-1960s. Billy Zantzinger, who comes of very fine, old Maryland family, came up from southern Maryland for the Spinster's Ball. You should know that southern Maryland is rural, out of the way. People live there in another age. The area hasn't the sophistication of a city like Baltimore or the people in the Green Spring Valley.

The Spinster's was a bash, with lots of liquor flowing, and dancing, laughing, and people pattering about the hotel corridors having fun. And late, late that evening, Billy

Zantinger, who felt uncomfortable anyway, probably, and had had a lot of drink, Billy turned in jest to a black barmaid, an old woman, and with lordly manner demanded a drink. It was a role he was playing, you see, the hick from the sticks; and when she didn't leap into the part with a swift "yassah," he shouted again for a drink and hit her with his cane. I don't know how hard he hit her. I've heard it was pretty light.

Anyway, later that night, after the party was over, the old woman had a heart attack and died, and Bill Zantzinger was brought up on charges of manslaughter, and he was tried before a judge and convicted and sentenced to serve some time in jail. The judge kindly permitted him to begin his sentence after the tobacco crop was in.

Bob Dylan wrote a song about it, called "The Ballad of Hattie Carroll," which took the view that Zantzinger's action was intentional, a racist act, when, actually, it was a pathetic, foolish gesture of fun that ended in tragedy.

It was not my parents alone, then, who misled my sister and me through the maze of class. Oh, it is a formless mass of general humanity, beginning with the immediate family and proceeding through layers of instructors and teachers, all conspiring in the defense of an indefensible system, all optimistically putting "the best face forward" on the one hand, and on the other, giving in to . . . to racial slurs, or ethnic slurs, except with their own, to whom was always given "the benefit of the doubt." Is that common to every people? To every class?

Social conformity takes manifold forms. I remember one schoolmate. Awkward and ungainly, crippled with eyesight so poor that she was almost blind (for despite the media myths, the upper class are not always graceful, gifted, and lovely). She was crippled further by her lack of confidence. She had one talent. Her music. Her natural musical ability exceeded any-

thing I have ever run across since, and when she sat down at
the piano, leaning myopically into the keys, you forgot
everything in the rippling notes that poured from her plump
white hands.

Her mother, in marrying, had given up her career as a
concert pianist, for Catholic duty. She bore five or six children,
of whom my friend was one. Alice, I shall name her now.

Alice could only play by ear. She never took lessons, was
never taught the structure of chords or harmony or even, for
that matter, to read the simplest music. Can you imagine such
neglect, when the mother played herself? No matter: Alice
taught herself to play. Whistle any tune–a Bach prelude–and
Alice could pick out the melody, using all eighty-eight keys,
black and white, and composing her own variations and
harmony.

One day a friend of her mother's called at their house while
Alice was at the piano. She was picking out the Beethoven
sonata that she had heard her mother play earlier. As the
doorbell rang, she politely stopped.

"Oh, Jane," said the visitor. "I've never heard you play so
well!"

But it was not the mother she had heard, but my friend, the
child.

Do you know that her parents never gave her music lessons?
Oh, once when she was twelve she took music from the piano
teacher at Garrison Forest School, one lesson a week for about
three months, and when she could not read after that, the
lessons stopped.

"Oh, Alice can't read music," her mother would say. "I'm
sure she could never learn. She can barely read *English,* after
all."

I was appalled, though I never heard any adults criticize that mother. All grown-ups were defended when I was growing up, I think perhaps in part because they represented authority, which is the first line of defense on the battlefield of society and the bulwark against the beasts that children are.

Alice was never allowed to play on weekends or to spend a night out unless first she had completed certain chores. Often, I would drive to her house to pick her up—only to discover her scrubbing the kitchen floor or doing the household laundry. This out of no need. The family had two cooks and a maid in their kitchen and a day laundress and a yard man. Sometimes Alice would be vacuuming the downstairs, and I would pitch in with dusting so that we could finish quickly and leave.

Her mother spent her days on the satin chaise longue in her pale blue bedroom, her back propped up by lace and embroidered pillows. In one languid hand she held a novel; the other hovered over the box of chocolates at her side (chocolates, I must add, that were never offered when we came upstairs to make our devoirs). It took me years to understand that she was crazy. We were told that she was ill.

She eavesdropped on all phone conversations. After a time, I learned to put her off: "Oh, it's me," I would say brightly. "I wanted Alice, thank you. And she's got the phone. . . . She has the phone now, thank you."

I would wait until I heard the extension click.

Yet, never did anyone around me say a word about this monstrous mother, mean and manipulative. Criticism of one's equals was not, I think, quite socially acceptable.

"Jane's sick, poor dear," you would hear. Or: "How that woman loves her second daughter!"

It was as if the expression of an angry thought about one's class would burst the bubble of refined pretense, and yet, this stop-think, this confining of thought to "nice," noncritical

paths, was balanced by such open anti-Semitism, such antago-
nism to outsiders as would make you gasp.

A lesson in class. The place: her mother's office, just off the
bedroom, a beautiful corner room, where the sunlight from a
southern exposure floods onto the Oriental carpets. Here is her
mother's American pine desk, where she keeps her accounts, as
well as certain favorite first-edition books, her sewing basket,
her favorite photos of the family.

"Pearl's a nice lady," said the little girl, speaking of one of
the army of maids who took their anabases through the house.

"Pearl is not a lady," the mother corrected her child.

"Oh." She was surprised. "She's not?"

"She's a woman."

The little girl thought a moment. "What's a lady, then?"

"Well, Mrs. Banker is a lady," said her mother slowly,
naming one of the neighbors. "And Mrs. Foster. Most of our
friends—"

"Oh." She considered the matter. "Well, is Mrs. Crawlspace
a lady?" she asked, naming yet another neighbor, prone to drop
in unexpectedly in her big Buick. She chainsmoked, spoke only
in a stentorian roar, and favored conversations about kikes and
Jew-boys down the road.

"Yes," said the mother bravely. "She's a lady, too."

On my grandmother's farm, we played with the farmer's
children, boys our age. They had odd mountain names: Kelsey,
Darcy. We crept under the floorboards of the porch where, in a
murky light, the boys dug out of the hard-packed earth for my
inspection their father's bag of gold dust. We poured the tiny,
glowing powder on our hands, smelled and tasted it. I had

never seen anything like it—gold. It impressed me immeasurably.

We played in the barns where the Percherons stomped on hooves as large as dinner platters; where the barn cats skittered around the feed bags hunting mice, while, high in the rafters, swallows maintained a continual twittering, swooping like bats; motes danced in shafts of light. We rolled in loose hay in the hayloft, listened to the munch of cows eating grain or the splash of their urine into troughs: nothing so wet as cow manure.

All day long, we could play with the farmer's boys. But after five P.M. it was forbidden. I remember going down at dusk one summer evening after dinner and being told on my return I'd done wrong. I was never to go down after dark again. Whether it was to protect me, a lady, as I somehow inferred, or whether it was an act of courtesy, in order to leave the farmer's family with free and private time, I do not to this day know. The rule represented another of the distinctions in class, for at dusk in my grandmother's house the grown-ups were gathering before a seven-thirty dinner over their old-fashioneds, waiting for the cook to announce dinner. Down the hill, the farmer's family had already finished eating and was sitting on the front steps of their house, still in their work clothes, each adult picking his teeth and the children walking around the yard, practicing the slow swagger peculiar to the countryman's walk.

There comes a time, it seems, around the age of forty, when one needs to come to terms with his past. Originally, I had thought this probing was my personal vendetta, drawn from individual need. I find in researching this book that this moment of re-examination is a common experience.

One woman remarked to me: "You've come at the right

moment. I'm hemmed in by certain things I've never overcome. It's now or never. Now my children are grown or, at
least, they don't need me the way they did before. And it's my
life. If I don't come to terms with it...."

I think this explains why so many people spoke to me so
openly, each questioning his life. It seems each had an
adjustment to make in childhood to his privileged class, some
accepting the position without question and others bothered by
distinctions they did not understand.

I don't know why it should be, but the women more
frequently than the men see their adjustment to the past in
terms of class. The men talked in abstractions, analyzing,
observing the same phenomena as did the women but
interpreting these events in an entirely different way: the men
see the conflicts with the past arising from their relationships
with their mothers.

Here is William van Petten again, in Los Angeles. Van
Petten's family derive from the Hudson River landholders, and,
in fact, his sister still lives on the ancestral property along the
Hudson River. But van Petten himself is a writer and novelist
in Los Angeles, concerning himself, to a degree he finds
annoying, with the family oil business.

Raised in Pasadena, he grew up in the privacy of a family
compound, a walled city, worked by five servants, not counting
the gardeners, and broken by vacations elsewhere. He speaks of
an existence that is "completely feudal," of the protected
enclaves in which he was raised, where the chauffeur, if a
stranger approached the car, would flick a button to lock the
children's door.... And then, on the edge of a shadowed
perception, he backs away: even the development of tracts in
southern California, he notes, are built on the Spanish style,
with the houses turned in upon themselves and walls encircling
the whole. They are set down in a controlled environment,

internally. "And that's the way everyone has always lived." He dismisses the thought. "You have to live that way. This leads to feudalism."

Did he ever question his background?

"What do you mean, question?"

"Wonder, who am I? And why am I rich and others are poor?"

"No," he said, sipping his after-lunch brandy. "No, never. But I did wonder—and my cousins and I often talk about this—about the Byzantine life in which we were raised and how it is impossible for anyone else to understand the games that are played to this day in our family, among ourselves." He went on to talk of the "vicious" competitive relationships and of his conviction that if one member of the family does not "watch it," he will be pushed out of his legitimate property by the others.

Others, however, do question the matter of class. Here is a woman from the East, who, though she has cast aside her background, asked, nonetheless, that her name not be used.

She grew up on a 300-acre dairy farm. There was a dairy farmer for the cows, a chicken man who looked after the poultry and fighting cocks, a man for the horse barns, a vet in residence. She and her sisters rode endlessly through the forest paths and on wide ribbons of dirt roads.

"There were few other kids to play with," she remembered. "The foreman's son was my age, and when I began to get the sense that there were classes of people, or had a sense that I belonged to the ... upper class—I mean, I could be friends with Rusty, but only to a certain extent."

"But you knew that, didn't you? Right from the earliest period?"

"*Of course* I did. Yes."

"How? How did you know?"

"Well, of course, it's very easy to know. My father—His father called my father 'boss' ('What are we going to do this morning, boss?'). And then, we lived in a big house and he lived in a tiny house. I went to private school, he went to public school. I mean, it's all there. His grammar was bad and mine was good. There was no way of *not* knowing it. There was always a cook, a waitress, an upstairs maid who lived in the house, a laundress who came in by the day, and my sister's governess from Germany and. . . .

"And then, just the places . . ."

We were sitting in the St. Regis Hotel in New York as we talked, and she looked absently around. She was talking to herself as much as to me. "Driving with my grandmother in New York City," she continued. "In The Car, which was a chocolate-brown Packard with a chauffeur, and the—you know—and being aware at some level of people looking at me as I descended from the car to go to Bendel's or Bergdorf's or whatever."

"Were you embarrassed at them looking at you?"

She looked at me curiously. "I'm trying to remember. It had to be right, because that's the way it was; but there was also a sense that there was something wrong, a little mixed, of being conspicuous somehow, and I think growing up in that way sets you apart from people. Ordinary people. I mean, your whole life is based on going through gates into places where other people can't go.

"Tuxedo Park, where my grandmother lived, has a wall around it, and there is a guard there, and you have to say who you are to get in, right? And I was always one of the ones who got in. Right? So, there must have been something right, because you always have this sense of the innocent child who . . . you know . . . is struggling against adverse circumstances, but, nonetheless, your family is one who's properly dressed and goes to these places. . . "

We fiddled with our drinks, let the conversation wander with our eyes to the Maxfield Parrish painting of Old King Cole behind the bar.

"Why are we so terrified?" she asked again, for the past weaves its strands and skeins about us, tying us down. I do not think the terror looms at any individual memory. Rather that childhood looms over us larger than life-size, so that one part of our minds is still inhabited by a time when we had no resources to control or comprehend our lives.

"It's only now that I'm able to love my mother," she stirred her drink thoughtfully. "To *see* my mother, to understand how vulnerable she was, or to recognize the emotional paucity of my father, who spent his days playing sports. To him, form is everything. If it's a nice day and you are playing tennis on grass courts with your family, you are happy."

"And is he?" I asked, that certainly being one possibility.

"I don't know," she answered slowly. "I don't know."

The Boarding School

The final step in the care and training of the propertied class occurs in the boarding school, a fact which is so completely understood all over the country that parents from Lake Forest, Illinois, or Pebble Beach, California, send their children automatically East to school. They say there is no equivalent education in the West. One San Franciscan has her son at St. Paul's. "It's so good for him," she told me. "One of his classmates is black. You'd never find that in San Francisco."

"What?" I answered in surprise. "I've always heard of the open, classless society of California! What do you mean, it wouldn't happen?"

"Oh no. You wouldn't ever find a black person at anyone's house for dinner. I don't know why. But you never do. And there aren't any in the schools here, and certainly not *rooming* with your child. I think it's wonderful. That's why we sent him East—to have this broadening experience."

The good boarding schools are concentrated on the East

Coast. For girls there is Madeira and Foxcroft in Virginia,
Garrison Forest and St. Timothy's in Maryland, Rosemary Hall,
Miss Porter's or Ethel Walker's in New England. . . . The boys
attend Choate and St. Paul's, Deerfield, Andover,* Groton,
Exeter, Kent, Middlesex. . . . In the 1950s, they were known in
composite as St. Grottlesex. No Southern schools approach the
reputation of these New England boys' schools, but in Virginia
we find Episcopal High, and elsewhere a dozen military
academies, for which Southerners have a particular fondness. As
for why the children are sent to school, the parents are honest.
"The friends you make at boarding school are the friends you'll
have all your life."

It is true. Lifelong friends are made, but some alumnae never
recover from the golden haze of joyous school years. We find a
core group where the Best Man in the wedding was the eighth
grade boarding school roommate. Others are cynical, even
bitter, about their boarding school. I think of one man, now an
alcoholic, who was kicked out of four schools, each worse, he
says, than the next. Or a Midwesterner, heir to a large and
famous fortune, who was sent in eighth grade to Brooks. One
sister went to Dobbs Ferry and another to Foxcroft. He hated
school, and his passive resistance to compulsory soccer or
hockey had already resulted in his getting kicked out of three
elementary schools. He didn't like the people at boarding
school, he says, he didn't like being sent away. Why go, then,
to a boarding school?

"Well, where else *would* you go?" he snapped. Mere
attendance was all that was required of him. That in itself gives
the Dun & Bradstreet seal of approval; you have been passed on
in advance and nothing you do in later life can diminish the
honor of this accolade. Certainly his attending had nothing to

* Philips Academy in Andover, Massachusetts.

do with getting an education, he said (you can see why I quote him anonymously):

"Education is dangerous. Education widens your horizons. Maybe through education you'll see more than you should—like black people outside of Granny's chauffeur, or Puerto Ricans who function outside of the delivery man.

"We got Latin and the Classics, but I still can't add, subtract, or spell. When I got out of school, I knew nothing of the real world, about leases and mortgages or how to send the laundry out. But I knew all the best restaurants in New York City. I was supposed to get out of school, go to Princeton, and set the world on fire. Only, how do you do that," he added bitterly, "when your father is already at the top. That's why so many men you know are alcoholics ... run through three wives. Too much is expected of them. They maybe did well, but they had to do better."

This is a young man speaking, just at the brink of life. He was thirty-two when we talked. Already, he had retired to his country estates, embittered by society and the requirements of excelling within boundaries too limited for creative activity.

"As for what you were expected to do with an education"—he was stuttering with emotion—"you're expected to be interested in everything, but do nothing well. If you like art, you can go to a museum, or music, you can go to a concert—but don't play or paint a sketch or sing. You have to be culturally well rounded. It's cute if you dabble in sculpture, but God help you if you try to be good at it. That's true of everyone in this group, with a few rare exceptions. Like Flicka van Staedte, who went to Farmington, and is now an opera singer. A wonderful singer. But she came from a poorer family. Once a friend of our family wrote a book, and I read it and told my grandmother, who knew her family, that it was really very, very good. Do you know her response? It was, 'Oh, well, she's always had emotional problems.' In other words, nice people don't write."

He paused a moment, mentally pacing up and down the rooms of his mind, then turned again: "Do you know Diana Oughton, the girl who blew herself up in a house in Greenwich Village? The response to that was typical: 'Oh the poor Oughtons. They are so sweet and nice. *Think what she did to them!'* "

He returned to the subject of boarding school.

"There was only one thing of value I learned in all this crap and garbage and shit instilled in me. And that was manners. To be polite. At six years old, I could get to my feet and pass trays at my parents' cocktail parties before going off to bed with Nanny. I had the proper upper-class American social upbringing.

"Well, that's important. It sounds stupid, I know, fatuous. But manners makes life just that much easier. Life is so difficult anyway, I wish everyone had manners: 'Would you mind' ... 'Please' ... 'Thank you' ... Just a little courtesy extended to others. That's the one thing left in this Formica, throw-away world we live in now, manners. And it's nice to know there are people who have them. But that's the only thing of value I learned in school."

Many people will disagree with the Midwesterner. Many will tell you that they loved boarding school, their classmates, the teachers, and masters, that at boarding school they were first introduced to a love of learning. To this Midwesterner, however, the point of school was to create yet another controlled environment for the child. "It's one more way to put on blinders and pretend the rest of the world's not there. It's another example of isolation and insulation. If you don't like the neighborhood, move. If you don't like the noise on the street, make it go away. Everything is controllable."

Yet, even this man, on reflection, apologizes for his attitude. His was a personal dissatisfaction, he says, and anyway, schools have changed since he attended in the early 1960s. You hear this all the time: the boarding schools have changed. They are often coeducational now. The uniform code has relaxed, and the students are often allowed to go off-campus for weekends. The students are mobile, intellectually stimulated. They work at jobs during the school year. Neither are they sexually ignorant, as we were in the 1950s and early 1960s. Schools in those days didn't need to cope with drugs or alcohol: smoking a cigarette was grounds for expulsion. Today, the courses offered in a large boarding school read like the curriculum of a small university, and parents will tell you how different are the schools from those we knew. But I am not so sure.

In the fall of 1976, a sophomore at Miss Porter's School in Farmington, Connecticut, had a baby. She delivered it herself, alone in her room, after which it disappeared. Somehow the fact was discovered. The headmaster, Warren Hance, called the police and reported that a baby had been born and no one knew where it was. It was found under a dormitory bed, a newborn boy, dead, and wrapped in a plastic baggie.

Everyone in our group was horrified by the story. How could such a thing happen? people said. Poor child, they murmured, and, How is such a thing possible? And one tall gentleman blurted out, unthinking—"It can't be good for the school!" But most people shook their heads with suffering. They spoke in undertones, aghast. Her parents didn't *know?* The teachers didn't *see?*

Apparently, she had been sent to school, this fourteen-year-

old child, seven months pregnant. The school was unable to
cope with the situation. All the teachers ignored it, and the
child earned straight A's and took basketball, it is said, right up
to the date of delivery. She explained that she had an
abdominal tumor that would soon be surgically removed.

It is said that some teachers recognized the girl was pregnant
but did not report her condition. No help was given her, and
neither was she sent to a nearby hospital to check on her
pregnancy or alleged tumor—as if we lived in some Victorian
time. Afterwards, the headmaster called the 290 students
together and asked them not to discuss the matter publicly. He
closed the ranks of class and school with loyalty.

Things did not end there. A month later, a sophomore at
Notre Dame, in Middleburg, Virginia, delivered her baby.
Again, she was alone in her room, isolated and afraid. Only this
time the baby was born alive. Later, it was found dead in an
incinerator.

It seems incredible that such a thing could occur in this day
of sex education, birth control, and legal abortion. But I
understand. I went to one of these fashionable girls' boarding
schools, a finishing school. I can understand how a girl can
parade, belly swelling, for two months and how the teachers
would not observe her, the administration close its eyes, the
students be unable to help. The Notre Dame student left
school and was prosecuted before the juvenile court. I do not
know these two poor girls, and the particulars of both cases
were hushed up, the press handling each with the finesse and
discretion usually accorded to the family of the publisher
himself. At other boarding schools nearby, the girls heard not a
word of the scandal. No one mentioned it.

Massive changes occurred in the 1960s, we are told, what
with the civil rights riots and the university riots and the

Vietnam War riots, and the general unease of that agitated decade, the loosening of the reins of discipline.

It is true today that you see evidence of change. It hangs on the walls of the half-million-dollar gymnasiums, as year by year the sequential photos record the varsity teams. Football, hockey, soccer. The teams are peppered with increasing shades of black. A single black player marks the photo of the early 1960s, then two, then three, until, by the present day, you find five or six a year, an acceptable quota in a school where tuitions range from $4,000 to $6,000 a year. Yet, basically, the foundations of the schools, their character, cannot change.

The boarding school I attended, Foxcroft, typifies most such institutions both in what it was when I attended and in what it has become today. Congresswoman Millicent Fenwick went to Foxcroft, and the Rockefellers and Mellons, the McCormicks of Illinois, and Anne Armstrong, who was a Legendre before she married into one branch of the King Ranch family and became chairperson of the Republican Party during Nixon's term, and finally ambassador to the Court of St. James's.

Foxcroft was designed for the education of the very rich. Moreover, Miss Charlotte, the founder, epitomized the Virginia aristocracy and, for that reason alone, her school deserves a place in this book. The concepts she taught, corrupted though they became, represented the first ideals of the gentry. In my family almost all the girls went to Foxcroft. My grandmother was a friend of the headmistress. It was a feminist finishing school, a girls' paramilitary army base. It was run with West Point discipline.

The school in Middleburg, Virginia, is forty miles from Washington, D. C., set in the foothills of the Blue Ridge Mountains. Its woods and farms are laced by low stone walls and wide, slow, muddy creeks. The country is beautiful, not so manicured as the horse farms of Kentucky, not so dry and dramatic as those of California; but the air is filled with blowing white apple blossoms on a green spring day, and it is sharp and crisp as a November dawn.

To my sister and myself, sent off at fourteen, it might have been a prison. Once on school grounds, no one left. We lived, approximately thirty to a class, for three or four years, until we achieved in this enclave, entirely removed from the outside world, our own customs, principles, and social structure.

The first thing that strikes a visitor is the extraordinary richness of Foxcroft, visible in the tennis courts, gardens, stables, orchards, and servants, in the boxwood walks and eighteenth-century brick house, in the classrooms, art rooms, photo lab, and dorms. One alumna donated a $500,000 stable and indoor riding ring to the school in the 1960s—to the annoyance of other alumnae, who prided themselves on riding outdoors even in the drenching rain. The stable has paneled tack rooms, and in its courtyard peacocks strut and spread their gorgeous tails.

We accepted the wealth as natural. We didn't even see it. Just as we accepted the grooms who brought our horses to us, already saddled and bridled, and the gardeners trimming the formal walks, clipping the hedges, and mowing the grass. We did not speak when passing them, but grunted, eyes grounded in pride or shyness, as they touched their caps.

There were about 120 girls in the school when I was there. Now there are about 200. The names meant nothing to me at the time: Mellon, Crespi, Guest, Watson, du Pont, Paepcke, Fell—they were simply girls. They came from Tuxedo Park and Oyster Bay, or from the environs of Baltimore, Philadelphia, or Wilmington. One came from Houston and two from California and one (engaged her junior year: we were fascinated) came from Batista's Cuba. But what was remarkable about them was—they were unremarkable. They were bright, dumb; pretty, ugly; sweet, foul-tempered.

At Foxcroft everything was reminiscent of the Hunt. The two athletic teams were named the Foxes and the Hounds, the alumnae paper was *Gone Away*, and the names of the houses were Covert or Sput & Spoon. Fox hunting formed the focus of the school, and social rank depended to some degree on who owned her horse and boarded it at Foxcroft, who had fox hunting privileges, and who was a member of the Riding Club. Oddly, almost all the girls who boarded their own horses at the school were considered good enough to fox hunt. (Today dressage has also been added to the riding instruction, but the school has always specialized in the haute couture of show-ring riding: the emphasis is on formality.)

Not all the girls liked riding. It has taken me years to understand the arrogant, cold expression of one of my classmates, as she lifted herself into the saddle of her handsome roan—she was an awful rider. Her horse's ears would flatten on its neck as she turned it toward the riding ring, and she would give me a glance of such supercilious distaste that I would cringe. I always took it personally. Since then I have often seen that look. It is one of pure suffering. She hated her horse, I think, as much as it disliked her. She was, however, in the Riding Club. This was called the WOP Club, because the Italians were the internationally acclaimed show-ring riders of the 1930s and 1940s; wop, like spic, being a term of derision: it was an involuted class joke. WOPs wore shining black boots, white shirts, and black Mussolini-type hats with tassels. As a sign of the times, the name has been changed in recent years to the ROCs, the Riding Officer's Club: the uniform remains the same.

Next to riding, the most important thing at Foxcroft was

military drill. Miss Charlotte, the headmistress, believed in drill. Tuesday and Thursday afternoons, rain, snow, or shine, we marched. We wore khaki corduroy skirts and green jackets and Confederate-style caps, and carrying our wooden rifles—our "pieces"—we marched around the drill field in three platoons to the wind-swept squalling notes of recorded Sousa Marches.

Left face. To the rear ... march.

At graduation one of the Joint Chiefs of Staff would come down from Washington to review our Commencement Parade. We would wheel and march past him, saluting in full review.

It's hard to explain to people about the marching. It was hard even for us to understand, though Miss Charlotte explained it many times. Military drill taught good posture, discipline. ("You cannot learn to give orders until you learn to take them.") It taught team spirit and cooperation. Moreover, it didn't hurt.

"We drill," she told one classmate, "so that we women will understand what our men have to endure in war."

Military drill had begun in a burst of patriotic fervor during World War II. It ended in 1968, after Miss Charlotte had died, a new feeling having developed in America toward martial endeavor. But when we were there nothing stopped drill. I remember one winter day, when a bitter wind whipped the snow across the parade grounds so hard that we were blinded. We couldn't hear the music. We were shivering with cold, complaining and frustrated, when Mr. Merle-Smith, our acting headmaster, strode out in his infantry boots and army parka and exhorted us to think of the boys freezing in Korea. He said that if they could fight a war over there, we could drill for forty-five minutes in Virginia without complaining.

After drill we would run thankfully to our houses and go to tea, hoping for sticky sweet cinnamon buns.

How ugly we were in our heavy brown ground-grippers and

rough corduroy uniforms! In the early years the school had required no uniforms, but eventually it was found that some girls brought trunks filled with scarves, pearls, skirts. My mother recalls one girl in the 1920s, when she was there, who had twenty-eight cashmere sweaters. And another with thirty-six silk nightgowns.

"Thirty-six silk nightgowns!" my mother exclaimed to her roommate. "I've never even had one."

"It doesn't matter," said the girl, the most beautiful girl in that class. "My mother only buys them for me to make herself look good."

Uniforms were instituted as a way of democratizing the wealth, and there were strict notices of exactly what clothes you could bring to school. But even when I was there, we were aware of a social hierarchy constructed on the number of extra cashmeres, stockings, high-heeled shoes, and furs you kept in storage for a "privilege."

It was to overcome the inequities of wealth that Miss Charlotte had also instituted the strict, almost penal code of Foxcroft. We slept on open sleeping porches, the beds lined up as in an Army barracks. We roomed, three to a room, and changed rooms every term, so that by the end of senior year we had roomed with almost everyone in the class. The rule was intended to break up cliques and demonstrate that "anyone can learn to live with anyone"—though it did nothing to lower the subsequent high divorce rate.

Our rooms were used only for dressing and undressing. We each had a bureau with a mirror. We each had a closet. Excepting one couch, no other furniture graced the room. Clothes were folded in drawers or hung in the closet in a regimented order. *Top drawer:* hairbrush and comb, personal trivia, gloves. *Second drawer:* six pairs of underpants, six bras, six pairs of green socks rolled a particular way, six pairs of white socks rolled the same way. *Third drawer:* six khaki shirts, six white shirts....

The clothes in the closet were likewise hung in rigid order. We had uniforms for drill, for dress, for work, for summer, for winter. Three times a day a "whipper-in" inspected the rooms. The "whips" were juniors. Inspecting with two white-gloved fingers, they gave demerits for everything. Not a puff of dust under the couch, not a hair in your hairbrush. Your laundry bag was hung on the left-hand hook of the closet; shoes were shined and lined in the closet, pieces gleamed with polish.... It took half an hour to clean a room and bath. "Whipping" gave unlimited opportunity for sadistic expression. There was no appeal. I remember one "whip" who handed out demerits for leaving drops of water on the side of the tub. There was a lot of sucking-up to "whips."

You can imagine the relief when, the final term of our senior year, we were allowed to choose our own roommates. Housemothers instead of "whips" inspected seniors, and we learned that adults are more rational than teenagers in dispensing justice.

We almost never left the school. Once a semester your parents could visit and take you off the grounds for a "privilege." With divorced parents you got two visits. Almost everyone's parents were divorced and sometimes several times, so that the girls spoke, to my astonishment, of stepbrothers, and half-sisters, and "my step-grandmother's brother."

When parents visited, we could eat lunch at the Red Fox Inn in Middleburg. There was almost nothing else to do. We would dress up carefully in high heels and stockings, sweaters, rings, rouge, and beaver coats, and traipse into that sleepy Southern village to eat an expensive lunch, smoke cigarettes, and wonder at the knots of black men lounging under the "No

Loitering" sign on the street corner. We would buy stacks of love comics at the drugstore and then return to school.

Seniors got one weekend a year.

For me the girls themselves were hard enough to cope with. They arrived in cashmeres and furs. We, in Maryland, wore heavy tweed skirts, fanny-sprung, and dowdy with good taste— the kind that your mother urges on you as "lasting a lifetime" and that, to your horror, do. We wore cloth coats and we listened agape to the New York girls who dragged out their sophisticated syllables. "N.O.C.D.," they would drawl: "Not our class, Dear." Long and gangly as colts, they ranged beside mothers wrapped in furs and fathers who worked themselves stiffly out of Jaguars or Cadillacs, and you knew that those mothers had never decapitated a chicken in their lives, or hauled a tractor around a seven-acre lawn. What work the fathers did, not even their daughters always knew; it was impolite to ask. One did not speak of parents at that school.

I remember one girl who raced squealing to her room every noon, clutching to her breast the blue envelope that enclosed a letter from a boy. Later I learned (her mother told my father) that the girl spent most of her holidays addressing envelopes to herself, which her mother would dutifully mail out, one a day.

And another roommate, whom I found one day washing her underpants with my toothbrush. She shrugged. She didn't know why I was shouting, screaming at her so that everyone came running down the hall. Her apology was not for her act, but for annoying me.

"Well, if I'd known you'd be so upset...."

One girl returned to school after one vacation, wrists bandaged from falling, she said, "through a taxi window." As for our own efforts at friendliness, they can be grasped by one game we played our junior year. "Frank Hour," it was called. It consisted of sitting in a circle and choosing, each girl, another's name from a drill cap. One by one around the circle we told what we thought of each other.

"Frankly, Andrea, I think you're a pig."

Such was the social development at Foxcroft, the school of Miss Charlotte Haxall Noland.

Miss Charlotte.

I remember the portrait of her that appeared in *Town and Country* in the 1940s: a full-page photo of Miss Charlotte, dressed in black hunting garb, her crop in one gloved hand, the whip end lacing down across her black sidesaddle skirt, her head raised with that proud tilt we knew so well. Her white hair billowed around high cheekbones. Black and white. She was arrogant. Beautiful.

Miss Charlotte was twenty-nine when she founded the school in 1914. She herself was relatively uneducated, and well aware from the age of sixteen that she would have to earn her own living. She had only that poor Virginia farm and her wits to help her out. She must be given credit for doing this at all. Her first idea was to start a drunk farm, with her friend Mildred Skinner, for rich Northerners. Mildred was to walk brightly about Foxcroft, posing as the *cured* alcoholic, in order to brace the spirits of the other "guests." Eventually, Foxcroft was transformed into a school for girls of means. I asked Miss Charlotte once about the drunk-farm story. Not unexpectedly she denied it, but Mildred Skinner swears to her own kin it is true.

When my mother and aunts attended Foxcroft in the 1920s, Miss Charlotte was in her prime. I gather those days were all fun and fox hunting, coon hunting, and wildly inaccurate Bible studies under the tutelage of the young and enchanting headmistress. You hardly ever find anyone from this period who didn't think the school was wonderful. Miss Charlotte had vitality and joy of life and charm, as well as the unwavering instinct to persuade the rich to hand over their daughters and their fortunes to her care. Merely being with her could spark a man with energy.

By the mid-1950s, though, Miss Charlotte was in her seventies, her virtues hardened into the arthritis of old age. She had raised two generations and was starting on her third. So confident had she grown of her ability to "develop character" that she was picking up strays, the tormented offspring of cast-aside marriages, whose parents, impressed by the idea of anyone "developing" their daughters, were glad to hand them over.

The students themselves seemed no less devoted than ever, and gave her the adoration that she felt was only her due. She moved regally amongst us, taking pride in knowing each girl's name and background. Evidence abounds of her lapses of memory.

I have only two recollections of Miss Charlotte actually speaking to me during my three years at Foxcroft, even though, as a "grandchild," an "It," I held a favored place. One of these conversations happened like this:

A sophomore, I was walking dolefully to my dorm one day, staring in vague dreaminess at the gravel drive, when I heard a voice behind me.

"Child!" she called imperiously. "Child!" Everyone knew the voice of Miss Charlotte. I turned.

"Child, I've just noticed the way you walk with your toes pointed in—pigeon-toed. It's very unattractive. You must practice turning your toes out when you walk."

"But I can't walk like that," I murmured humbly. We were all overwhelmed by Miss Charlotte.

"Of course you can!" She was decided. "When I was a young girl, I used to turn my right foot out at quite an extreme angle, and when it was pointed out to me, I simply practiced, and now it goes straight." She gestured to her own elegant, fine foot in its sheer stocking and tidy brown pump. I looked at my bare, white legs set stumpish above my green socks and sensible brown oxfords.

"Yes, Miss Charlotte," I said hopelessly.

"Try. Decide to do anything," she said, with a pat to my shoulder, "and you will achieve."

The school made no sense to me at all. The time had passed when the girls were taught, as in my mother's day, to make a proper court curtsey, one by one dropping to one knee before Miss Charlotte, as they would later when presented to the English court. But it was by deliberate intent a finishing school. Seniors, for example, could take a housekeeping course in Cook House. No cooking went on in Cook House. Instead, we filled our notebooks with

— the order of servants in a great household
— how the butler should answer the telephone *
— the proper place-setting for a twelve-course dinner
— the difference between high and low tea and what to serve at each.

Cutting down the Yule log was fun, and dragging it back to school with a team of horses; and so was the Coon Hunt, when we trekked through the woods by night (though weaker stomachs turned as the coon was treed: dogs leaping and barking, while the coon huddled in the branches, his fierce, frightened eyes glittering in the beams of the flashlights; then the coon jumped and the dogs lit into it in a great snarling heap, snapping, and the men moved in too, hooting with

---

* This information was useful later when I got a job. You say: "Miss Noland's residence ..." (Is she in?) "One moment, I shall see. Who shall I say is calling?" You *never* say: "Who shall I say is calling? One moment, I will see if she's in." (The implication being that she was in until she learned who was calling.) It is a lesson more secretaries could learn.

laughter, and pulled the dogs away). The coon usually got away, and the walk in the autumn woods at night was always interesting. But what was one to think of May Day, for example, when the trees were hung with lollipops and the gym teachers bounded over the meadows, dressed in gauzy costumes, while the girls hunted for the lemonade fountain in Miss Charlotte's yard? Then Miss Charlotte put one hand to her ear (her "children" assembled adoringly at her feet):

"Listen! Listen! Is that a fairy bell?"

You could get an extremely good education at Foxcroft, but academic achievement was not the purpose of the school. Most girls did not go on to college. Those who did rarely graduated. Today most seniors attend a college of some sort, for customs have changed, but subtly it was presented to us that our purpose in life was not to be found in academic learning.

One day Miss Charlotte told my mother she didn't know what to make of me: all I liked was to study. If only I would *do* something. "Give, child. Give," she would say. But I was much too frightened. I was horrified at the fact that one South American heiress was expelled for smoking, while a girl on the Honor Board went unpunished for cheating on her final exams. Not even the other girls seemed to notice the double standards.

Listen. I'm not telling the important thing. The institutionalization of cruelty. I make it sound exotic, this school. What we were taught at Foxcroft was a corruption of values as extreme as I have ever seen. It was institutionalized hypocrisy.

The basis of our education was class. There is no question of equality in a system where seniors dominated juniors, who in turn had absolute authority as "whips" over the freshmen and sophomores; where seniors "hazed" the New Girls and New

Girls were encouraged to have "crushes on" and "slave for" a senior. Prejudice was likewise implicit in a system where one of the two secret societies bore the initials of the Ku Klux Klan, and stood for something like Kourtesy, Kindness, and Kompassion.

We were taught nothing of compassion. I do not think this was intentional. Merely that the spiritual and physical discipline to which we were subjected reinforced the tendency toward arrogance.

Hazing was commonplace in all boarding schools until recently. According to one Middlesex alumnus, it remained at that school until the 1950s, when one boy tore a tendon or ligament while being paddled down a row of seniors. At Foxcroft hazing has been replaced by a "New Girls' Initiation," but this drew so many complaints last year from outraged parents of trembling freshmen that once again the school was considering doing something about–perhaps even stopping altogether–the seniors' prerogative.

When I was there hazing lasted for a week. For a week the New Girls wore black hairnets and had to obey any senior's order. They were Rats: Rat Chubb. Rat Giles. One favorite order was to make them fly airplanes, and all week you would see fleets of New Girls, hair bound in black, or tied into twelve or twenty pickaninny braids, buzzing, arms extended, to lunch or tea or sports. Others hopped like frogs. Or wore their jackets inside out.

At the time I knew only that I wanted no part of such behavior. Today I see it as the breaking of a human spirit, and as destructive to the instigator as to the victim on whom it is inflicted. The point of hazing was to destroy the freshman's identity. In a subtle way it killed something in her, so that soon afterwards she could give unyielding loyalty to the school and to the headmistress, who used to stride up and down before us, singing her favorite song:

I am the Boss. I am the Boss.
I am the Governor General, but no Hobo. No Hobo.
I'll letcha know who's the Boss of this Show
And it's me, and I'm Charlotte Haxall Noland.

How busy we were kept! The bells, the lack of privacy, the constant intrusion of rules all exacted their own punishment. Bells clanged for bed, for breakfast, for classes, for church, assembly, riding, gym, or drill. Distrust of friendship, of intimacy, was likewise institutionalized. Intimacy could lead to emotion. Or lesbianism, I suppose. We moved in gangs, in packs; the school preferring to see us as a mass, like bear cubs rolling in play. The pack was regarded as proper social adjustment. And the pack, this mass psychology, created its own convention, in which to excel, to draw attention to oneself (beyond the acceptable bounds, I mean, of winning a horse show or being drill captain), indicated a subtle betrayal of the whole. To choose one friend was unacceptable.

There was a reason. Miss Charlotte hated cliques. Excepting our two secret societies, she wanted no clubs in the school. This has changed since her death, and clubs have multiplied. Today you can join the art club, the photo club, the drama club, the poetry club. There is a club for any interest you may have, and this though Foxcroft is a tiny community by comparison to Andover's 1,114 students, for example, or St. Paul's 496. There is even at Foxcroft a secret club called the EATS, composed of select upperclassmen. Its purpose is "to be nice to" homesick New Girls. Do you understand the implications? A club so secret that seniors who are not members have never heard of it; a club that institutionalizes the pitiful act of being kind.

Miss Charlotte had some good ideas. She instructed us in our duties of noblesse oblige by obligatory community service.

Some seniors worked in the Middleburg Clinic and others taught at the public school.

It was also part of our training to earn five dollars for the poor during Lent: not an easy task in a community where everything was taken care of for us by servants, gardeners, grooms, and staff.

In presenting the school I suppose I must remember that by the time my sister and I arrived, Miss Charlotte was old and resentful of retiring.

"You are the most selfish child I've ever met," she told one of my classmates.

On another occasion she had the unpleasant task of informing one girl that her mother had been put in a mental institution. An extraordinary task, and we are left appalled that the child's father could have shucked his own responsibility, though, yes, it would have entailed a trip to the school. Or a telephone call at the least.

Miss Charlotte called the girl to her office and set about the task with her usual aplomb:

"I have something to tell you, uh ... child," she said firmly. "It won't come as any surprise to you. You know your mother. You know the kind of person she is. She should have been sent away long ago."

"Sent away?" murmured the girl.

"She's been sent to a mental institution. Finally. It should have happened long ago—"

"My mother!" the poor girl gasped.

"Your father asked me to tell you. I doubt if she'll ever get out."

"What are you saying!" the girl screamed. "My mother!? My mother!" She was hysterical.

"Now don't get upset," began Miss Charlotte, but then, as if remembering something, began to shuffle through the papers on her desk. "Wait, wait—" she mumbled. "What? Oh." She looked up accusingly: "You're not the girl I want. It's not you. Go along outside and send me Alexandrina," she concluded, calling for another girl. And the poor child ran hysterically from the room, pushing past Alex, who was waiting in the antechamber, eyes wide with horror at the muffled screams emerging from behind the heavy oak door.

"It's not my mother!" screamed the first girl in passing. "It's yours! It's your mother! It's yours!"

The final authority of the school rested on an honor system. We were on our honor not to cheat or steal or smoke or break a rule or tradition. We were also on our honor to tell on anyone who did, so that even here the ideal was degraded, the girls demoralized by the virtue of turning in their friends.

The head of the honor system was also head of the secret society to which every girl in the school eventually gained admission by her senior year. To gain entry was considered an honor, though I've never heard of anyone who was not taken in.

It was another of the confusing principles of the school that this society was so secret that no one talked about it. No one uninitiated into the mysteries knew what the secret Greek initials—XM—stood for, and no one knew exactly what special qualities were being rewarded by initiation. You could tell who had gotten in, because each girl suddenly sported her XM pin on her green corduroy jacket. Certainly initiation seemed chosen by no rhyme or reason except the usual favorites—the military captains and WOP members were usually in early.

Our first act upon initiation was to vow to uphold the secrecy of this society, meaning in particular the significance of the initials. This I regret, because they stand for a code of the highest dimension. I made my vow, however, and I shall keep it. Let it be known, however, that the ideal centered on compassion and understanding. It was the execution, like so much else in this education, that left something to be desired.

I was one of the last in my class to be invited to join the XM. One day Skippy Carew took me aside in the library, murmuring that she had good news of great significance. I wondered vaguely what it was.

"You have been asked," she lowered her voice respectfully, "to join the XM."

"Oh."

She then told me the date, what I was to wear, and not to mention the invitation to *anyone in the world.*

The ceremony took place at night in the living room of senior dorm, Dillon House. The novitiates (each of us surprised to discover someone else had received the same secret summons), huddled in a room down the hall, waiting with nervous laughter as each was led away, one by one, by a stern, unsmiling senior. Once gone, no one returned.

Time passed. Laughter changed to talk. And talk to silence.

We knew that secret mysteries were involved. The lack of joy associated with this ceremony, the disapproving air, the discipline of those straight, military backs leading away our classmates, austere, severe, attested to the awesomeness of the occasion. Whatever it was, was not to be taken lightly.

Finally my turn came. I smiled shyly at my guide and received in return a reproving scowl. The door to the living room was thrown open just enough to let me through.

A raised dais. A long table draped in white, on which were silver candelabra. An enormous Bible. The flickering flames cast shadows in the room, but facing me, behind the barrier of the table, was the entire XM membership, forty or fifty girls all in identical dress uniform. And there was my gentle sister, Anne, smiling timid encouragement. In the center stood Miss Charlotte, her white hair like a halo, her white robes, like a druid's, gleaming in the candle's glow.

"Kneel."

I fell to my knees, and she began the intonation of the solemn prayers and ceremonies, while for one horrified moment, the thought flashed through my mind that she would produce a white rooster—and slash its throat, its hot red blood flowing over the white robes and cloth. . . .

This was a dream—the product of a fevered imagination. Instead, each initiate was given a word signifying (true to Foxcroft form, emphasizing the negative) her most grievous flaw.

In some cases this might be a fault such as *pride* or *timidity*—something to be overcome. In other cases it represented a quality lacking in her character: *perseverance,* or *equilibrium* (This latter was the flaw of one classmate who, despite having had it brought to her attention, proceeded to fling herself into six marriages.) Oh, Miss Charlotte had us pegged. Mine was *sarcasm.* (Sarcasm?! Because of sarcasm I am kept out of the XM until the last minute? For *sarcasm?*)

I was led away to meditate on these things, while the next novitiate fell to her knees before Miss Charlotte, abject subject to the queen.

People in our circle will tell you that such an upbringing as this at Foxcroft was unusual, that it has nothing to do with those two poor girls who delivered their babies, frightened and alone, last fall in their boarding school rooms, unassisted either physically or emotionally. But I say the pieces of the jigsaw form a picture of the whole.

And where were the parents who sent their girls, seven or eight months pregnant, to a boarding school? Were they in

Europe at the time? At home? These parents, whose children could not talk to them.

And the doctors who gave their preschool physical exams? Each child contacted her family physician, I suppose. "Oh, lovey, it's such a bore" (she'd say). "You know I just *had* a physical last year, and now I've an invitation to the beach. I'll just send you the forms, lovey, and do fill them out like a dear man..." Shame.

Shame on the school administrators, who turned their heads, not seeing that the child was pregnant. ("Oh, well, you know, she arrived here already fat, and you really can't tell all that well.") Who, blinded by horror and fear, permitted themselves the indulgence of believing in a stomach tumor (but who never telephoned the parents or guardians to question such a tale). Shame on the parents for neglecting their children. Shame on us all for not looking in their unhappy eyes, not caring, not looking, not touching.

On Power

You see the pattern, the grooming of the propertied class. We were being instructed in our station at Foxcroft. Certainly there was no expectation of work, a career. Or even of college. We were conditioned to no higher ambitions than to sit on a volunteer board or the back of a horse. We were in the process, in other words, of learning Social Power.

Social Power is not in fashion these days. You hardly hear of it, though power itself is as much in vogue as ever. The media slink around that stench like dogs at a garbage can, and being largely New York-based (where Social Power is nearly defunct), they isolate with keen noses the manifold components of the whole, never noting the absence of one bone: they find Business Power, Political Power, Financial Power, Fashion Power, the Power of Flamboyant Behavior, the Power of the Pen, Celebrity Power....

For Social Power, you search in small cities, where a tight-woven social fabric is still intact. There, men who bring world leaders to their knees stand trembling before the force of Social Power—which as in the larger cities, though for a different reason, is largely ignored by the press or reported in the local society pages as a marriage, birth, or debutante dance. The media show no comprehension of its importance at all.

Social Power is what keeps society intact. I mentioned earlier my European friend who thought that in marrying an American she was marrying beneath her class—and rejoiced, I should add, rejoiced at giving the finger to her background, the triumphant fist to class. In her country, everyone *knows* what class each person occupies. You can't hide it. Voice, carriage, dress, the length of your fingernails, the size of your diamond ring (male or female) attest to your class.* In Europe, if my friend wants a favor done—a telephone installed—she calls her father's friend who is head of the telephone agency, and—poof!—a telephone arrives the following day.

---

* The same attributes reveal class in America, subtle signals passing back and forth, though many people refuse to recognize them. One day I was in a taxi when the driver stopped for a second fare (this being permitted in Washington, D.C.). A nice-looking young man in a soft gray Brooks Brothers' understated suit got in the front seat.

"Wow, not much traffic," he observed.

"Not too bad," answered the driver.

"I'd have expected more at this hour," he said amiably.

"That's because you're from New York," I said from the back seat. He turned, surprised, with a half-laugh:

"How did you know?"

"It's easy," I answered, exulting in the perfect knowledge that occurs so rarely in life. "You live on East Seventy-third Street . . . between Lexington and Third."

He swivelled round. "Seventy-second."

"And you went to Buckley and then St. Paul's. . . ."

"Do I know you?"

"Hey," laughed the driver. "How do you know all that?"

"And Yale," I said—and overshot the mark.

Little did she think to find the same social interests operating here. One day her children were turned down at the New York school she wanted them in. She was distraught. She went to lunch with her husband's father just after she had heard.

"What's the matter, Fifi?" he asked. "You're not eating."

"My children can't get into the school I had wanted for them."

"What school?"

And when she named it: "Well, don't think anymore about it. Come for dinner tonight.... And by the way," he continued, "who are the trustees there?"

"Trustees!" she cried, astonished. "I don't know.

"Can you get a list?"

And that night, puffing on his pipe after dinner, he idly ran his eyes down the list. "Oh, yes." Puff. Puff. "I remember him. Knew that one's father." Puff. Puff. "Porcellian." Puff.

Entry for her children was assured.

Social Power is the ability of a class as a unit to maintain itself. Social Power enfolds and promotes its members on the one hand, and on the other, it excludes or downright kills. Social Power is rooted in money, but only of the right kind. Yet, because it is evasive, visible only in the reflection of its acts, we easily lose sight of or misread its strength. Or we arrogantly underestimate it, contemptuous that the sword of Social Power is wielded by women, our Mnemosyne, who pass down cultural values generation to generation. Don't be fooled.

"Brown," he corrected me. "Have we met?" He peered at me suspiciously.

"Nope. I can just tell." And I paid my fare and got out. It wasn't really fair. The East Seventies are a cinch.

Military, political, or economic power bows to social force. Let me give some examples.

Soon after we graduated from Foxcroft, Mitsi Hatcher (who was a du Pont) met at a debutante party in New York a young Marine lieutenant, just graduated from Yale. She turned his head. He was stationed at Camp LeJeune at the time, on the North Carolina border, and he was doing everything in his power to get up to Washington every weekend to meet Mitsi, who was attending Mt. Vernon Junior College. One day at a party, he mentioned to a visiting Marine commandant from Washington that he had recently been riding with the Hatchers in Middleburg. This commandant had a place nearby in Warrenton, Virginia, and he wanted more than anything to fox hunt with the Middleburg Hunt, where Miss Charlotte had served as MFH, to move in these rarefied circles.

Privates and corporals were ordered out to Warrenton to maintain the commandant's lawn and gardens in style, and because Miss Charlotte had promised full scholarships for the commandant's daughters in return for officers to drill her girls, majors and captains were assigned from the Marine barracks in Washington to go teach drill at Foxcroft. The commandant, therefore, was delighted to meet this charming young lieutenant who travelled in such a set, and he immediately had him transferred to the Marine barracks in Washington, D.C., where he pursued Mitsi with increased dedication. Everyone was pleased except Mitsi's mother, in Middleburg, who thought her daughter too young, at nineteen, to marry. She called Miss Charlotte. Miss Charlotte called the commandant. Can you imagine how his heart leaped up on hearing who the call was from? Or how he squirmed at hearing why?

"Well, we do *not* like having him about...."

A captain hauled the lieutenant to the mat. My lord, he was

scared! Even today, at the age of forty-four, and two wives later, he still dreams at night about being recalled into the Marines. He begged me to use neither his name nor that of the commandant, lest the government take some vengeance on him, twenty years later, for this story.

"I don't even know if the commandant's alive," he said. "And the government can be ... really, you know—well, you don't mess with that."

Rigidly at attention he stood throughout his ordeal. The captain shouted in the belligerent monotone affected by all drill sergeants:

"Andrews! Your activities in Washington regarding a Miss Mary Hatcher have come to the commandant's attention. He is not pleased! Andrews! We are sending you far, far away from Washington!"

Instead, he was transferred to Parris Island, Georgia, where officers were needed. He spent his time duck hunting and playing golf, and Mitsi flew down to Charleston, where her grandmother had a place, so that the affair did not completely end until her mother packed Mitsi off to Europe. She married one English lord and then another for the next few years.

And what was Miss Charlotte's power over the military? The same power that could attract the daughters of admirals to her school and bring down the Joint Chiefs of Staff to graduation review. It was social influence.

Political power bends, likewise, to its call. Jake L. Arvey, leader of the Cook County Democratic organization in Chicago, the man who groomed and developed Adlai Stevenson for political office, once defined politics as "the art of putting people under obligation to you." At its base level, this is patronage. When the King Ranch maintains and protects its kiñenos, it commits, in a broad sense, a political act. If the local gentry contribute to the election of the local sheriff, they engage in political action, as does Douglas Dillon and his wife when each contributes $1,000 to the congressional campaign of their friend Millicent Fenwick, Republican of New Jersey. When the Rockefellers recommend a position for their colleague and former employee Henry Kissinger or suggest for the head of the National Endowment for the Arts their competent associate Nancy Hanks, they deliver patronage, a political act. When the landowners of California determine that votes on water rights shall be settled according to the size of each individual's acreage, they flex their political muscle.

Among the propertied class, the exercise of political power is accomplished with subtlety, as befits a group whose greatest need is the preservation of its place. Often political power is expressed as a negative quantity, like a minus digit in mathematics, which takes the shape not of action but of blocking action to protect from poaching and intrusion. Often it's exercised so quietly, so discreetly, at the local country club or over a Saturday game of tennis, or on the terrace at Royal Orchard, that it is hard for anyone to know—especially the principals—that a political act has taken place. This is especially true when the act is negative, an act of omission.

Once, I was the guest of a couple who run a farm in the Midwest. They are in the cattle business, and the wife entertains so frequently that, at the beginning of each year, she goes over several menus with the caterer, selecting three basic meals that she will call for in that year. One Saturday night, a group of friends gathered. It was easy and relaxed, and, after a while, the conversation turned, as happens with good food inside and a fire at your back, to the macabre.

A murder had recently been committed. "You ought to do an article on the murders around here," said the host. "We have phenomenal murders: Manson-type gang killings." Then nodding heads and comparing names and correcting each other with details about the victims and the crimes, the story evolved.

A young woman they knew had gone to pick up her children at the local private school ("Car number 22 may now approach.... Alexandra and Christine, your mother is here. You may walk to the door ... *slowly*"), when two convicts jumped into the back seat of the car—right at the school!—and at gunpoint forced the woman to drive them to her house. There they tied her up, together with the two little girls, and then murdered them. And roads are named in shocked whispers, roads right nearby, to indicate the violation of an entire neighborhood. Cold-bloodedly they murdered, and the husband came home that night to find his wife and children dead.

"We're none of us safe anymore."

"It was the guards' fault. What were they doing, leaving two convicts alone in a room with a window they could escape from?"

I don't remember if anyone that night added the stricture that rapists should be castrated. Perhaps I've heard it said so often that the expostulation merges into one generic conversation, like voices in a dream.

"If I had anything to do with things—"

"Then they'd think twice about—"

"It's the courts. They just let them go—" And heads nod and seats are shifted in their chairs and shoulders hunch with horror. This murder, however, brought another crime to mind, this time committed by a doctor in their own social set. The details seemed known to all, and no one in that room appeared to doubt that the doctor, their acquaintance, had killed his wife with drugs. The story had much about drinking in bars and flashing of bankrolls and then the little children walking into the bedroom next morning to discover their mother dead. To make matters worse, the death occurred on the very weekend that all the coroners were out of town at a convention. The doctor signed the death certificate himself, and his wife's body was hardly cold before it was in the ground.

"But what happened? Was he brought to trial?"

"Oh, no," murmured an elderly white-haired woman, sitting back straight on her straight-backed chair. "What purpose would that have served?"

"And then the children," broke in another. "They'd had enough to deal with, poor things, discovering their mother dead."

"He's a horrible man," said a third. "But that would have just stirred up trouble."

Was the story true? I don't know. Quite possibly the husband was acquitted of the charge. What is interesting, however, is that a roomful of friends, gathered over drinks, were convinced of his guilt and of the rightness of dropping charges. Yet I am sure that not a person in that room considered himself less than of the highest moral stance.

Class unity is nothing new. Do you remember how, in 1791, Richard Randolph of Virginia and his wife's sister, Nancy Cary, had an affair that resulted in an illegitimate child, a murder charge, and a trial? The lawyers for the two lovers were Patrick Henry and John Marshall, and Randolph's wife rushed to the defense of her husband and her sister. Thomas Jefferson's daughter Martha was married to another Randolph and wrote details to her father, who returned her letters with admonitions on how to behave with propriety. The walls of Social Power, of family power, of family association, were raised. Such walls shield everyone in a household, family and staff. Here is one lady talking of her upbringing in the Deep South. She was roughly my age, so this would be just during and after World War II.

"And the children of the overseer were my closest friends. I grew up with them, and I played with them and the children of the house servants, and it gave me a very rare understanding of the colored race, and probably a totally different viewpoint from that which most people that I know have, because I never looked upon them as somebody who came in once a week to clean my house. These were my friends. They were my playmates. I went down to their house and I ate at the table with them. The only thing, I was told not to drink Jack's water, 'cause he was poisoning Betsy, which he was, and finally Betsy died of it.

"So I stayed away from that one ... but Betsy wasn't too popular.... And little ploys would take place that I was completely cognizant of, such as Albert did have a sort of wild disposition, and one night he stabbed his wife and, in a very drunken state, came up to the house and told us he had tried to kill his wife, and we went down to her, and she swore she'd fallen over a knife that was sticking up over the boards of the floor, and we had to take her to the doctor.

"And I also remember when Lester found out that his wife, Annie, was having a wild affair with Luther, who was devastatingly handsome and half white, on the lower part of our place; and when Annie came from town one Saturday, her husband lay in wait behind the crepe myrtle bushes and took a razor on her and sliced her to pieces.

"He didn't tell anybody what he was going to do. But he'd made me promise that I would not come out at that hour. So he was lookin' out for me....

"But Jack did kill Betsy, and he killed two other wives, too. He was on his fourth wife when my children were little, and I took them on home to visit. And I remember I brought some friends of ours down with us. We were out at dinner at somebody's house, I remember, and Jack was babysittin' with my children, and I started tellin' them about my childhood and how Jack had poisoned his wives, and they said: 'But he's a *murderer!* You've left your children with a *murderer!*' But I said, 'But *Jack's* not a murderer! It's a totally different situation. . . .' "

Murder is perhaps an extreme example of social protection, but it does illustrate the double standards that apply when one's affections are engaged. Nothing–not even economics–can withstand the force of Social Power. An example occurred in 1973 in the Valley when Clark MacKenzie announced his plans to build a twenty-acre shopping center and 1,000 houses (or "homes," as he called them) on his 800-acre place.

Clark MacKenzie, a developer, was in his mid-thirties at the time. He got an architect, who drew up plans for schools and shopping island, housing and sewage–a mini-city that he would build in the midst of the horse farms.

The Valley was incensed. A meeting was held at the Butler Fire House that drew 150 or 200 people, depending on whom you believe, and resulted in the formation of the Central Baltimore County Planning Association. To observers of the social forms, the formation of this association was itself remarkable, given the general belief that almost any concerted action can lead to Communism.

MacKenzie was ostracized. His children were not invited to play with other children at school. His wife was dropped from the car pool, and at church the family sat isolated in the air bubble of their pew. And after the service, when the congregation gathers in the churchyard to greet each other cordially and invite one another for a drink or perhaps a round of golf, at that time, which is surely one of the pleasantest of a summer's morning, the MacKenzies were ... invisible. People turned their backs.

"Well, it's not as if he *needed* the money," said one Valley resident.

"It's inexcusable," said another. "One doesn't *do* that sort of thing."

The family underwent, said Clark MacKenzie, a "continuing personal harassment" for nearly ten months.

Eventually, MacKenzie called off the plans for a development. He put the property up for sale. Some people say the decision not to develop was based on economics rather than social factors, but Clark MacKenzie, when I tried to reach him, refused to take any telephone calls or to talk about the matter at all.

The girls in our set in the mid-1950s and early 1960s were serious about their work. Their work was marriage, which is basically the way that a woman of a certain group increases her property and rises in the world.

Diane Guest flew every weekend, I heard, to France to go stag hunting with a nobleman, and Gilly Wister, and Alice Grey, and my own sister, and Mimi Mills, and Didi Ladd, whom Michael Scully worshipped, and Evalina Hollins, and any number of others, married Europeans—English, French, or Belgian—and went to live abroad. Joan Dillon did the best of all, marrying a Prince of Luxembourg, messy though that situation was for a divorcée. It took all her social influence to effect, because her first marriage had been celebrated with great pomp in Notre Dame Cathedral when her father, Douglas Dillon, was ambassador to France.

Many other girls got pregnant and married according to the

social imperative. It was the only way to solve the problem safely in those pre-Pill days. I know of one poor child who got pregnant at fourteen by a sixteen-year-old boy and was dutifully married off by her parents; she, a tenth-grader, smiling bravely and choosing her white gown and silver and china pattern as if it were a game. Poor parents! At the time, I thought them cruel. It is only now that I understand the torment they must have undergone. She was divorced two valiant years later, leaving her parents to raise the babe, who grew up under the impression that her mother was an older sister. The story has a point: it happened all the time, and people's wishes were squeezed to fit the corset of society.

I know a girl whose aunt married because the trousseau initials fit. She had been engaged when very young, had bought her trousseau and broken the engagement. Several years later, when another suitor appeared with the same initials, the arguments of thrift were too strong to withstand.

I am told that in small villages of Europe in provincial societies, sex is more restrictive than in urban centers. Certainly our upbringing was antisexual, although sex and life itself were understood to combine in the same creative juices. These things were complicated. There were different standards for the young and the mature, the married and the underage.

I remember as a child going to the parties at the Upper Club, where the riders met. Both men and women were dressed in fine cream britches and black boots, their white ascots pinned to their throats in a cornucopia of tucks and folds. Some wore their heavy formal pink coats, and their spurs gleamed at the fireplace; their boots clattered against the bare boards of the floor. The clubhouse was very old; the cracked plaster walls were hung with faded photos of old hunts and former masters with their packs, or of the field ranged before some house, posing stiffly for the photographer. A fire burned in the massive stone fireplace in the dining room and on the bare wooden table would be hams and turkeys and biscuits for sandwiches. White-coated waiters poured the drinks. The voices rose in a sea-roar of joy that was drowned periodically from upstairs in the antique thunder of a flushing toilet.

I was shy at these affairs, for children were tolerated like dogs, ignored though underfoot. More than shy, however, I was made uncomfortable by an overt sexuality that has taken me years to comprehend, the heat of men and women flushed with physical exercise, their pleasure heightened by hard drink. Their granite laughs, their diamond glances. I've not seen such sensuality in our urban centers, not even in the twin sin-centers of New York and Los Angeles, where a mechanical pornography passes for sex. It is found in small societies, is repressed, and flares more fiercely from repression. It lurks in the laughing eyes.of matrons, who entice men confident in their role of male domination.

There were different standards for the married and unwed, as was explained by C. Z. Guest.

"We are what we are from our environment," she told the *Washington Post.* "I had the most fantastic environment. We were all brought up strictly. I went to Aiken to school, to Fermata [an exclusive girls' boarding school, now closed]. I was tutored most of my life. You can have affairs—God knows I've had plenty. But you *always* marry somebody from your own environment."

When we were children, sex lay all around us with an explicitness and crudity that today is termed liberated—where animal matings were as common as birth and death, and therefore "natural." As children, we were subject to attack by the dogs—the Chesapeake Bay retriever mounting us in an ecstasy of love whenever he found us unguardingly playing on the floor—while we beat at his head and ears in rage. It was accepted as natural. Only the "natural" was not the ideal.

(Actually our experiences with animals were very different from that of the Algoncourt children in the Nancy Mitford novels, who wept over mice and worried that dogs could be bored. Our animals were enemies: the horses that maliciously stepped on our feet, the dogs that refused to come to our whistles except at dinner, the pony that bit, the donkey that ran down the stable path, slamming our kneecaps into every dogwood tree with unerring aim. Our relations with animals, with our natural environment, constituted a state of warfare, a political struggle that required unflagging concentration to win.)

Nature was the enemy. Since it acted "naturally," then human love should logically be repressed. Animals and men, we learned, do not behave the same way. True, in those pre-Pill days real reasons existed for repression. Marriage, abortion were the consequences of a mistake. Both were dangerous. Girls today hardly know the terror of the threat that a single act can "ruin one's reputation." It happened. If word went round that a girl was "fast," her marriageability dropped. Some "nice" girls did not get into trouble. And all of this was accepted, just as it was accepted that high-spirited boys, operating in a near-perpetual state of rut, would attack. It was their role, as it was the girl's to ward them off. If she did not, then both paid the price of momentary pleasure.

Does it make more understandable the odd marriages you see today? The couples, who after years of living together, still do not seem to fit? Link it to a social fear. The necessity of putting on a bold face, of holding up one's head in public, of bravely maintaining place. And link it to loyalty as well. The feudal dedication to vows made and kept.

I saw a photo once of a couple at a country club lunch. They were in their thirties. Such silly, fatuous faces, so smug and proud in their Lacoste shirts, with their gin and tonics set on little napkinettes before them. How could you feel anything but distaste for such two faces? Until you learn that the man had been fired from his job the previous day. Man and wife, they wrapped themselves in Face, which is the mask of social pressure. Losing property is serious, for with its loss goes loss of Social Power. Nowhere are the rules so rigid or so clearly enunciated as in a small city, a local society.

I heard of a family in one Southern city, for example, who could not afford to give their daughter a debut. The clan was enormous and entirely crippled by the requirements of living up to its name—of taking only certain kinds of cases, for instance, if one was a lawyer. They were hard put as well to maintain the town house in the proper district and the country place to shoot. The town house had a central hall and off of it a parlor with heirloom rugs and cheerless ancestors glowering from the walls, while down the hall all pretense was discarded in a shambles of skates and bikes and broken chairs that the family actually used. The family could not afford a dance for Mary-Anne when she was eighteen. Or again at nineteen. Do you imagine I am making up some apocryphal tale? I tell you, Social Power and the pressure it applies are not to be denied. Years passed, and finally the money for a coming-out was found. By then Mary-Anne was in her twenties and had a job and was a decade older than the other giggling debs. It made no difference. Mary-Anne came out.

Women in the propertied class are more liberated than women in other classes in our society, which explains their aversion to the Women's Movement. Their power is immense. Women like Joan Irvine, who bring the moguls of Mobil Oil to their knees, squeezing an extra $136 million * in offers from them for the purchase of her property—and then refusing anyway to sell! What a lark! Single-handed, she gets Congress to change the law governing what property a charitable foundation may own, thus forcing the Irvine Foundation to sell off the Irvine Company, of which she and her mother are principal private stockholders, thus increasing her interest in the company and changing, thereby, the tax structure of millions of Americans. Ah, Erica Jong, you should see the women of the propertied class, women with offices and empires, chatelaines. They may appear to be delicate flowers around their men, deferring at times so modestly, begging, wide-eyed, the indulgence of masculine advice. They control their own money, their own investments, and often their men, whom they pull like bulls by their nose rings. Only in politics does their power historically seem small. And here too appearances may deceive.

There was, for example, Mistress Margaret Brent, who arrived in the colony of Maryland in 1638, three years after its founding. She was a thirty-seven-year-old spinster. With her came her family and nine servants, a number that entitled her to 800 acres of land. She took her allotment in thousand-acre units instead. She was the first woman lawyer in America, and she initiated more lawsuits than anyone else in the colony, both on her own behalf and on that of others. Usually, she won. She was attorney for Lord Baltimore (who was the absolute ruler of Maryland, with powers greater than the King's). She collected his rents and managed his estates. She was sole executor to the

---

* The first offer in 1974 was for $200 million; by 1977 it had been raised to $336.6 million.

estate of his brother, the governor, Leonard Calvert, who on his deathbed delivered himself of his last will: "Take all," said the laconic Calvert to Mistress Brent, "and pay all."

Finally, it was Mistress Margaret Brent who, after the governor's death, put down a revolution in Maryland and kept the little colony from war with Virginia—a war it would certainly have lost. In effect, then, she kept Maryland from being absorbed into Virginia.

Later, Margaret petitioned the assembly for two votes as a member, one as Calvert's executor, and the second as a major freeholder of land. No women belonged in the assembly. The members agreed that no one in the palatinate was more suited for admission than Mistress Brent, but Lord Baltimore, who was back in London, denied her request, being annoyed that she had sold his cattle, as he said, to enrich herself. From his point of view, three months' travel away, the impression may have been justified; but her fall from favor was also caused by the political necessity of favoring Puritans in London over Catholics if Lord Baltimore wished to preserve his colony.

Bitterly stung, Margaret moved to Virginia, settled near what is now Alexandria, on her estates (named Peace) financed more settlers, and retired from public life. She died around 1671, having lived long enough to see a shift in the position of women from Elizabethan dominance toward the myth of Victorian submission. Ha! Submission! They submit to no one in the propertied class.

Social Power is evidenced in the lawyer's son who is not booked by the police when he has an auto accident; or the zoning case, where the airtight lower-court decision is overturned, without explanation, at the appellate level after the judges—landowners themselves—make an unauthorized and illegal personal inspection of the site. Social Power influences business decisions, which take place in old-line clubs that exclude women, mavericks, Jews, outsiders, blacks. Their political power may be deduced from the Maryland law that permits a country club to take a tax deduction for the "open spaces" of its private golf course–so long as the membership is not "restricted!"

How elusive is Social Power! How it abhors publicity! How it scutters quick as a cockroach under the kitchen sink! You catch the shadow of its action, like a movement glimpsed from the corner of your eye–and gone as you turn your head. From its actions, you guess at its presence.

You look at the voluntary boards of our charitable institutions: of museums, hospitals, schools, and universities, of garden clubs and associations dedicated to historical preservation or conservation of land. And whom do you find? The cream of the propertied class. They exercise the prerogatives of the very old, very solid, and very respectable established wealth. To this extent, their values and behavior affect us all.

The institutions themselves betray our reverence for social caste. To sit on the board of a cultural institution (an art museum) reveals the trustee to be of a higher rank than if he sits on the board of an educational institution (a university), which, in turn, reveals and bestows more clout than an institution of health (a hospital). To serve on the board of any of these three bestows more prestige and reveals it more than to serve on the board of the PAL or the YMCA. There is a simple explanation. The higher one rises on the social scale, the less controversy one can stand, the less publicity, the less mud and dirt of life's unpleasantness. Therefore, the fewer decisions he cares to make and, therefore, his preference for the rarefied world of art, where a decision has less consequences than educating someone's children or warding off a death.

But no power on earth can protect against the savagery of life, the fear, guilt, disease, anxiety, repression that ends so often in alcohol or suicide. Two forms of self-destruction and despair. Suicide. Alcohol. The curse of this class. Alcohol is disguised in the overly hearty laugh, the hospitable tippling that begins a bit earlier with every day (oh, happy suns over yardarms). Brother, uncle, husband, wife, sister, father, mother, aunt—or you, yourself—are no better than a drunk in the gutter, except that money permits a tax-deductible drying-out in a fashionable sanatorium named something like Silver Hill.

No power in society can fend off fraternal quarrels, incest, lawsuits, and money squabbles. The pain is intense. The only preservation lies in camouflage. Therefore, you barely see the member of this class, so quietly does he live, like a salamander slithering on a branch, the pale, translucent body blushing green against a leaf, or brown on bark, and only the shy heart battering in its throat (that pulsing glottal tissue) to catch your eye and betray the creature hiding on the twig. The least he asks is to be let alone.

How many stories I have left to tell. Stories! They aren't stories, but fragments, with neither character nor plot, lest any living man be hurt. I haven't told you of the virtues of my class, the aspirations, the moments of happiness that are all a man can anticipate in a lifetime of moments; I haven't told of honor or discipline, abstinence and thrift, of friendship, generosity, altruism and love. I haven't told you of the old women, the dowagers, wonderful in their strength and aptitude. One down in Virginia who is ninety-five now has recently built an apartment over her garage for her old age, though she hasn't moved there yet.

I haven't told you of my mother, who can stop a mule with

294 THE LANDED GENTRY

her cry: "HEEAAAAAYYYYY YOU! What do you think you're doing?!" A workhorse. I have seen her stop while mowing the lawn and look out across the valley, down the sweep of the pasture and up the other side. She draws in strength from the earth.

I haven't told about my younger cousin, who was killed a few years ago in a fall from a horse she was breaking. She was hardly thirty. Her funeral took place amidst sheets of rain, one warm spring day. Then you saw the strength of social form, with my aunt, regal as a Roman matron, greeting the mourners like her guests at the church door, and remembering all the right things to say:

"How sweet of you to come."

"Do you know Mrs. Smith? She has just written the most beautiful book...." Her eyes were dim with pain.

Afterward, we went to a relative's house in Warrenton. The bluebells, tulips, and daffodils dripped with water under a cloudy sky. Stone fences bounded the fields. The house had been in the family since the 1700s, and behind it stood the plastered log cabin that the family had originally lived in while they waited for the Big House to be finished.

"Now don't everyone flush the toilets, please," was our greeting. "You know what country water's like."

The mahogany dining room table was spread with a Virginia ham and cucumber sandwiches and deviled eggs and salad and coffee, and there were also sherry and drinks. The ninety-year-old mistress of the house told how she'd been bitten by a copperhead while gardening and drove herself to the hospital, after chasing off the snake with a rake. Otherwise, the talk was of crops and farming and the Buddhist religion, because one member of the family had found out who she had been in an earlier incarnation in India.

Everyone tried to be gay, and no one could take his eyes off the little children, aged six and four, all golden hair and blue eyes, whose mother had been buried. The boy was dressed in jacket and tie and the girl in a pretty dress, and they solemnly balanced their plates with deliberate concentration on their tiny laps.

Too many things to tell. They jumble up my brain. I can only think of things I haven't said.

Odds and Ends

After school I went away to college, and never returned to the Valley to live. I watched my landed friends marry at eighteen or nineteen (the biological urgings of strong young bodies not to be ignored), and when I ran across the prototype of the gentry of my youth, I hurried off the other way. Until now, twenty years later, when I feel the need to re-examine what I knew. There's so much I haven't said.

I haven't told about the goodnesses of my class. This is hard. Goodness is visible in little acts of kindness—a glance exchanged, a squeeze of a hand, a moment's understanding in the isolation of life. Beyond that, goodness is an abstract term, depending to large degree on how an act is received, for any act leaves trails of good and bad behind.

Mrs. Lucy Ferguson, of Cumberland Island, Georgia, remembers, according to one family member, that her mother, a Carnegie, gave a formal dinner party, smiling, gracious, in every way the perfect hostess, though her baby lay just dead upstairs—

and never from her small talk did she betray the fact. Who dares interpret such an act? Or say it really shows no heart? It derives from training, from a discipline and reserve that is instructed from birth, the purpose of which is simply this: to put others at their ease.

Manners. Courtesy. They are intended to make more bearable the harshness of life, to reduce its pain. Thoughtfulness is the ultimate act of kindness, and kindness is at the root of regulation, too. There is a need for rules.

Looking back on this book, I wonder if I've been too harsh on rules. Rules teach us not to hurt each other, not to steal, not to invade another's privacy with indiscreet warm questioning (no matter how well intentioned is the prying source), and not to inflict one's own emotions in another's path—spilling fear, pain, anguish, depression, or even joy all over him.

I remember coming down to breakfast one day and commenting: "I don't feel well." To which the answer came: "Well, don't tell us about it. No one wants to know."

Rules serve a function. In the absence of a perfect inner regulation, a spontaneous morality, then rules can substitute. Rules are easier to teach than virtue. The problem arises when we replace the virtue with the rule.

There is no intentional abuse. The training of children is undertaken in this class with no more rancor than the training of a dog. Or horse. A showhorse is taught to step smartly by cracking his ankles with a pole as he jumps: why should he know the reason why? If the pain is severe he will learn to lift his feet, and if not he will fail—a show-ring reject. The same holds true for the child, who is likewise being trained to a specific, limited, and practical goal.

I had an idyllic childhood, a wonderful life! But autobiography is not the purpose of this book and I haven't told of that, just as I haven't shown the characters I knew. They are real people. They sit under pyramids to ingest that power, they read gothic novels, play with their children, repair their houses, have affairs, and rush off in all directions whenever they get upset. They have dreams of honor, pride, heroism, generosity, conservation, care. Many feel deep responsibility. There is something touching about the anxious desire to please that influenced my schoolmate when she married at her mother's request. I find a certain heroism in that straightening of the shoulders, that steadiness in taking up the diurnal drudgery of responsibility. It is so unpretentious.

So the ideal of the landed gentry is not the worst one we could find. It motivated Thomas Jefferson, engineer, artist, politician, architect, who drove himself into debt to build his beloved house in the Virginia mountains, and devoted himself to the study of plants and agriculture. Jefferson warned against the dangers of a hereditary aristocracy. He called for an aristocracy of merit and saw in a system of established wealth the principal danger to our republican ideal.

Many still share his image of the country gentleman as an ideal way of life. We also live now with the reality he foresaw— of a caste system based on hereditary wealth, self-perpetuating, privileged, private, educated, and powerful.

Surely if there is anything we need to know about, it is our land—not in a romantic way, senselessly setting out to save an endangered entity, but with ruthless concern for truth. Begin with its ownership. The issue is more controversial than school busing or abortions: decisions on land—or what is more common, the lack of decisions—affect every person in the nation. It is no accident that no land census has ever been taken. It is no accident that the Department of Agriculture collects information only on farm operators and almost none on owners of land. The staff of the Economic Research Service are well aware of the deficiency, have made repeated budget requests for ownership studies, and discovered every time that their requests go no farther than the secretary of agriculture. They are not even fowarded as a budget line for the consideration of Congress.

The matter of the Westlands Water District still continues, with Congress winding itself up in rhetorical promulgations on the need for the redistribution of our land, and with the situation apparently quite safely stable and set. Mr. Carter comes out softly against redistribution, and one assistant secretary of agriculture lobbies in Congress quietly "as a personal citizen" to keep the thousands of illegal acres in that rich farm valley that his family owns.

By the end of the nineteeth century all of the agricultural land in the country was in private hands. Three-fifths of the land mass of the United States, 1.3 billion acres, is privately owned today, and the quantity of land in farms has remained relatively constant for the last thirty years. It is not our farmland that has declined, but the number of "operators" who own their land: 3.9 million in 1945-50, 2.4 million in 1969, less than 2.2 million in 1974. Therefore we deduce the increasing concentration of land ownership and the trend to landlordship.

And is this new? A change of any sort? It is tautology to state that the wealthy few own most of our income-generating wealth. In 1810, one percent of the people owned 21 percent of America's wealth. Today they own 25 percent of "all personal and financial assets," according to Professor James D. Smith—eight times the wealth owned by the bottom one-half. Corporate stock, tax-exempt state and local bonds, notes and mortgages, real estate are concentrated into the hands of a relative few. What we remark on is the constancy of the ratio between rich and poor. And the hereditary pull. And what we remark on is the need for a land census, a detailed study of land ownership and land needs; and we remark on the absence of such studies.

I was once asked about the future of the propertied class—a word, "future," that its members hardly recognize. In fact when they are not busy denying their own existence, they predict an imminent demise. Gloomily they foretell vast change. It is always for the worse.

"Look at England," they say, "where the upper class is being taxed right out of its property." It is a prospect that fills the gentry heart with horror. But I'll stake my cards on the propertied class. They've been on the planet longer than recorded time, well settled in every cranny there. Not always in the same fashion, perhaps, not always with the exact same principles, but with surprisingly similar ones. Read Mencius on the behavior and ideals of a prince of China in 300 B.C., and you're reading the ethics of the present age: they do not change. Read of how hard he found it to get the princes to practice his doctrines—concerning land tenure and rents, concerning war, concerning respect for the elders or the forms of courtesy—and you learn how changeless are the patterns of princely life.

In our country chances are we will not redistribute land. The few will monopolistically get more, the poorer landed lose their land, and they will turn to other forms of financial support and continue anyway. And so will our class system. And so will our philosophical system of ethics and values that deplores the way we live.

The propertied class, however, in considering the future, gets bogged down on change.

"Not even the land looks as it did when I was young,"

comes the mournful complaint. "You didn't have all these houses around."

This is true. Forty years ago in 1936 the population in America was only 100 million. In that short time it has more than doubled to stand today at 218.5 million. And swelling. The press of people flows out from the cities, pushing, populating the land. But does that show any change? It seems more along the lines of a continuum, marked not by a new direction but by the increase in existing trends. And slumminess has always sprawled along some roads.

As for the absence of ready cash, well, that too is nothing new, while the absence of servants has been discussed with relish for as long as I can remember and with less insight into its endurance than one might expect from avid readers of the past.

"A good servant can't be found anymore."

"What's the matter with them? No one wants to work anymore. I just don't understand it."

On the servant question, I go along with Parmenides that there is no change in life, but only the appearance of change.

Of course things change. They grow and die out all the time, and among the propertied class as well there is a constant, almost imperceptible shift, an accommodation, in order to preserve the status quo, for preservation is the first responsibility of any species, and is never accomplished except by adaptation to the new.

I know a lot of people for whom even physically the world has little changed, though others of my friends would ridicule the statement and say I have some unnamed compulsion to put a halt to time. Communications, roads, TV, papers—ideas press in: the landed world is not so far removed. Things change. And all remains the same.

One year ago–that's all!–an acquaintance returned to her hometown for an Assembly Ball. This woman had lived for some time in New York, and she was one of the most vocal in insisting things had changed: the entire emotional climate of our times, she said, was new. So she did not hesitate to bring a friend back with her for the ball.

"The man was Jewish," she told me. "Only he didn't look Jewish," she added quickly, and gestured in a vague fashion to her hair. "He looked black. Very dark skin. Kinky hair. I guess I was naïve. I just thought things had changed."

They sat at her family's table, and no one said a word about her date. Everyone at the ball showed the finest manners imaginable. What she did not know was that as the evening progressed and the liquor flowed and some of the men got tight, a movement started to throw the black man out. At one point, after he had danced with one woman, a man took her aside: "How *could* you dance with a Negro?" he asked. "*How* could you do it?"

My friend was shaken when she learned the truth. To her it indicated that no change had taken place at all, no softening of the prejudice. She was hurt. But think. The man was not evicted from the ball, drunk though some members were. Some people will say that manners have always been highly prized in this group, so that this story demonstrates nothing; that to eject the guest of a fine old family would constitute an intolerable breach of etiquette. But others will argue on the side of change, for didn't the girl, herself a product of her class, invite the outsider in the first place to the ball?

Surely on an individual basis we all agree that change occurs. Eve Pell is one of those who has left her past behind. She lives now in California, radicalized, and has for years written about the minorities and poor, including the Jackson brothers and, most recently, Wendy Yoshimura, who travelled with Patty

Hearst during her wild, fugitive career with the remnants of the SLA.

One day George Jackson, the black radical prisoner, said to her: "If I had been a groom on your mother's estates, would we have fucked?"

To which she answered, amused: "If you had been a groom in my mother's barn, the closest you would have come to me would have been to put out your hand for my boot, to give me a leg up to the saddle."

And they laughed.

Index